THE CIVICALLY ENGAGED CLASSROOM

READING, WRITING, AND SPEAKING FOR CHANGE

Mary Ehrenworth | Pablo Wolfe | Marc Todd

HEINEMANN
Portsmouth, NH

Heinemann

361 Hanover Street

Portsmouth, NH 03801–3912

www.heinemann.com

Offices and agents throughout the world

© 2021 by Mary Ehrenworth, Pablo Wolfe, and Marc Todd

The author and publisher wish to thank those who have generously given permission to reprint borrowed material:

Figure 2.4 from "Narrow your Results: Advance Search" on Booksource: https://www.booksource.com/search.aspx. Reprinted by permission of the website.

Figure 3.7 from "Information Disorder, Part 3: Useful Graphics" by Claire Wardle. From *First Draft Media* (July 9, 2018). Reprinted by permission of author.

Score in Figure 5.4 created with "Flat:" https://flat.io. Reprinted by permission of the website.

Excerpts from Common Core State Standards © Copyright 2010. National Governors Association Center for Best Practices and Council of Chief State School Officers. All rights reserved.

Library of Congress Cataloging-in-Publication Data

Names: Ehrenworth, Mary, author. | Wolfe, Pablo, author. | Todd, Marc, author.

Title: The civically engaged classroom: reading, writing, and speaking for change / Mary Ehrenworth, Pablo Wolfe, Marc Todd.

Description: Portsmouth, NH: Heinemann, 2020 | Includes bibliographical references and index.

Identifiers: LCCN 2020021752 | ISBN 9780325120430

Subjects: LCSH: Civics—Study and teaching (Middle school)—United States. | Critical thinking—Study and teaching (Middle school)—United States. | Culturally relevant pedagogy—United States. | Social justice and education—United States. | Democracy and education—United States.

Classification: LCC LC1091 .E53 2020 | DDC 372.83044—dc23

LC record available at https://lccn.loc.gov/2020021752

Editor: Tobey Antao

Production: Hilary Goff

Cover design: Suzanne Heiser

Cover imagery: © Getty Images/subtropica, © Shutterstock/Amitofo

Interior design: Monica Ann Crigler

Typesetter: Shawn Girsberger

Manufacturing: Steve Bernier

Printed in the United States of America on acid-free paper

1 2 3 4 5 6 7 8 9 10 MPP 25 24 23 22 21 20

September 2020 Printing

To my son, Jackson,
with hope for his generation

—•—

To my children, Julien and Lucia,
you remind me daily of what's at stake

—•—

To my mother, Mary Ellen, who made me
believe in the democratic process
and the possibility of change

CONTENTS

INTRODUCTION   *xvii*

Our greatest fear in these turbulent times is that our young people will disengage. It's not our job to tell them what party or which candidates to vote for. It is our job to instill a sense of civic engagement. It's our job to help them become citizens who seek knowledge from multiple sources, who are alert to bias and injustice, who are critical—and engaged—consumers and producers of media.

CHAPTER 1 Engaged Citizens Explore Their Identities and Their Biases   *1*

This is a crucial time for our students, for as they grow they will have greater and greater capacity to understand how different aspects of their identities—those that are part of their upbringing, those imposed by society, those that are with them from birth, and those they've chosen themselves—affect their lives. In this chapter we'll explore how students' identities can be affirmed in civically engaged classes, and then begin exploring the biases that reside within and around us. We will help you to:

CHAPTER 2 Engaged Citizens Build Background Knowledge   *37*

Responsible citizens are informed; their participation in society is grounded in what they have learned through wide-ranging inquiry. They know that there is no single source perfect enough to provide them with the depth, nuance, and complexity to match reality. In this chapter we'll offer suggestions for helping kids build background knowledge in response to contemporary news events, for creating in-depth units of study, and for everything in between. We will help you to:

CHAPTER 3 Engaged Citizens Question Their Sources of Information *75*

Questioning the motives and credibility of sources of information gives students the tools to consume media intelligently and satisfies their growing desire to be a partner at the table rather than an object of adult whims. In this chapter we'll work through the skills that contribute to reading with healthy skepticism. We will help you to:

CHAPTER 4 Engaged Citizens Come to Nuanced and Receptive Stances *105*

Truly engaged citizens don't just pick a side; they get to know the ins and outs of a topic, listen carefully to learn (even from those with opposing viewpoints), and explain their positions in their own authentic voices. This chapter lays out lessons to help students to do just that. We will help you to:

CHAPTER 5 Engaged Citizens Rise Up

As educators, we've witnessed student walk-outs, sit-ins, and strikes. Who hasn't had a student refuse to do work? That's a strike! Who hasn't had a student grab the hall pass and storm into the hall when denied a chance to go to the bathroom? That's a walk-out! As civically engaged classroom teachers, our challenge is to guide this instinctive activism rather than fight it. In this chapter we will help you to:

CHAPTER 6 Feedback and Assessment Strengthen Engaged Citizens

Engaged citizens are assessing all the time—judging a candidate's speech, an ad's effectiveness, a phrase that a colleague just used. At the same time, assessing gives us, as engaged citizens, opportunities to grow our understandings and improve our actions. In this chapter we will help you to:

ONLINE RESOURCE CONTENTS

RESOURCES FOR CHAPTER 1

» Resource List: Educator Activists
» Resource List: Understanding Bias
» Classroom Tool: Bias Centers
» Video: Consciousness Time Lines

RESOURCES FOR CHAPTER 2

» Student Work Example: Essay Researched in Multiple Languages
» Student Work Examples: Lean Notes
» Student Work Examples: Recursive Notes
» Student Work Examples: Synthesis Pages

RESOURCES FOR CHAPTER 3

» Classroom Tool: Common Persuasive Techniques
» Classroom Tool: Understanding Misinformation
» Video: Conducting a Read-Aloud

RESOURCES FOR CHAPTER 4

» Student Work Examples: Personal Arguments and Identity Essays
» Student Work Examples: Writing About Social Issues
» Student Work Examples: Adjusting Register
» Classroom Tool: Flash Debate Protocol
» Video: Helping Students Envision Their Personal Essays
» Video: Helping Students Consider a Social Issue from a Personal Perspective
» Video: Helping Students Connect Their Own Stories to Social Issues

RESOURCES FOR CHAPTER 5

» Resource List: Teens Who Made History
» Resource List: Contemporary Teens Who Are Changing History
» Classroom Tool: Sample Rubrics

Online resources for *The Civically Engaged Classroom* can be found under Companion Resources at: http://hein.pub/CivicallyEngagedClassroom.

ACKNOWLEDGMENTS

We are grateful to every teacher and principal who has tried to move kids to care, including those who taught us and those whose classrooms we have collaborated in. There are also a host of people whose ideas and vision have inspired and informed the particular work in this book.

Whole parts of the book pay tribute to the work of C. Aaron Hinton and Akeem Barnes, whose love for young people, belief in social justice, and willingness to experiment created the conditions for their students to seize their civic responsibilities. Pablo notes: "Aaron, thank you for your time and energy and for inspiring me with each conversation. I can't thank you enough for all that you taught, and continue to teach me, or for the way you helped our kids see their community with new eyes. And, Akeem, over the four years of our work together, I was always moved by how much you cared for your students and how much they reflected that love back to you. Students were brave and vulnerable in your room because of the supportive tone you created. Thank you for allowing me into that space and for being open to learning new ways of teaching together. I've been shaped as both an educator and a person by the time spent in your room."

We thank Sonja Cherry-Paul for reading large swathes of the manuscript and giving detailed, specific, supportive, critical feedback. Sonja's sense of outrage at injustice, her commitment to anti-racism and anti-oppression in education, and her belief that people can improve moves through this work. We love to learn from you and to collaborate with you, Sonja. Thank you, too, to Sara Ahmed, who spoke at Teachers College again while we were in the midst of writing this book, and riveted us with her 2012 talk, "When the World Hands you a Curriculum." Sara's work on identity exploration, especially in her book *Being the Change* (2018) as well as her prior, equally significant book with Harvey "Smokey" Daniels, *Upstanders* (2015), informs a lot of this work. Thank you to Cornelius Minor for sometimes disturbing our thinking, sometimes moving us to tears, and always showing us what it means to teach with both outrage and love. Thank you to Audra Robb for her friendship, insight, and barbaric wit.

Doug Reeves of Creative Leadership Solutions read and made tremendously helpful suggestions for our chapter on assessment. We thank Doug for the feedback and for the work he does to limit punitive grading practices and promote generative ones. We also thank Ray Pecheone of SCALE at Stanford for the wisdom he imparted when he came to Teachers College to help us with performance assessments, checklists, and rubrics. It changed everything for us. And we thank Paul Deane at Educational Testing Service (ETS) for always pushing our thinking in terms of nonfiction skills and assessment.

Deepest gratitude to Kisha Howell, whose generosity of spirit is unmatched. Pablo notes: "Kisha, your guidance and insight helped me take steps toward becoming the kind of educator I would like to be. The way you listened, questioned, and offered suggestions challenged me to interrogate my own biases in the classroom. There is no better thought-partner in the world than Kisha Howell!"

Pablo thanks Kenya Harmon, Rashad Mack, Meg Wheeler, and Chris Wade, who are the kinds of leaders that our educational system needs. Balancing firmness with compassion, high standards with empathy, they are an administrative dream team.

We've, each of us, come of age as educator–activists with particular colleagues who have challenged us and conspired with us, whom we admire and love, and whose work we admire and love. In the places where we have most worked, they include Audra Robb, Katy Wischow, Cornelius Minor, Kelly Boland Hohne, Amanda Hartman, Kate Montgomery, Chris Lehman, Kate Roberts, Maggie Beattie Roberts, Carla España, Colleen Cruz, Emily Strang Campbell, and Katie Clements—the many beloved colleagues with whom we first worked on this kind of material while we were all at or around Teachers College Reading and Writing Project (TCRWP); Ellen Foote, Christina DiZebba, Jaclyn Maricle, Patrick Hector, Brian Gordon, Mari Mannino, Carol Shirai, Heather Freyman, Jennifer Brogan, Keisha Adams, Gianna Caramonica, Ray Selinas, Chi-Man Ng, Yelena Berdichevsky, Daryl Grabarek, and Andolyn Brown—all of whom helped originate a lot of this content literacy work at IS 289; and Stacy Goldstein and Katherine Messer, who planned and plotted with us in our time at School of the Future. We could write books about each of these people, how much they have meant to us, how we admire the work they do in schools with such joy and compassion, and how they have made us laugh.

We also need to thank the entire current middle school team at TCRWP, who think, laugh, and work with us in such generous and thoughtful ways. They include Heather Burns, Laurie Burke, Dwight McCaulsky, Cheney Munson, Kat Schechter, Mandy Ehrlich, Janet Steinberg, Sara Gretina, Philip Seyfried, and Angela Forero. Sara, Phil, and Angela, your optimism and insight have given us all new energy in dark political times. And an honorary member of the middle school team, André Martin, needs mention. André films, documents, and gives tech support. You're a superhero to us, André.

There are some educators at schools that are dear to our heart whom we'd like to name, because at different times we have seen the work they do to fight oppression, instill life-changing study habits, and build kids up. They include Mark Federman, Elisa Zonana, and Chantal Francoise, whom we know from East Side Community High School, a hotbed of anti-oppressive education; Sharon Larpenteur and Ann Karakas of Southridge High School in Beaverton, who create a kind of collaboration that is a model for teachers, kids, and colleagues; and Carol Mashamesh and Stacey Fell at Thompkins Square Middle School, whose quiet and not-so-quiet brilliance illuminates their work with kids. They also include Principal Dina Ercolano, Assistant Principal Janice Liao, coach Laura Stein, and the entire faculty of PS 158, for making teaching into an art and covenant; and Principal Susan Felder and the entire staff of PS 40 for making the study of social justice part of the every day curriculum. We have learned an enormous amount with these women and their remarkable teams.

They include special educators at Gahanna Middle School—Tia Holliman, Kevin Misheler, Kristi Griffiths, Tyler Bradford, and their merry band of instigators and change-agents; at Wilton public schools—Will Mathews and Susana Prata, who constantly inspire us with their openness to new ideas; and in Cleveland Riverside Schools—Abbey Hartman, who said of Marc, "you are the Cornelius to my students." We know what a compliment that is!

They include all the faculty at the American School of Barcelona (ASB), and for this book, particularly, Jennifer Killion, Johanna Cena, Mark Pingatore, Danny Crescenti, Steve Gnagni, Micah Cook, and Taylor Bingle. At ASB they have taken up high-leverage study habits with zeal. These educators shared student work, shared their classroom work, and made us think. Thanks especially to Micah for sharing images, to Danny for sharing the ibuprofen problem, to Taylor for sharing his experience with kids researching in multiple languages and Nico's work, and to Jenny for being one of the most beautiful high school teachers in the world. Thanks to all the students for being so open, caring, and daring. Thanks also to the team of English and humanities teachers at the American School of Madrid, led by dauntless coach April Stout, for letting us try out things together.

They include all the faculty we have worked with at Avenues, and for this project, especially Todd Shy, Ivan Cestero, and Stephanie Shore—inventors of innovative humanities curriculum, who have focused on teaching kids to read critically, even suspiciously, while still remaining open and alert to the beauty of text.

They include the staff of PS 126 in 2001, when we all used to teach there, including Karen Lowe, Jenny Bender, Christine Holley, Sarah Picard-Taylor, and principal Daria Rigney. They also include then superintendent of District 2, Shelley Harwayne, who put Mary in PS 126 and IS 289, making lifelong friendships and collaborations possible.

Marc and Mary thank Zeynep Okzan, principal of IS 289. Zeynep championed the spirit of this work and the labor it took. She embraced lab-sites and curriculum piloting. She opened classrooms and conversations. Perhaps most importantly to us, Zeynep was proud of this work, and that makes us so very happy.

Marc especially wants to thank Gordon Ostrowski, who co-leads the monumental work of composing and presenting an all-grade, seventh-grade opera each year at IS 289. Gordon gives his time, his expertise, his years of work in the theater, and, mostly, his belief that art is a vehicle for social protest. Gordon taught us all to believe that kids can create art that speaks up and speaks out. And Karen Scher of Facing History and Ourselves, for always being willing to discuss ideas about essential questions that lead to civic engagement.

Thank you especially to the entire Heinemann team, including Hilary Goff, Paul Tomasyan, Marjorie Glazer, Suzanne Heiser, Patty Adams, Elizabeth Silvis, Sarah Fournier, Steve Bernier, Val Cooper, Catrina Swasey, Jillian Sims, Roderick Spelman, Brett Whitmarsh, Lauren Audet, Vicki Boyd, and every person at Heinemann who makes the work of writing books for teachers such a joy. We are always thankful to the sales team, to the creative team, to the digital team, to the business team.

We especially want to thank Lucy Calkins, leader of the Teachers College Reading and Writing Project. Lucy brought us together by sending us into schools with a covenant to promote literacy as an act of social justice. She gave us opportunities to speak and to write, to research and to inquire, around the globe. She gave us colleagues we treasure, access to speakers who have influenced our work, classes to teach and a university to teach in, and a think tank in which to grow. What a gift.

There aren't enough words to thank Tobey Antao, our editor. For readers who are also writers, you'll know what it means to have someone pore over your writing, attending to every word, suggesting large- and small-scale changes, cheering on the work. We literally couldn't have written this book, in this time frame, with three writers who weren't often in the same state, without Tobey's incredible support and expertise. She not only brought all her writing knowledge, she also brought her intense engagement with political activism and education to this work, and it is better for it. Tobey is a truly great editor. Thank you, Tobey. Really.

Finally, we need to thank our dearest families.

Mary wishes her parents, Kay and Paul Lohnes, were still with her here on this planet, but they are here in her heart. They were educators and activists, and she thinks they would have really liked this book. Dear friend Marjorie Smith, state representative, acts as a friend and mentor politically and personally. Mary wants to say: "Thank you, Marge, for your influence and your love." And also, always and ever, thank you to Rich Hallett, partner extraordinaire. Rich had the idea for this book when the 2016 election occurred. And thank you to our kids, Jackson and Lauren, who strive to see injustice and to not turn aside.

Marc wants to say to his mother, Mary Ellen Todd: "I know I may not be the son you expected but I hope you are proud of who I have become. Thank you for believing in me. It let me be true to myself. I hope this work makes you proud, and that you see some of yourself and your influence in it. I do." And to Cy Orfield: "You honored the space to make this work possible. The gift to create is something so rare and so valuable. And to create in order to make change is something incredible. Thank you, Cy. You are my everything."

Pablo can't do enough to express his gratitude to his wife, Virginie. He wants to say: "Virginie, without your love and support I would never have had the strength to see this project through. You are the kind of leader I hope to become: a social justice warrior who never shies from putting in the work needed to create the world our children deserve. Thank you also to Mami, Pops, Rebecca, José, Stephan, and Brigitte, whose cheerleading gave me the final push to cross the finish line."

Dear Educator,

Thank you. By picking up this book you must be ready to create change. Good for you. Our world and our students will be better for it. Change will come. Our hope is that with this book in your hands you will be encouraged to be brave and begin this work now. As Cornelius Minor encourages us all with his brilliant mantra, "We Got this!"

Change will come if critical conversations are happening in our classrooms. Change will come if personal stories are encouraged and shared. Change will come if the conversations and the stories we tell about ourselves are honest. Change will only come if we are equipped to use critical lenses to sift through the daily onslaught of information and data our students consume alone on their devices. We need to create classrooms as a space where truth is practiced or exposed or accepted or challenged or embraced or resisted.

It is okay to be afraid and struggle with this work. The work can also be uncomfortable at times. And that's okay, too. It is uncomfortable to talk about and realize the barriers that people encounter. However, left unacknowledged, the barriers remain unseen and securely in place. That matters because we are teaching young adolescents who are developing their own precious identity. That identity will influence their behavior and sense of self for the rest of their lives. If you are teaching middle school and high school, then your students are in need of this work. The aha moments we know so well as educators now need to include the "oh wow!" moments when we all look at ourselves.

We teach who we are so we must do all we can to know who we are. I am a gay, cis-gendered, white, middle aged, middle class, male teacher, with pre-revolutionary settler privileges working in the most segregated school system in the country. Please don't put the book down because of who I am. Keep this book in your hands because of who you are. I came to education from an undergraduate and master's degree in theatre. In theatre we seek the truth of the characters we play and in the moments shared on stage with other performers. In theatre, both our actions and our feelings must be present and equal in order to be believable. In our classroom the truth is who we are as educators, the words we use, the relationships we have, and the community we create with our students.

As Cornelius's mantra, "We got this!", plays in my consciousness, so does Paulo Freire's, "The teacher is of course an artist, but being an artist does not mean that he or she can make the profile, can shape the students. What the educator does in teaching is to make it possible for the students to become themselves."

Mary, Pablo, and I, thank you for picking up this book and being ready to create change.

In admiration,

Marc Todd

Dear Reader,

All right coconspirator, are you ready? This book is not a curriculum, it's not advice on classroom activities, it's not a pedagogical treatise; no, this book is a call to arms. Grab your laptop, make those remote-learning links, pick up your markers, chart paper, and document camera—and get ready. "For what?" you ask? Well, in the words of James Baldwin, to "achieve our country, and change the history of the world" (1993).

Yes, that's the task set before us.

It has always been the task set before us, but in light of the COVID-19 pandemic and the murder of George Floyd, it becomes even more essential that we work deliberately to create a better world. Of course, we won't do it alone—we'll combine forces, collaborate, and steel each other with outrageous love for the struggles ahead. And, it goes without saying, we'll partner with young people who, ultimately, will do the hardest work of re-envisioning our nation. We won't be alone, but this won't be easy.

It was never meant to be easy; after all, democracy is by its nature difficult, but tyrants and demagogues as well as nativists and racists would have us believe otherwise. They promote an illusion that this country was purer, better, in some utopic past. They peddle a dulling nostalgia that lures people to sleep while racist gears continue to grind. They lie and obfuscate. Either you fall to the narcotic and are lulled into passivity, or you're so enraged in response that you exhaust yourself shouting at the car radio in the morning or complaining to like-minded friends. As teachers, we can't fall into either camp; we can't detach and ignore, nor can we fool ourselves that complaining is the same as action. Our society, and our young people in particular, can't afford to have teachers watch the proceedings from twenty thousand feet.

So, instead, we will embrace complexity; we will embrace discomfort and failure. We will embrace the challenge that as citizens we have duties to uphold, not just rights to claim. We will recognize that if we are to claim any rights at all, it is only after we have upheld our duties to one another, for how can we have a social contract from which people only withdraw and never contribute?

The COVID-19 pandemic has laid bare the injustice at the core of our society and the ineptitude of many of our leaders. It is plain that our system must change. The road ahead is long; for while the virus itself may be novel, the crisis of our democracy isn't. We must acknowledge that we live in a house built on a rotten foundation. Racial injustice exposed by the pandemic is not an ugly aberration—it's a founding principal. The hypocrisy of proclaiming freedom for all while pursuing a genocidal campaign against Indigenous Peoples and enslaving Africans has infected all facets of American life. We aren't in a new catastrophe; it's just that more of us who have been privileged enough to live at a comfortable remove are becoming aware of what has raged from the beginning. To them we say, "Join us in preparing the next citizens who will make this country what it should be!" And to those of us who have been painfully aware of the poison coursing through these American veins, those who are like, "You see it *now*? All right, better late than never, I suppose. Can we get some shit done, then?" To them we say, "We're with you, willing accomplices, in the work ahead."

I'll start with the challenge to myself. I find it so easy to be comfortable, to sit back and coast on the privileges that have been placed in my lap through no exertion of my own. Parents who were professionals? Check. Light skin? Check. (White dad. Puerto Rican mom—although compared to my mom or sister, I'm still woefully melanin-deficient.) Fancy-pants private schooling? Check. Graduated from a liberal arts college, debt-free? Check. Married, two healthy children. Professional. Homeowner. I check the boxes and realize how fortunate I am as well as how easily I can slide into comfort and let it envelop me as I ignore the injustices around me. What good are antiracist thoughts if not met with antiracist actions? What good is there complaining about the state of our country and world if these thoughts are not tied to work? I return to Baldwin, who reminds us "that a civilization is not destroyed by wicked people; it is not necessary that people be wicked but only that they be spineless" (1993). Nothing melts the spine like comfort.

So, this book is a call to *work*. Throughout it we've included a feature called "Practice What You Teach," a regular reminder that the work in these pages is for all of us to take on, not just our kids. We can all do more to be better citizens; we can all do more to re-envision our democracy. This is not about indoctrinating children, but it is about our duty as educators to help them realize that they have a lot of responsibility in this society and that if they don't take it up, or aren't adequately prepared for it, they'll continue to perpetuate grievous harms to themselves and to others.

I can't wait to walk this path with you. Let's put in this work together.

Yours in struggle,

Pablo Wolfe

Dear Colleagues and Collaborators,

I offer this book, with my beautiful and disruptive coauthors, Pablo and Marc, out of a sense of horror at the hate speech and rabid propagation of misinformation that have menaced this nation and spread around the world, at the violence done to families, at the despair of young dreamers. And I offer this book out of a sense of wondrous love for the young political candidates, the teen activists, the coalitions of civically engaged citizens, and especially, the teachers who strive to protect people who need champions and to better conditions, every day, for the students and families in their care.

I am a white, cisgender, bi woman with degrees from Ivy League universities, and my current professional position is Senior Deputy Director of an influential nonprofit think tank at Columbia University, the Teachers College Reading and Writing Project. For many years, I saw the teaching of literacy as itself an act of social justice. To help young people find their voices, to instill in them the love of reading that will make books and ideas central to their lives, to teach them to write through trouble and to hold onto beauty—that seemed enough. But it isn't enough. The world needs us to teach an explicitly anti-oppressive curriculum. Young people need us to acknowledge the kinds of oppression people suffer daily and to teach anti-racism, antisexism, and anti-homophobia. And the world needs us to teach students that civics matters—that their words and actions can make a difference; that being civically engaged is not only worth it but critically important to the lives they will live; and that it is vital to pay attention to the events that unfold around them, the voices that shape people's thinking, and their place in this chaotic, often painful and sometimes spectacularly beautiful world.

It's not fair that kids have unequal access to education in this country. It's not right that young people are vulnerable to violent speech and action because of their skin color, their culture, their religion, the places their families came from, and the places they live. It's not fair that some children go to schools that are full of books and interactive whiteboards and artwork, with teachers who love their work and their students, while other children go to schools that seem devoid of human compassion. We need to do more in the service of equity. We need to instill a sense of respect and even awe for the lives people live, for the remarkable strength and beauty of the human spirit, for the interconnectedness of humans. Part of this work is instilling in young people a sense that they matter; that they can be part of changing things for the better; that their vote, their voice, their outrage can fuel change.

With humility and hope for the influence of teachers and the future of the generation we teach, we offer a vision of classrooms where teachers and young people know that the world is not good enough, and act daily to confront injustice and to hone their minds and spirits for the work of making it better.

All the best,

Mary Ehrenworth

INTRODUCTION

Do the best you can until you know better.
Then when you know better, do better.

—Maya Angelou (2015)

Thinking about our thinking, imagining things for ourselves,
seeking a community of concern in a public space: These may
be the phases of our striving for social justice, our striving for
collectivity, our striving for what is always in the making—what
we call democracy. These may be our ways of reaching toward
each other in safe and unsafe spaces, seeking equity, seeking
decency, seeking for a common world.

—Maxine Greene (2000, 303)

I would unite with anybody to do right;
and with nobody to do wrong.

—Frederick Douglass (1855)

The Challenges Facing Our Democracy and Our Students

COVID-19 exposed every flaw and crack in our society, and education and protest have never mattered more. While rich and poor alike are susceptible to the virus, there is no question who has been dying at greater rates. While some of us sheltered in and continued to collect paychecks, many exposed themselves daily to the virus in order to maintain their income. As unemployment numbers ballooned, many struggled with no income at all. Access to healthcare has been unequal and unfair, with BIPOC and immigrant families enduring racial injustice in our healthcare systems. Immigrants were detained at the United States-Mexico border in inhumane conditions that continued to spread the virus. As the country with the highest incarceration rate in the world, the United States saw the virus tear through its prisons. The litany of injustices revealed by the virus is long and sobering and it doesn't take rigorous analysis to see that its consequences are felt in vastly different ways across racial fault lines. Faced with this oppressive reality, which is just one in a list of injustices that haunt the daily lives of so many citizens, our great fear is that our young people will retreat and disengage.

There are reasons for them to feel disenfranchised and disillusioned. And, for most of our young people, there is reason to distrust the world that adults have made for them. In her piece about Ibram Kendi, journalist Lonnae O'Neil describes the climate in the United States as one where "the threat of shoot-you-down, run-you-over racial violence feels as close at hand as the peril to the republic from fake facts and revisionist history" (2017). If that description feels overstated, then probably your privilege protects you from these conditions. That happens inevitably. We seek places to live and to work where we can be safe and productive, where our colleagues are like-minded, where we are protected from bigots and hate-mongers and those who are afraid of anyone who is not just like them. But that sense of security also isolates us.

As teachers, this moment calls on us to examine our history in light of the current disturbing tides of xenophobia, police brutality, racism, and sexism, with our colleagues and the young people in our care.

The antidote to creeping hopelessness is action. In our classrooms, whether virtual or brick-and-mortar, we must look collectively at the resistance movements, the moments of light and possibility when things changed for the better, when people spoke up, marched, wrote, formed coalitions, and voted—and take example from their investment in bettering our society. Our young people can't vote yet, but they will. It's not our job to tell them what party or candidates to vote for. It is our job to instill a sense of civic engagement. It's our job to help them become citizens who seek knowledge from multiple sources, who are alert to bias, who are critical—and engaged—consumers and producers of media.

Here's a little of what we're up against. In the 2020 election, the very possibility of fair elections is cast into doubt by COVID-19. States are scrambling to improve their capabilities for mail-in voting while some politicians attempt to impede such efforts. Even in the best of times without the pandemic preventing our public gatherings, according to the Pew Research Center, compared to other highly developed democracies, the United States ranks 26th out of 32 in voter turnout. Only 56 percent of eligible voters voted in the 2016 presidential election. Voter participation in the United States is notoriously low, especially among young people, minorities, and those living under the poverty line—and there are concerted political efforts to further suppress turnout. The very core of democracy, the freedom to vote, is under regular attack. Just think about the rollback of parts of the Voting Rights Act in 2013, the voter ID requirements that disproportionately target Black and brown citizens, the outright conflict of interest of elected officials overseeing the recounts of their very own election results, rampant gerrymandering, an antiquated electoral college system that elects presidents who lost by millions of votes, a president who said openly that he welcomes the aid of foreign powers who provide dirt on his opponents, social media networks that widely disseminate misinformation and hate speech, and the disproportionate influence of corporate money in elections. Put together, these attacks from within pose as dangerous a threat to our democracy as any foreign power.

Phew. As Shakespeare said in *Hamlet,* "Something is rotten in the state of Denmark." If our students are to become the citizens our society needs, we need to prepare them for this struggle—first, by raising their awareness of injustice, then by helping them develop the critical thinking skills to coherently critique our societal ills, and lastly, by helping them practice the civic virtues our future as a nation will depend on.

What We Can Do

For all the truly frightening oppression and bias that infuse the very air we breathe, let's also look at the signs of transcendent possibility and power that make it possible to teach with hope. Picture fifteen-year-old Greta Thunberg going from her sit-in outside her school to talking to the entire United Nations about the climate crisis. Picture fifteen-year-old Xiuhtezcatl Martinez getting fracking banned in his county. Picture sixteen-year-old Mya Middleton and seventeen-year-old Emma Gonzalez each speaking to thousands of protestors at the March for Their Lives. Picture the many children who shared messages of hope and demonstrated fortitude during an international pandemic, and who joined Black Lives Matter protests in hopes of a better world.

We live in a time that shows us, perhaps more than any time prior, the remarkable possibility of youth. In the adult-created mayhem of civic strife, it is remarkable how many young people are taking up activism.

Yet even as young people become more politicized, teachers remain unsure about their own political status in the classroom. Because we want to be careful about proselytizing, we sometimes remain quiet about public figures and policies. We avoid classroom discussions of current events. The problem with that approach is that silence is not neutral. Silence props up existing power hierarchies and does nothing to protect vulnerable students. We have a responsibility to respond when our President calls nations "shitholes," mocks the disabled, or engages in name-calling. Silence in these circumstances signals consent. It is not surprising that the Southern Poverty Law Center reported an upsurge in hate language and bias attacks and harassment in schools. Their report is sobering: "on the upswing: verbal harassment, the use of slurs and derogatory language, and disturbing incidents involving swastikas, Nazi salutes and Confederate flags" (2016).

It's not okay for teachers to ignore that a president and his political and social allies have made young people more afraid. It's not okay that it is increasingly dangerous for young people in this country to identify as immigrants, Muslims, BIPOC, or LGBTQIA+. So, part of our job, regardless of our political affiliation, needs to be that we make our classrooms and our schools places where we stand up to hate speech, and where we encourage students to bring and embrace their whole identity. That means explicitly doing antibias work and identity exploration. We dedicate Chapter 1 to this work, because it feels so important, especially in times of strife and discord.

If part of our work is to support students' identity construction, and their ability to express and celebrate all the parts of themselves, another part of our work is to teach in such a way that kids are educated for participatory democracy. In his speech accepting the Paul H. Douglas Awards for Ethics in Government at the University of Illinois, Former President Barack Obama addressed America's youth this way:

> To all the young people who are here today, there are now more eligible voters in your generation than in any other, which means your generation now has more power than anybody to change things. If you want it, you can make sure America gets out of its current funk. If you actually care about it, you have the power to make sure we seize a brighter future. But to exercise that clout, to exercise that power, you have to show up. In the last midterm elections, in 2014, fewer than one in five young people voted. One in five. Not two in five, or three in five. One in five. Is it any wonder this Congress doesn't reflect your values and your priorities? Are you surprised by that? This whole project of self-government only works if everybody's doing their part. Don't tell me your vote doesn't matter. I've won states in the presidential election because of five, ten, twenty votes per precinct. And if you thought elections don't matter, I hope these last two years have corrected that impression. So if you don't like what's going on right now—and you shouldn't—do not complain. Don't hashtag. Don't get anxious. Don't retreat. Don't binge on whatever it is you're bingeing on. Don't lose yourself in ironic detachment. Don't put your head in the sand. Don't boo. Vote. Vote! (2018)

While our classrooms are not the only place where young people will learn how to interact with democratic society, they are an essential space for them to experience what it means to live in community with others, to balance their own interests with those of the group, to challenge themselves to overcome differences, and to ask the questions that help them understand the crux of an issue. These are civics lessons that must be lived in our schools today, and we need a committed corps of teachers to deliver them.

You are one of these badass teachers.

And to you, our fellow badass teachers, we have a similar exhortation. Under the current conditions facing our country, the teacher cannot sit idle; the teacher must be an active proponent of reason, logic, empathy, and passionate inquiry— none of which should be the exclusive province of a particular political party or ideology. You must get out there and teach. Teach!

There is a perception in the United States that teachers must remain apolitical, but we argue in this book that we have a responsibility to be exactly the opposite: we have a duty, as part of our profession, both to defend democratic values and to fight alongside young people as they shape the future they want to live in. In these pages we hope to offer a rallying cry for, a guide to, and examples of, civic education that spurs teachers and students alike to be active participants in society. You can be a political being without sharing your voting record!

Currently, education reformers push the raising of standards; they tout the importance of making sure that schools be measured on how "college and career ready" their students are. The current educational paradigm calls for a view of school as a training ground for future workers, whether their work is intellectual or manual; and reformers are looking at education through a largely economic lens. We all experienced, though, during the COVID-19 crisis, that schools need to be places that address issues of connection, of equity, and of visibility. We argue for the type of education that not only teaches students how to write clear, concise sentences and well-organized essays but also ensures that those essays are directed at the moral issues of the day, to the causes that need to be addressed. Amy Gutmann, in *Democratic Education,* reminds us, "Education, in great measure, forms the moral character of citizens, and moral character along with laws and institutions forms the basis of democratic government" (1999, 49). Our teaching must ensure that our students are more than "college and career ready," they must be "citizen ready," and that means we have an obligation both to teach in democratic ways and to have students produce work that allows them to practice civic virtues through real-world experiences.

When we became educators, we entered into a covenant with young people. We promised to sustain and protect, to teach and inspire. Maxine Greene, Professor of Philosophy at Teachers College, writes: "There is no question but that our schools must educate for a range of literacies today. Everyone (including those classified *at risk*) has a claim to be able to seek some sort of status, some sort of security in a society as unpredictable as ours" (1993, 223).

We must be brave. We must find our courage to do this work. Change making does not belong to one group of people. We must be courageous enough to create a classroom, grade level, or school of students in pursuit of social justice. Students and teachers engaged in this work see themselves differently, listen to their peers and colleagues differently, and experience the collective power of activism that is needed to create change. The New York Public Library's exhibit *Love and Resistance: Stonewall 50* reminds us that society changed because people organized and participated in politics passionately and personally. Those individuals protested, organized, wrote, argued, and embraced each other through it all. They were brave. They created change. As educators, we have to provide an opportunity for our students to be brave enough to care.

It may be scary, but there's no doubt about it: teaching is a political act—not because we name our political party, or tell our kids how we'll vote, or whom they should vote for. It's political because we live in the world, and all our decisions and actions, what we say and what we don't, implicitly empower some and disempower others, whether we mean to or not. This book isn't suggesting that we lead kids toward one or another political party. It *is* suggesting that we lead kids toward the voting booth. This world needs young people to engage with voting, activism, and the empowerment of their generation. We hope, here, that you find out more about how to create a civically engaged classroom that teaches the skills necessary to be an alert and active citizen and that models what it means to be a member of a democracy that is full of both pain and potential.

This book and the work inside it overall exist in the wake of John Dewey and Maxine Greene's work on the role of public school as formative to participatory democracy. These philosophers—both of whom taught at Teachers College—believed that teaching ethics, orchestrating participatory experiences, and studying ways to engage with the world are central to schooling in a democracy. We especially love Dewey's *Democracy and Education* (1916) and Maxine Greene's *Dialectic of Freedom* (2018). Since then, Bettina Love's *We Want to Do More Than Survive: Abolitionist Teaching and the Pursuit of Educational Freedom* (2019) calls into question how schools continue to fail Black and Brown students, and thus fail at the democratic covenant of public education.

Then there is Gloria Ladson-Billings' *The Dreamkeepers* (2009). When this text came out, it was the first time we were pushed to rethink our liberal practices and our liberal identities. Ladson-Billings' work remains essential to helping teachers really think about, research, and connect with the students in our classes, including their histories, cultures, and dreams. Her work sparks much of the identity exploration of Chapter 1.

Finally, Randy and Katherine Bomer, Smokey Daniels and Sara Ahmed, Carla España and Luz Yadira Herrera, and Cornelius Minor help us conceptualize our literacy curricula as sites where important social justice work can happen. If you didn't read Bomer and Bomer's *For a Better World* when it came out in 2001, read it now. It is relevant and useful and beautiful, showing us how to position book clubs and literacy discussions as places where kids will engage with important social issues. Pick up *Upstanders* by Daniels and Ahmed (2015) as well, if you haven't already. These two activists help us harness the sense of outrage, urgency, and awakeness that teens are capable of, and show us how to activate and keep that sense alive in our classrooms. And you've surely read Cornelius Minor's *We Got This* (2019). Keep it by your side, to fill you with faith that you can tackle tremendously important work if you believe in your students and yourself. Most recently, Carla España and Luz Yadira Herrera came out with *En Comunidad: Lessons for Centering the Voices and Experiences of Bilingual Latinx Students* (2020). It is an anthem and a protest, a call to make our classrooms ones where all kids' histories and their voices are celebrated.

All of these thinkers and educators are concerned with injustice in the world and ways to position oneself toward resisting injustice and embracing liberation. In the upcoming chapters, we offer specific guides to other significant current readings that have shaped our thinking and that feel important for educators to engage with at this moment. We thank our many colleagues in the field who constantly recommend, produce, and challenge us with their texts.

Our goal is to create more alert, thoughtful, engaged, inquisitive, and active citizens by reframing teaching so that it's not only about content and standards but also about *civic virtues*. We promote teaching methods that are democratic and that encourage teachers to create experiences that allow students to practice what it means to be a citizen in our democracy. Some of these experiences feel immediately liberating, others create initial discomfort.

The theory of allowing discomfort as part of learning will be a thread throughout this book. Being civically minded and striving toward ethical interactions is not always comfortable. When Lisa Damour, author of *Untangled* (2017) and *Under Pressure* (2019), spoke at Teachers College about the process of change and growth, she reminded her audience that, "stress is crucial for change, and change is crucial for growth" (2017). We believe that. We believe that to create conditions in which growth is possible, there will also be periods of uncertainty and discomfort, for us as well as for our students. Uncertainty is better than complacency. Distress is better than ignorance. And imperfection in this work is okay. Awareness is an ongoing process of learning, of putting aside old selves and trying out new selves.

How This Book Is Structured, Conditions for This Work to Succeed, and What's Offered in Each Chapter

The chapters in this book are each dedicated to crucial civic virtues, from acknowledging identity, bias, and privilege, to seeking and building background knowledge, to close and critical reading and ethical research skills, to composing nuanced stances in writing, to building coalitions and engaging in activism. In each chapter we describe classroom structures, curricular possibilities, and specific lessons or teaching methods that have made a difference. We've also included student work and teaching charts and tools. We hope this collection will make it easier for you to try this work inside your own classroom and with colleagues.

Below are the civic virtues we attempt to foster throughout this book. We see this list as both a guide and a pledge:

In the process of becoming an engaged citizen, I:

- celebrate my own identity and the identities of those in my community
- become alert to my own biases
- realize how my bias might shape my consumption of media
- resist the "echo chamber" by recognizing how modern media can solidify my biases
- recognize the gaps in my knowledge
- care enough to research deeply and ethically
- attend to a balance of perspectives
- seek out missing voices
- look for complexity within a topic
- critically consume media and texts
- question sources and pursue further research
- resist resignation and cynicism
- find my voice through writing
- engage with urgent social issues
- revise my thinking willingly and openly
- become a radical listener
- identify social causes
- build coalitions

- inform myself about local government
- advocate for social change.

As we take on the teaching of these civic virtues and the application of them to our own lives, it helps to think about the conditions that make learning and exercising these virtues possible.

Conditions for a Civically Engaged Classroom

- belief in one's own power to change systems, expose oppression, and influence others
- social networks that extend through, and beyond, the classroom to the community
- access to texts and sources, to mentors and media
- knowledge of skills, strategies, habits, and behaviors that help one engage critically with texts, ideas, events, and each other
- a class culture of care and respect
- awareness of oppression and injustice, and hope and liberation
- willingness to find out more about local issues and activism, systems of local government, and nongovernmental institutions that are designed to amplify individual voices
- awareness of rights and responsibilities and the distinction between the two
- love.

If we can establish these conditions, our classrooms will become the places of civic training and discourse that our society needs. The Knight Commission on Trust, Media and Democracy has issued a report titled *Crisis in Democracy: Renewing Trust in America,* which cautioned:

> Today, Americans need to strive for a stronger vision of democracy and citizenry. It includes the right and obligation to voice one's beliefs and to grant the same to all fellow citizens in search of shared truths. As Supreme Court Justice Oliver Wendell Holmes wrote a century ago, "The best test of truth is the power of the thought to get itself accepted in the competition of the market. . . . That, at any rate, is the theory of our Constitution." The marketplace for ideas, though, presumes an electorate willing and able to search for the truth. (2019, 19)

The creation of an electorate that is willing and able to search for elusive truths falls to us, the teachers. So, enough preaching, let's get started.

Onward!

Civic Virtues Addressed in this Chapter

- celebrating one's own identity and the identities of those in the community
- becoming alert to one's own biases
- realizing how bias might shape consumption of media
- resisting the "echo chamber" by recognizing how modern media can solidify our biases

Planning Your Time

We suggest devoting time at the very start of your curriculum—a few days to a week—to the initial work of affirming identities, building relationships, and introducing the concept of bias. This will set the stage for your work together; however, you will have to regularly return to this work as the year progresses. The lessons and tools in this chapter are designed to help students consider how implicit bias might affect their reading and perception as they read and do research throughout the year. No isolated activities, videos, or guest speakers will radically transform the perceptions we've spent a lifetime learning in a social curriculum seeded with racism, sexism, homophobia, and classism; however, by returning to awareness-raising tools regularly throughout future units, we can begin to establish the habits of mind that challenge entrenched biases.

ENGAGED CITIZENS EXPLORE THEIR IDENTITIES AND THEIR BIASES

There is an intoxicating buzz at the beginning of every school year, part thrill of anticipating all the new learning that will take place, part fear of the unknown. With the unstable educational conditions kids and teachers experienced around the globe during COVID-19, any new year also now raises questions of how the classroom will build and sustain community, and how it will respond to crisis together. The night before the first day of school, children and teachers alike wonder who will be in their classroom this coming year. What will they be like? How will we get along? How will we respond to trouble? At the heart of this questioning is identity. We are asking ourselves, "Who am I? How will other people accept, challenge, and shape who I am? Who will I be in the space that we share?" We all seek to be understood by those around us; and the classroom is one of the first places where children explore and mold their identities with peers.

As teachers of adolescents, we know how many transformations take place during these vital years. Our students are moving through stages of adolescent development and identity development. In terms of adolescent development, accrued experience, emotional maturity, and physical change all mix to recreate our students year to year over this span. Kids seem to slip in and out of stereotypical roles: video game nerd, team captain, skater dude, drama queen; they experiment with clothing choices we might find confusing; they emulate social media personalities from around the world. In terms of identity development, the process can be more painful, as our students bump into oppressive discourse that works to silence or marginalize parts of their identities. It's a time of self-exploration and identity construction that is equal parts beautiful, silly, joyful, anxious, bitter, and cruel. Our students are perhaps at their most vulnerable during these years, and we have the daunting responsibility of affirming and protecting our students as they undergo their unique metamorphoses.

As our students grow they have greater and greater capacity to understand the ways in which different aspects of their identity—those that are part of their upbringing, those imposed by society, those that are with them from birth, and those they've chosen themselves—affect their lives. Students will become more and more capable of articulating the intersecting factors that shape their identities; the injustice with which they may be treated by society because of these factors; and the ways in which these factors strengthen them, sustain them, and make them who they are. We all know from today's social and political currents how identities can be both celebrated and vilified. If we are to create in our classrooms the type of society we'd like to see, rather than replicate the division and animus in the outside world, we'll need to address identity head on with honesty and courage. If we want our students to read widely and critically, to take well-reasoned positions, and to take action in support of their beliefs, they need to understand how their own identities affect their perspective and the perspectives of others.

See the online resources for recommended reading, including educator–activist twitter feeds and blogs.

In this chapter we'll explore how students' identities can be affirmed in our civically engaged classes; then we'll pivot to discuss how to explore the biases that reside within and around us. Finally, we'll consider how we move forward as engaged citizens with a better understanding of ourselves and others.

In this chapter we'll help you to:

- affirm identities and build relationships
- introduce the concept of implicit bias
- consider how implicit bias might affect our reading and perceptions
- teach kids to be alert to common biases with bias centers
- teach kids to be alert to how their identities and biases affect how they read
- involve families and communities
- be ready for anything
- practice what you teach.

This slim chapter only scratches the surface of identity exploration in the classroom. There are many educators doing comprehensive research and writing about issues of identity and personal history in our classrooms and we encourage you to study their work. Authors and educators, such as Ibram Kendi, Gloria Ladson-Billings, Django Paris, Christopher Emdin, Jamila Lyiscott, Sharroky Hollie, Ijeoma Oluo, Robin DiAngelo, Sara Ahmed, Tricia Ebarvia, Sonja Cherry-Paul, Carla España, Luz Yadira Herrera, and Cornelius Minor, have reminded us that at the core of our teaching and learning reside questions of race, ethnicity, orientation, gender, religion, and class.

Affirm Identities and Build Relationships

The work that we embark upon in this chapter is difficult. It's difficult for your students and it will be difficult for you. It will demand that you be vulnerable, it will demand that you be trusting, and it will demand that you attempt and fail repeatedly as you forge a path along with your students.

We'll begin with an admission. In 2019, Pablo, a nine-year veteran of the classroom and four-year veteran as a Staff Developer at the Teachers College Reading and Writing Project (TCRWP), found himself taking over for a teacher. Filled with enthusiasm and ideas about effective teaching, Pablo began his work by reading poems to his students that he'd used successfully in the past and showing them videos of slam poetry that he thought would excite them, and—he failed completely to capture his students' attention. A student wandered the room, occasionally slapping a peer's neck. Another farted intentionally, causing the table to clear in hysteria. Another stood and improvised a dance in the middle of a lesson. "Look down below, it's Pa-beh-looo!" he crooned to the laughter of his peers.

With bruised ego, Pablo would fall back into his chair during his preps and try to piece back together what had gone wrong. In a moment of desperation, Pablo even tried "tough love" by holding the class for a silent lunch after a particularly disastrous lesson. An all-out mutiny resulted.

What was he doing wrong? And how could he make it right? As if by divine intervention, Pablo received a call from Kisha Howell, a friend and colleague from TCRWP.

"How much time have you spent getting to know them?" Kisha asked.

"Umm . . ." During their long conversation Kisha also advised Pablo to explore why he was taking on this work and what he hoped to achieve. She pushed him to examine the self that he was bringing into the classroom so he could understand what he was communicating implicitly as well as explicitly to his students.

Pablo, who was the school's Dean of Instruction, had become the class's teacher suddenly and, desperate to pick up a dropped baton, Pablo had wanted to move on with the important work of learning but had neglected the far more important work of relationship building. In his fervor to get to the work of engaged citizenship, Pablo had not taken the time to get to know the very citizens he wanted to reach, nor to know himself as their teacher.

The only antidote to this dynamic was to delve into identity, to explore what made Pablo who he was and what made his students who they were. Pablo shared his own identity map in which he explained aspects of himself and then encouraged his students to do the same (more on this process follows). He also wrote poetry that explored aspects of his identity that the students would never have been aware of otherwise. For example, he wrote an *I remember* poem (inspired by Joe Brainard's book of the same name) in which he highlighted facets of his Puerto Rican heritage and the childhood memores that shaped him:

> *I remember calle Orquidea*
>
> I remember the smell of *arroz con pollo*. Just off the airplane
> and starving, I ate plate after plate as abuela spurred me on, *"Come mas mijo!"*
> I remember chickens in the neighbor's yard
> I remember walking to Titi Tella's house, sitting on her floral
> printed couches, each one sealed in clear plastic
> I remember sawing down mangoes with abuelo. The fruit fell
> in the long grass. With pocket knife and steady hands, he sliced off
> the skin while I waited hungrily
> I remember *coqui! coqui!* the sound of tree frogs after summer rain

While Pablo's students, all of whom identified as Black, didn't share a cultural heritage with him, his openness with his identity made it easier for them to share aspects of their own identities. One student came up to him afterward to say that she was Dominican; another volunteered that she was half Cuban. The beauty of this activity is that it is relatively simple and yet can open up rich conversations and opportunities for connection. Pablo had students examine the breadth and variety of the memories that Brainard (2001) recounted in his work, scraps of images both powerful and mundane that come together to make him who he is. Soon his students had pages of memories that they could mine for future memoir ideas or for deeper reflection.

Pablo continued the work of getting to know his students outside of the classroom. He asked them to join him individually for a few minutes to chat after class. He volunteered to meet with many of his students in a tutorial group after school. He texted images of laudable work home to proud mothers. Very slowly, protective barriers on both sides began to come down. He began to both share, and learn, about hobbies and passions, favorite artists and TV shows, and eventually, about attitudes toward school and about traumas that informed some behaviors. The path was hard and continuous, but as Pablo and his students learned about each other's identities, they were more able to consider each other's perspectives, and to see each other as people.

If we are to proceed with the work of supporting our students as responsible young citizens, we're going to need to dive headfirst into an exploration of who we and they are. We will have to question our assumptions about our students and spend the time to know them as individuals. In *Why Race and Culture Matter in*

Schools, Tyrone C. Howard (2010) describes the necessity of considering race and culture in order to have sustained, critical conversations. He talks about finding out not just who students are, but what drives them. As Ijeoma Oluo writes in *So You Want to Talk About Race*, "Each of us has a myriad of identities—our gender, class, race, sexuality, and so much more—that inform our experiences in life and our interactions with the world . . . [P]rivileges and oppressions do not exist in a vacuum . . . and they can combine with each other, compound each other, mitigate each other, and contradict each other" (2019, 75).

As with any good teaching, we'll want to do the same work that we ask of the students. Just as kids' identities matter in this work, your own identity also matters. The suggestions below will be just as helpful for you in unpacking your own identity as they are for your students in unpacking theirs. As Parker Palmer so beautifully illustrates in *The Courage to Teach*, "Face to face with my students, only one resource is at my immediate command: my identity, my selfhood." He goes on to explain, "My ability to connect with my students . . . depends less on the methods I use than on the degree to which I know and trust my selfhood—and am willing to make it available and vulnerable in the service of learning" (2017, 10).

Mapping Identities

Sara Ahmed's social comprehension work, outlined in *Being the Change* (2018), begins by asking students to sketch identity maps, in which they place their own name at the center and create a word web that names aspects of their identity—*sister, daughter, cousin, granddaughter, reader, second-generation American, babysitter, gamer, Instagrammer,* etc. Below we share some of those created in our classrooms (see Figure 1.1). As Sara explained in her 2020 address at Teacher's College, identity maps "are not ice-breakers"—they are living tools that will be useful throughout the year to help students consider how their identities intersect with the curriculum. Because of this, you'll want to ensure that students can access their individual maps easily: have students create them across a spread in their notebooks. Students might refer to their map as they read or as they consider research possibilities in future units, they can return to it as they brainstorm memoir ideas, or they can simply add to it periodically as they learn more about themselves over the year.

Marc uses a similar activity in which students create identity trees to explore both their lived and their virtual selves. The roots represent the past: people, places, events, and the art/media that has had a lasting effect on who we are. The trunk represents who we are now. Inside the trunk represents who we are on the inside and how we see ourselves; it may even include secret identities that we hold inside. On the outside of the trunk, on the left, is how other people see us. "Other People" can include family, teachers, peers, friends, coaches, siblings, and strangers. On the

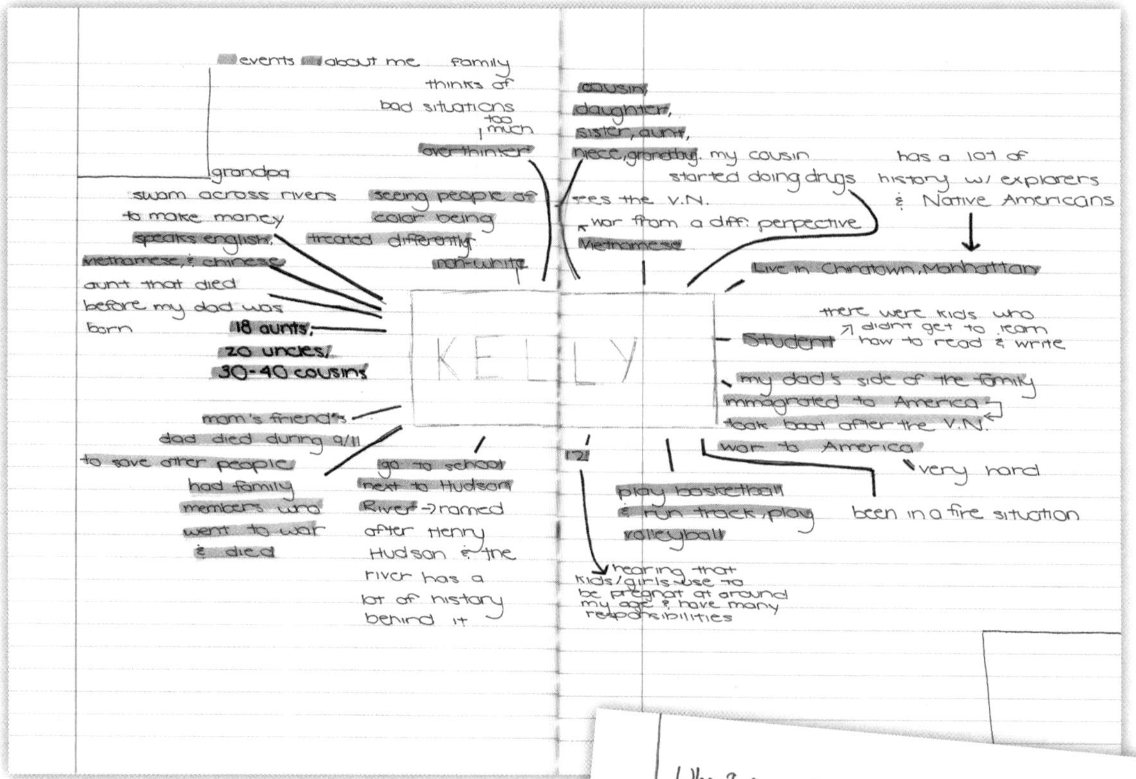

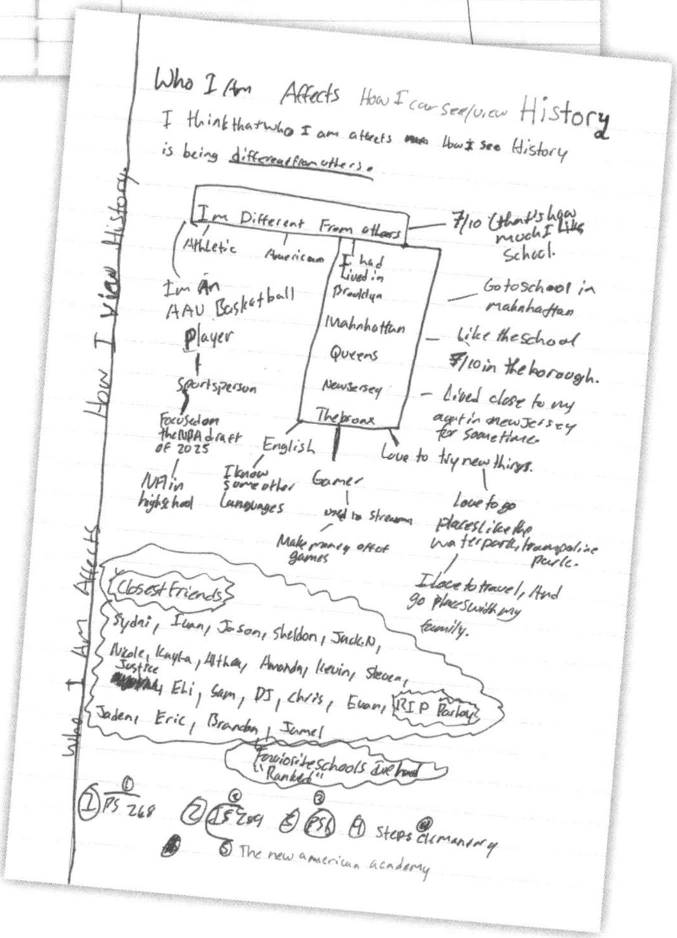

FIGURE 1.1 These seventh graders explore what makes them who they are, or at least, the parts that are on their mind and that they want to think about and share right now. Kelly (top left) names her Vietnamese heritage and growing up in Chinatown. Dayvon (bottom left), a Black student, thinks about being different from others in his current school, and he ranks the five schools he has gone to in terms of belonging. Lucy (top right), a white student, reflects on being an LGBTQIA+ activist. Arnaud (bottom right) reflects on his white male privilege. These students express the parts of their identities that are on their mind, that they are willing to share, and that they have language for, as they prepare to consider how their identity might shape how they view history. Kids may translanguage, or use multiple languages together, in this work and in their conversations. Give kids explicit permission to do so, as sometimes these conversations, which are nuanced, need to be in the language that allows for nuance.

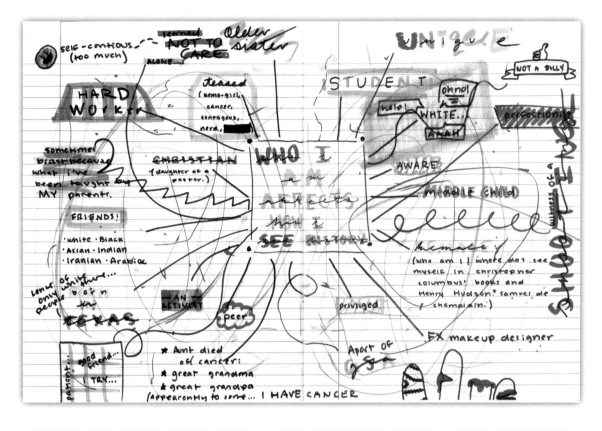

right, is our "Virtual Selves," the social media image we create of ourselves and post out in the world for others to see. The branches, leaves, and sky represent our own hopes and dreams for the future as well as legacies and changes we want to see in the world.

You'll see in Figure 1.2 that kids are cautious about what they choose to share and not share, reveal and cover. Their maps and trees, because they are made in school, are a way to recreate themselves as well as to reflect.

When you invite kids to do any kind of identity mapping, your modeling, your risk, and your own show of trust matter. You can make deliberate decisions about both what you reveal and the pacing of what you reveal, in a kind of rolling demo. You can also adjust your language depending on both the age of the kids and the work you've done or have not yet started on racial consciousness and other identity language. When Mary models, for instance, she might start with words, such as *reader*, *introvert*, or *white*, and only later add *bi, first-generation middle class*, or *secretive family*.

Through our own modeling, we can set classroom norms. When a cisgender educator simply names "cisgender" as part of their identity, it normalizes naming one's gender identity and de-centers cisgender identities. Of course, you can roll out the parts you share over time, and the language you use to describe those parts, as kids will as well. The main thing is that we don't want to leave all the risk to kids or to make some identities invisible.

If you look at some of the initial identity trees from Marc's classroom (Figure 1.3), you'll see that even as they open up parts of themselves to share, students are initially cautious about race, ethnicity, and religion. Often kids begin with things that they simply like, like soccer, which is slightly different than identifying as "I am a soccer player." Our colleague Sonja Cherry-Paul notes that while likes and favorites can be important to kids, it is our social identities that have greater impact on our worldview. For example, enjoying soccer will influence a person's point of view on some things, but it doesn't have the same impact as a person's racial, gender, or sexual identity on their world view or interactions with the world. We've found that starting with accessible points and moving gradually to social identity markers, can be helpful. In Marc's demonstration below, you can see that he started with identifiers, such as *NYU, New School, Columbia, and Teacher, Strict, Funny,* and then he began to layer in *Queer, White, Old.*

Our aim in this work is not to dare (or require!) students to share aspects of themselves that they do not want to share. It is to help students to begin to think about and affirm aspects of their identities. This work is effective even if not all of students' thinking makes its way onto the page.

Doing identity work can be used later in the year to coach students into connections not only with their classmates but also with historical figures, people involved in today's current events, journalists, and authors. You can coach students to ask

EDUCATOR SPOTLIGHT

Mary tried this work for the first time during reading in a classroom at PS 40 on the Lower East Side of Manhattan. She used sticky notes to jot down different parts of her identity in fourth grade (the same age as the students in front of her) that she felt were coming up as she was reading *Harry Potter.* She began by jotting *younger sister, struggled with popularity and fitting in, pressure to achieve,* and *over-achiever.* As she spoke and kids began to nod, exclaim, and write their own words, she described and added, *wished I were an only child.* Then she said, "and this one I think I want to keep secret right now," as she wrote the secret on a sticky note, which she then folded over. Kids were soon doing the same.

Then Mary made an unplanned decision about how much racially conscious language she'd teach in that one setting. In response to the work of kids and other teachers in the room, Mary said, "Oh, I see some of you are adding in race and culture and religion." The kids weren't yet, really; only the teachers were. Mary wanted to get to this, and so she said, "I should do that." She added, *white,* at which point a fourth grader said, "You're not white, you're pink with spots, like a giraffe." Kids began to add *brown* and *black* and *pink.* Sometimes what we mean by color and what kids mean is not precisely the same. Unsure whether to sidetrack into a minilecture on race versus skin color, and remembering that Cornelius Minor had warned her that this work could leave you reeling and unsure, Mary decided to add both *white* and *pink and spotted.*

Mary moved from this initial identity exploration to a digital read-aloud. Posing these critical lenses, she told kids to hold their maps on their laps and ask themselves: "Who do I sympathize with?" "Who do I admire?" and "Why?" The class then watched *The Supporting Act,* a narrative about a young girl who wants to dance and her single-parent father who seems to ignore her as he struggles with his own work. Pausing in the midst of this work for partner-talk, kids began to add to their identity work, as did Mary. She added in *latchkey-kid* and explained it. Kids added to their maps and began to talk about how and why they sympathized with one character or another. At the end of the story, Mary posed new critical lenses, suggesting that kids ask, "Who do we struggle to connect with?" "Who is invisible to us?" "How can we reread to open ourselves up to other perspectives?" Kids watched the story again, and one girl said, "I think I'm too hard on my mother. I need to be more supportive of her." Another said, "Maybe there are different ways to love someone." And all along, the kids were quietly adding to their maps, looking at them, talking about them. In Figure 1.2, you can see Mary's final map from the fourth-grade classroom and, later that day, from a seventh-grade classroom. It turns out that adjusting our identity mapping to the grade level we are teaching can be generative.

FIGURE 1.2

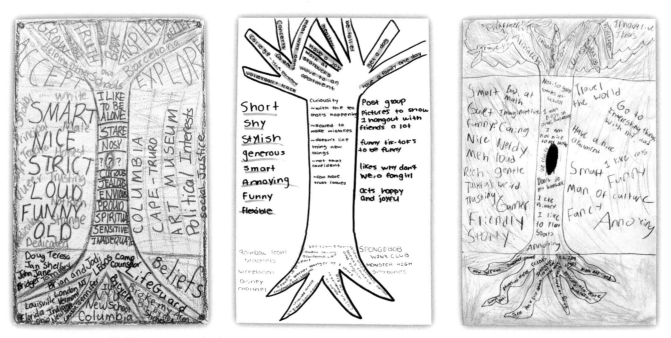

FIGURE 1.3 Marc's identity tree sets the stage for students to consider their own roots and branches of their lived and virtual selves. Be prepared for kids, at first, to share only the parts that they actually want others to see. As they map their own identities, they are also sculpting them.

themselves, "How does my shared identity with this person affect my response to this situation or text?" or "How can I better understand this situation or text by considering this other person's identity?"

Writing Creatively to Name Our Identities

In September 2001, in a small school blocks away from the World Trade Center, PS 126, experienced sixth-grade teacher Karen Lowe taught her new staff developer colleague, Mary, about how she began her humanities studies for the year by first exploring students' own identities in poetry, particularly in "I am" poems, inspired by George Ella Lyon's poem "Where I'm From" (see Figure 1.4). In the decades since the poem's publication, "Where I'm From" has become synonymous with explorations of identity, so much so that the author has even invited others to write their own "Where I'm From" poems on her website and as part of the I Am From Project (2018). There is a beautiful chapter in Carla España and Luz Yadira Herrera's book, *En Comunidad: Lessons for Centering the Voices and Experiences of Bilingual Latinx Students* (2020), called "Hearing and Sharing Personal Narratives / Mi Origen," which describes the work of writing stories about our family and cultural origins, including the intersectional connectivity of those origins. Other poets and spoken word artists have added to the "Where I'm From" and identity poem and story genres, gifting us with mentor texts with possibilities for mirroring students' racial and cultural identities. Some of our favorites are Daniel Beaty's "Knock Knock" (2010), and Warsan Shire's "Home" (2017), both of which are available on YouTube as video performances.

This work explores and affirms kids' identities, reveals sides of themselves that might never otherwise emerge, and reminds students and teachers that, as they are about to embark on a study of human culture in the literacy curriculum or human history in the social studies curriculum, the kids are the curriculum, too.

As your students produce this work, make sure to devote precious wall space or digital space to it when kids want to share. Bulletin boards, closet doors, extra whiteboard space, websites, padlets, classroom blogs can become galleries of your students' lives, a daily reminder to them that you value who they are and the individual beauty they each bring to this world.

Contemporary Identity Poems, Poets, and Spoken Word Performances

Daniel Beaty, "Knock-Knock" (2010)

Warsan Shire, "Home" (2017)

Noah St. John, "The Last Mile" (2012)

Zora Howard, "Bi-Racial Hair" (2013)

Mayda del Valle, "Tongue Tactics" (2009)

Belissa Escoloedo, Zariya Allen, Rhiannon McGavin, (Brave New Voices) "Somewhere in America" (2014)

Elizabeth Acevedo, "Afro-Latina" (2015)

Kobe Bryant, *Dear Basketball* (2015)

I am

the chocolate in the twix bar
the cookie crunch in the oreo cookie
not the creamy center
I am
B-ball and yoga and
books hidden under my bed
I am
not 'ho' or 'yo' or anything else
the boys in my neighborhood
call the girls they think are easy
girls who go with them to be somebody
I am somebody already

Imani

I am Alani
I am black like a berry
black like the night
I am Haiti
I am not AIDS
or hunger
or knives in the streets
I am pink flowers hanging over stone walls
I am women singing love songs
standing thigh-deep in cool water
In my heart I am a little island
where the blue waves break on white sand
I am so lost here
I thought Manhattan was an island
but I cannot find the sea
I thought there would be people like me
but I cannot find them

I am Alani,
black as a berry Alani
from Haiti

FIGURE 1.4 In 2001, sixth grade classmates Imani and Alani explore their own identities before embarking on the study of hierarchies, social stations, and gender in social studies.

Introduce the Concept of Implicit Bias

It may seem abrupt to turn from the joy of celebrating identity to the introduction of the concept of bias, but we include these ideas in the same chapter because in many ways they are two sides of the same coin. We exist at the intersection of many cultures and groups and it is their interplay that helps us define our loves, our passions, where we find beauty, and how we express happiness. These cultures, however, also inform the biases that we have about those who exist outside of our cultures: we and our students are all conduits of those biases and suffer from them in unequal measures. As Ibram X. Kendi notes in *Stamped from the Beginning* (2016), we are all inadvertently racist—and classist and sexist and homophobic—because the very air we breathe is infused with historical and current racism. We are embedded in a society in which oppression around race, gender, class, and sexual orientation is endemic.

The goal of this work is not that students (or teachers) divulge or confess biases publicly, but that they become aware of and interrupt the biases at work inside their own heads. Our minds create stereotypes as mental shortcuts in order to make quick judgments and navigate through life without being overwhelmed. However, these shortcuts need to be interrogated regularly so that we do not sacrifice the individual identity of the person in front of us to the generalizations our life experiences have fed us. Yet even doing this work internally asks students to be extraordinarily vulnerable. You might consider smaller groupings as kids try out this work. Partnerships, especially choice partnerships, where students are able to work with someone they are comfortable with, are more intimate and safer than larger groups or ones the teacher chooses.

We can also model how we interrogate our own biases. When we are the first to say, "Oh, my gosh, my response to that was racist," or "Thank you for pointing out that that was racist," (not, "could be perceived as racist," and not "hurtful,"), we model an openness to interrogating our own biases. This is especially important for white educators to bear in mind. In *White Fragility,* Robin DiAngelo says, "One of the greatest social fears for a white person is being told that something that we have said or done is racially problematic. Yet when someone lets us know that we have just done such a thing, rather than respond with gratitude and relief (after all, now that we are informed, we won't do it again), we often respond with anger and denial" (2018, 4). She goes on to say that "racism is unavoidable and that it is impossible to completely escape having developed problematic racial assumptions and behaviors." Mary can attest to many uncomfortable moments. We are so thankful for colleagues who care enough about us to address our language.

With your own admissions, help students understand that everyone has biases and that those who reflect and acknowledge their natural biases are best suited to combat them. This is a difficult concept for anyone—adult or adolescent—to accept; you'll want to carefully consider the types of activities you use and the partnership structures you put in place so that students will feel safe enough to truly reflect. They are going to be uncomfortable. That's inevitable and part of the process of awareness. Social bonds that students trust will help them move through stages of discomfort to learning. We recommend that students use notebooks as they self-assess and that they fold down pages if they want their writing to remain private. Respecting students' privacy and the emotional labor they may be involved in or protecting themselves from is important. If you have access to laptops in your classroom, you might want to begin by setting up stations devoted to implicit bias. You could have some students study the *New York Times* video "Peanut Butter, Jelly and Racism" (Reshamwala 2016) and then jot some notes on the meaning of implicit bias. Another group may explore gender bias by watching "Like a Girl" (Always 2020) and unpacking their reaction to the video. You might have one or two groups explore MTV's "Look Different" site, which has several quizzes, activities, and articles to help students identify their own biases. If you decide to include the implicit bias tests on this site, you may want to invite students' participation to be voluntary (see Young Citizens in Action, p. 20, later in this chapter). If students do use the tests, you'll want to clarify that the tests are not meant to label individuals as biased or racist. On the contrary, they are tools to help us name the implicit—and explicit—biases we have so that we can consciously combat them. The less aware we are of our biases, the more power those biases have over us. You'll want to assure your students that the discomfort they may feel is shared and that it is important to confront and question it rather than allow it to linger.

> See the online resources for a list of resources to help you study bias with your students.

The objective of engaging with any of these sites is to give students opportunities to self-reflect. A prompt like this one can get that process started:

> We've discussed how all of us have our biases and that the first way to combat them is to be aware of them. At this station you'll be watching: _____. After you've watched the video, respond to it in your notebook. As you respond, you may use the following self-reflection questions and prompts to spur your thinking. **Remember, your notebook is for your reflection only. You do not need to share what you write. If you'd like to keep these pages private, just fold down the corner.**
>
> 1. What are your initial reactions to the video? Why?
> 2. Name three things you learned from the video, two questions you still have, and one new realization about yourself that you're developing.

3. Was there anything that made you uncomfortable while you were watching the video? Explain.

(See Figure 1.5A–B for further thought prompts.)

This work on identity and implicit bias is really only an introduction. Our aim in this work is to prepare your students to read the content that lies ahead of them with an understanding that their own identity and bias may have a role in how they interpret what they are learning.

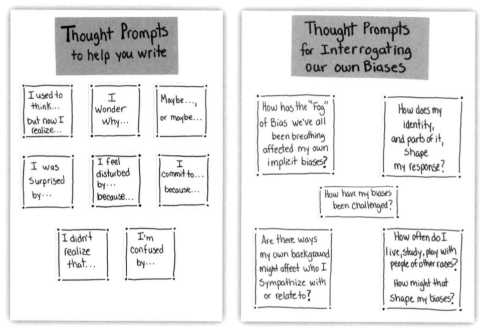

FIGURE 1.5A You might also find that students are ready for sentence starters that can help them begin to develop more critical language and self-interrogative stances—part of the process of racial socialization.

FIGURE 1.5B A posted list of prompts such as these can be adapted to use with videos, websites, and articles to spur student self-reflection. Remember to stress that the students are using these prompts to unpack their own thinking, not to complete an assignment. Coach students to think a lot and write a lot, but you need not read their pages if students don't feel ready to share.

Consider How Implicit Bias Might Affect Our Reading and Perceptions

As students become more accustomed to the productive discomfort of identifying and confronting their own biases, you can invite them to apply that new self-understanding to the topic that you are about to explore as a class. This work can be valuable at the beginning of a unit of study about a particular topic, or within the unit, as students are interacting with sources. Working through these prompts with students before diving into content related to the topic will surface some general dispositions, which can be valuable to know from the onset of the work, but students may not yet have the depth of knowledge on a topic to discuss it in detail. Considering (or reconsidering) these thought prompts in the middle of the work gives students more specifics to respond to and may help them to see if their implicit bias is affecting their research.

As with any good teaching, you'll want to model this for your students. Your students need to know that you too have biases that will affect your perception and that you will have to push yourself to think beyond your biases, just as they will. To avoid the risk of directly swaying and influencing your students' perceptions, model your answers with a different issue than what you will study as a class.

You might ask students to consider thought prompts like those in Figure 1.6.

Notice that these are *thought* prompts, not discussion prompts or mandatory writing prompts. Simply read each prompt aloud and give students a few moments to consider their own response to the prompt silently. This work is to help students consider their own thoughts, not for us to read, share, or grade. It may be powerful for students to write down their responses to these prompts and then return to them later in the unit and see how their thinking has evolved. However, in order to do this successfully, it is imperative that you remind students that their writing here is private and meant only for their own self-reflection. Again, you may want to remind students to fold down any pages not intended for your reading.

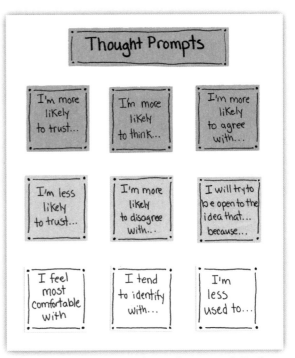

FIGURE 1.6 Exploring one's own biases is a difficult and emotional process. A list of prompts like these can help students to reflect and extend their thinking.

If we were to consider the issue of family separations at the Mexican border, for example, we might model responding to these question stems:

- I'm more likely to think . . . *that refugees from Central and South America should not be separated from their families because, first, I couldn't imagine having children taken away and, second, I know people who have come across the border as refugees and they are some of the hardest working, most honest people I know.*

● I'm more likely to trust . . . *these refugees and their personal stories.*

● I'm less likely to trust . . . *the government and its representatives because these stories put the government in a bad light and I think they'll try to make things sound better than they are.*

● I'm more likely to agree with . . . *the refugees and their families.*

● I'm more likely to disagree with . . . *the government officials.*

● I need to be open to the ideas that . . . *immigration policies need to be reconsidered or changed in our country and that allowing everyone over the border might not be the best solution . . . because . . . I feel really strongly that everyone should be let in no matter what, but I need to hear some people who think otherwise and to try to understand their point of view. I'll never agree that taking children from their families is justified, but maybe there are some reasons why immigration policies need to be changed or why people disagree on them so strongly.*

Once students are more aware of how their implicit biases are playing a role in their reading, they are better positioned to challenge them as the unit progresses. Suggestions like those in Figure 1.7 might help.

In teaching your students about implicit bias, you've not only laid the groundwork for more sophisticated reading and viewing in the unit to come, you've equipped them with an essential, if unheralded, prerequisite for civil discourse.

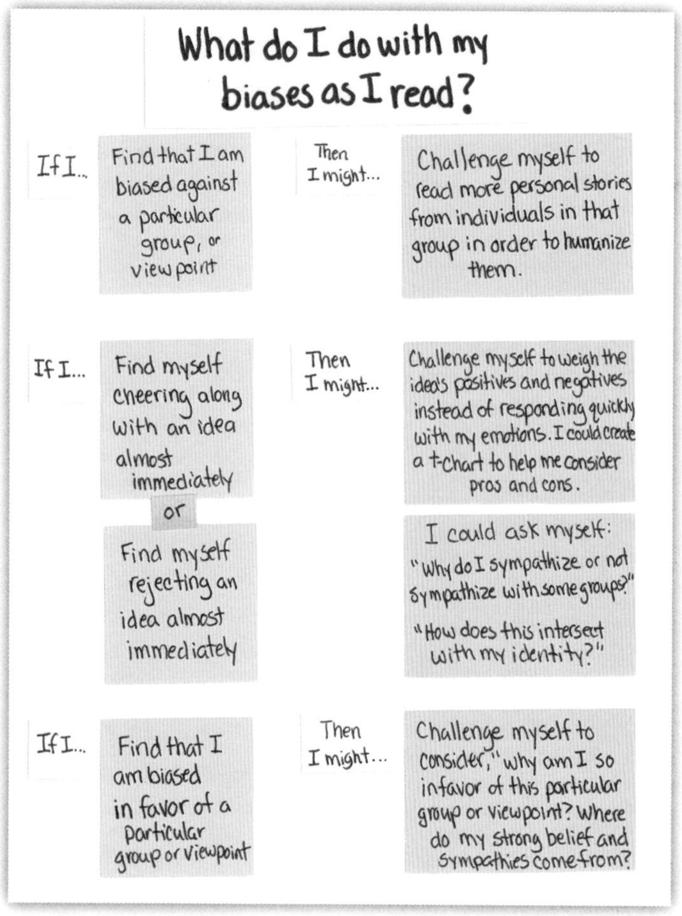

What do I do with my biases as I read?

If I... Find that I am biased against a particular group, or viewpoint

Then I might... Challenge myself to read more personal stories from individuals in that group in order to humanize them.

If I... Find myself cheering along with an idea almost immediately *or* Find myself rejecting an idea almost immediately

Then I might... Challenge myself to weigh the idea's positives and negatives instead of responding quickly with my emotions. I could create a t-chart to help me consider pros and cons.

I could ask myself: "Why do I sympathize or not sympathize with some groups?" "How does this intersect with my identity?"

If I... Find that I am biased in favor of a particular group or viewpoint

Then I might... Challenge myself to consider, "why am I so in favor of this particular group or viewpoint? Where do my strong belief and sympathies come from?"

FIGURE 1.7 It can be tremendously helpful for students to have some tools on hand that will help them monitor their own responses and coach themselves. We've found sticky notes helpful. You can make them by hand, or use printable ones.

Lesson: Building Background Knowledge

CONNECT: Remind students of the identity work that they've done in English Language Arts and/or social studies, and suggest that this work doesn't only help us to reflect on our own identities, see each other in richer, more nuanced ways, and consider how we respond to people and stories—it can also shape our interactions with history. Explain: "Our own histories, including our cultures and ethnicities, our experiences, and our sympathies and biases, will shape how we respond to history. It's worth exploring the intersection of our own histories with the history we study by asking: 'Who do I tend to sympathize with and admire? Why? Who am I uneasy about or outraged by? Why?'"

You might help students to hold on to these questions by making a chart like the one in Figure 1.8.

TEACH: Demonstrate how you might study your own identity map or chart and think about parts of it that you might extend/add to as you think about what you've been reading. For example, if you're reading about a character or historical figure, you might consider what aspects of identity (if any) you share with that person—gender, race, beliefs, interests, etc.—and whether those elements of shared identity make you more sympathetic to this person. Or, if you find that you have little in common with the person, you might consider how that may affect your sympathies. One's identity is not a map for one's beliefs or sympathies, but it is helpful to be aware of how a shared aspect of identity can affect our outlook.

FIGURE 1.8 This chart pushes the students into difficult, and likely unfamiliar, terrain. Anticipate "I don't know" responses. You might need to push students to reflect on personal experiences as they attempt to answer these questions.

ENGAGE: Invite students to consider the historical figures and perspectives that they have tended to sympathize with, or have been less sympathetic to; have them consider both what in their reading leads them to this response and what in their life experiences might lead to this response.

LAUNCH INDEPENDENT WORK TIME: Invite students to think back over what they've read and researched so far, asking themselves the questions in Figure 1.8.

Teach Kids to Be Alert to Common Biases with Bias Centers

You'll find printable pages for the Bias Centers in the online resources.

Once the initial work with implicit bias has begun, we can discuss additional biases. Bias centers can illuminate common biases and provide students with meaningful tools and resources to discuss bias, while giving students more privacy as they work independently, in trusted partnerships, or in very small groups.

For example, you might set up six bias centers—*Implicit Bias, Confirmation Bias, Anchoring Effect/Halo Effect, Selection Bias, Backfire Bias,* and *Choice-Supportive Bias*—with consistent structures (like the questions shown in Figure 1.9) to ensure an ease of use for students as they move from center to center. At each center, students preview the bias definition, preview the available sources, and read/watch the sources, pausing often to talk together about their thinking; they then try to explain the definition again by tucking in examples. In addition, students are given a sheet of specific scenarios and asked to identify what bias each scenario represents. The learning outcome is for students to discuss, understand, and distinguish types of biases.

We want students to realize that bias is all around us, it is often invisible, and it is at the root of many of the issues that matter to engaged citizens. The aim of these centers is to help students uncover their own biases and privileges, see the effects of biases in their own lives and in the world around them, and call out bias when they see it in themselves or in others.

Be prepared that this is emotional work. While all people hold biases, no one finds it easy to discover that they hold a bias. It is difficult for people of any age to be confronted with how others feel about them or to have their identity challenged and questioned. Additionally, students who have been negatively affected by others' biases in their lifetime may find that this work hits close to home. It's up to us to ensure that these students, in particular, are not made to feel responsible for educating others or for speaking for an entire group of people with a shared identity. Be alert for a shift in your students when something that was once implicit becomes explicit. With this new awareness there is also likely to be confusion, discomfort, dissonance, pain, anger, shock, stress, and shame. Let students know they learned bias in many ways without realizing it; however, they can also learn to interrogate their biases, open themselves to change, and strive to be more conscious.

FIGURE 1.9 Students can use notebooks to individually process the experience with the bias content by considering some critical questions. Creating charts or tools that document these questions helps the work live in the room and in kids' notebooks, increasing the likelihood of transfer.

Teach Kids to Be Alert to How Their Identities and Biases Affect How They Read

If we adults find the informational overload of today's society daunting in our own lives, it's even more menacing for our students, whether they realize it or not. Rahaf Harfoush has researched how a move from data scarcity to data abundance to digital intimacy has affected our society. In a talk at Teachers College, Harfoush said: "We need to teach kids how to navigate in an infinite information system, or it creates enormous stress" (2018). In *Hustle and Float: Reclaim Your Creativity and Thrive in a World Obsessed with Work*, Harfoush (2019) describes how we now have no barriers from media, from information.

Young people are consuming media at an extraordinary rate and are often largely indiscriminate with what they read, interact with, and "like" online. In doing so, they feed algorithms that continue to channel misinformation or even hate speech their way. As civically engaged educators, we have the responsibility to teach the youth in our care to question and critique the nonfiction that is fed to them, to be aware of their media intake, and to know that there are computers reading their inputs and corralling them into closed media loops.

The lesson starters that begin on page 22 offer some suggestions for how students can use their new understandings of identity and bias in their interaction with text and media as they read as engaged citizens. The work of understanding what we, as readers, bring to texts, and how media responds to us, is essential in critical reading and writing.

» YOUNG CITIZENS IN ACTION «

At IS 289, Marc and the student members of the Gender and Sexuality Association (GSA) sat together in small groups during lunch and took the Harvard Implicit Association Test (IAT). (See Figure 1.10.) No one was prepared for how emotional the work would be. The IAT begins with a series of thirteen demographic questions followed by a rapid digital questionnaire that measures automatic preferences. As students progressed through the test, gasps and outbursts punctuated the silence. "I did not mean that!" "This is a stereotype!" "This is stressful." On hearing the emotional reactions from students, Marc questioned whether diving into such work had been wise. Important work is difficult, Marc reminded himself. All he needed to do was to keep the students feeling safe and the work purposeful.

Then came the results. "I *am* homosexual. How can I be homophobic?!" one exclaimed. "I do not automatically prefer light-skinned people over dark-skinned people!" another cried out. Self-discovery, for some students, was painful. They panicked that the possibility of having unintended biases made them "horrible" people. Students, like all of us, don't want to know that we may not be who we believe ourselves to be.

To help process their experience, Marc asked the students to respond to two questions in writing:

1. Would you recommend other students take this test? Why?

2. Where do you see implicit bias at our school and what effect does it have?

Surprisingly, the answer to the first question was an overwhelming *yes*. Nearly everyone who took the IAT said that this is a test that everyone should take. One student commented that the results present an opportunity to change or grow. Another liked the idea of giving people an opportunity to realize they do have biases. Perhaps yet another student's insight said it best: "Knowing the results yourself will give you insight to change, which could prevent difficult conversations in the future." Sitting in small groups to have these discussions helped students feel safe and heard. Acknowledging their uneasiness with the results led to self-reflection. Most importantly, purposefully taking time to celebrate their courage in sharing the pain of self-discovery strengthened the community and their own resolve to continue this work.

The answer to question number 2 was insightful and determined the work the GSA would take on in the year ahead: confronting biased comments and the separation of groups of people. "Doing nothing will prolong bias," a student insisted.

FIGURE 1.10 Students work through the Implicit Association Test.

Lesson: Introducing Consciousness Time Lines to Confront Our Personal Bias Histories

CONSCIOUS-NESS TIME LINES

Watch Marc discuss the power of consciousness time lines and demonstrate how to help students set up their notebooks.

http://hein.pub/
CivicallyEngaged
Classroom

CONNECT: When you're working with a charged topic, step outside that topic for a moment. For instance, before diving into consciousness time lines around race, we can demonstrate *how* a consciousness time line works with a topic that feels safer but that still conveys emotional response. Sharks, rats, or wasps work well for this. Show, for example, some images of sharks, and ask kids to share their learning experiences around sharks with a partner by answering these questions: "What ideas and emotions do you have about sharks?" "How did you learn these? What were you taught?" Then ask them, "What experience have you had with sharks?" For those of us who are from the *Jaws* generation, no matter how many Seymour Simon books we read or Blue Planet videos we watch, no matter how much we admire these fierce and graceful creatures and want the world to protect them, they also make us anxious—all because of a horror movie. Explain: "Whenever you are researching a topic, a person, or an event, it's worth it to investigate your own prior experience with the content. Ask yourself: 'How did I learn about this? What ideas and emotions do I have on this topic? What shapes those feelings?' Often, we bring old histories, or what's called folk knowledge, to our studies, and those old histories, left unquestioned, shape our response, creating unacknowledged bias."

TEACH: Demonstrate how you might reflect on the learning experiences connected to your demonstration topic (your real one, not sharks), and how you investigate the history of those experiences. For instance, it might be that you read a novel, watched a film, or sang a song and your understanding about the topic began to take shape. It might be that you had an experience on a vacation or shared a conversation with family or friends that also added to your learning. Most importantly, show how you have to be extra careful to be conscious of evidence and perspectives that represent your content. Marc created a consciousness time line (see Figure 1.11) to help him share his experiences with his students.

ENGAGE: Invite students to reflect on their own educational experiences with the topic you are studying, and to think about when or how they were first exposed to it. You might suggest that they write for a moment in their notebook or record their experiences on separate sticky notes before sharing with a partner. It may be helpful, as you consider more charged, human topics, to think about forming affinity groups to support kids' identies as well. Have them think, as well, about films, books, songs, games that might have aided in their understanding of the topic. Arranging these experiences and influences on a time line helps students to see how their perceptions were formed.

LAUNCH INDEPENDENT WORK TIME: Send kids off to continue their research on the class topic, reminding them to be extra conscious of their history with the topic and how that might affect their reading. Caution them to think beyond their own experiences and to be on the lookout for titles, authors, and groups that might tend to misrepresent or marginalize the topic.

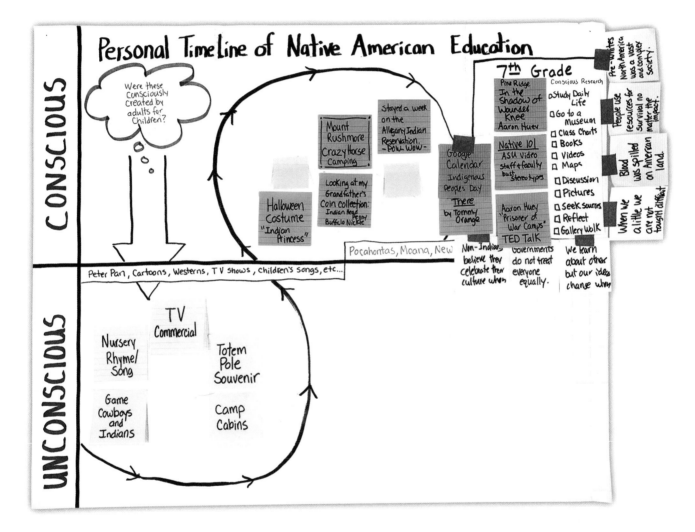

FIGURE 1.11 Marc demonstrates his consciousness time line for learning about Indigenous Peoples. The "7th Grade" box reflects discussions that Marc and his students have had together. You may find it helpful to try a consciousness time line on your own, about your own identity, as a way to be vulnerable and brave.

EXTENSION: While this approach can be a strong, quick lesson, it can also be used for a much more in-depth study of potential bias. Before embarking on a comprehensive study of North America's First Nations, Marc begins by having students jot down their initial beliefs and understandings about Indigenous Peoples—cultures that his students overwhelmingly have little firsthand knowledge of. He does not stop there, however: he pushes the students to trace the source of those beliefs to particular experiences. As the class researches more, writes more, and learns more about Indigenous Peoples, Marc has the students return to their consciousness time lines and add to them so that they can visibly track how their understanding of Indigenous Peoples' histories and cultures is evolving. (See Figures 1.12 and 1.13.)

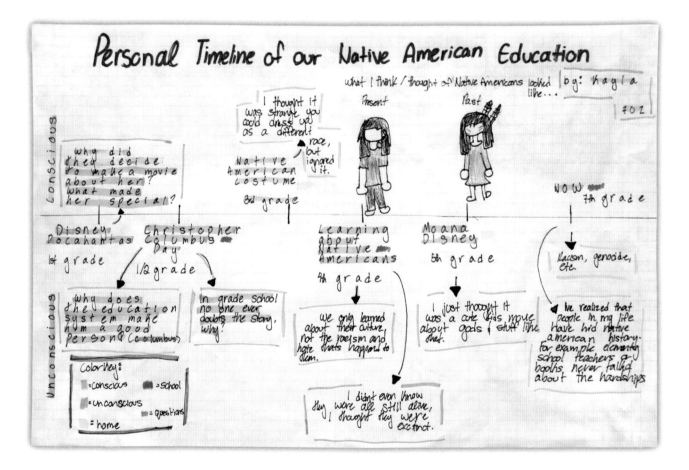

FIGURE 1.12 Looking closely at students' consciousness time lines reveals the power of popular culture in the formation of our ideas about groups of people. Disney's *Pocahontas* and *Moana*, the novel *The Indian in the Cupboard*, and the comic book *Lucky Luke*, feature prominently in students' time lines.

The regular returning to these time lines makes personal what can be abstract and cerebral reflection work. After students reflect on their time lines, they can consider when they were first aware of bias, marginalization, victimization, genocide. They can see how their perceptions of the world grow and change as they mature and as they learn.

While the topic in this example relates to cultures that are largely unknown to the students in this classroom, time lines can also be used to unpack topics that students know more about. While time lines for those topics may be denser, they offer students the same opportunities to consider how their perceptions were formed, reflect on their perspectives, and consciously decide to grow their understandings.

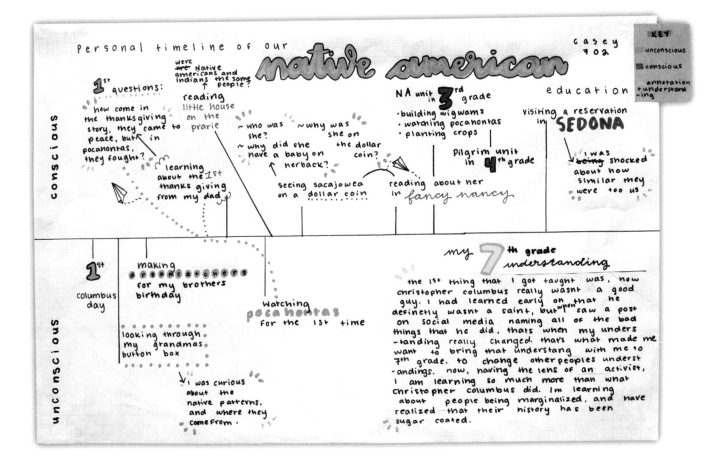

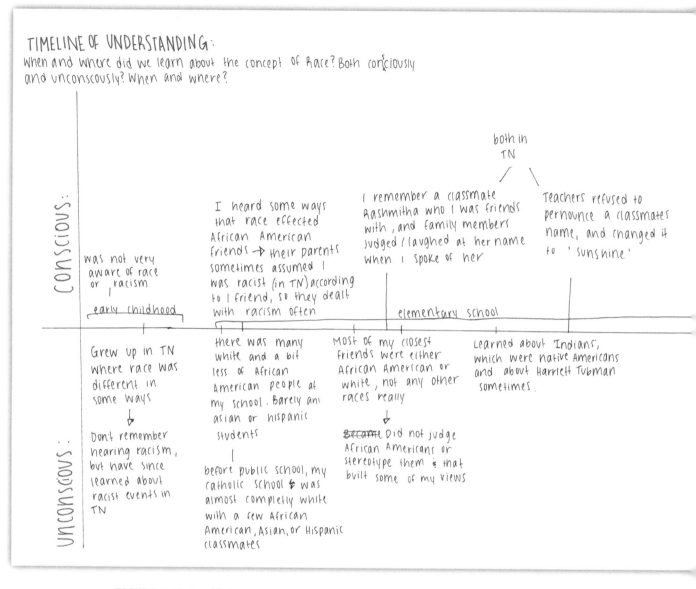

TIMELINE OF UNDERSTANDING:
When and where did we learn about the concept of Race? Both conciously and unconscously? When and where?

Conscious:

both in TN

was not very aware of race or racism

I heard some ways that race effected African American friends → their parents sometimes assumed I was racist (in TN) according to 1 friend, so they dealt with racism often

I remember a classmate Rashmitha who I was friends with, and family members judged / laughed at her name when I spoke of her

Teachers refused to pernounce a classmates name, and changed it to 'sunshine'

early childhood   elementary school

Unconscious:

Grew up in TN where race was different in some ways
↓
Don't remember hearing racism, but have since learned about racist events in TN

there was many white and a bit less of African American people at my school. Barely any asian or hispanic students

before public school, my catholic school & was almost completly white with a few African American, Asian, or Hispanic classmates

Most of my closest friends were either African American or white, not any other races really
↓
~~Became~~ Did not judge African Americans or stereotype them & that built some of my views

Learned about 'Indians', which were native Americans and about Harriett Tubman sometimes.

FIGURE 1.13 In addition, race consciousness time lines help students process the personal experiences from school and family that lead to the formation of the racial concepts we have. We've included an online collection of some student samples, as these often inspire students in any unit of study to try this work out.

when I started running on a new track team, I noticed that more African Americans were at meets than other groups → heard stereotypes & wondered if there was a reason for this

I started noticing that friend groups often consist of people who look similiar to each other & I wondered why

By 7th grade, I became more concius of the social issues involving race or the way people look
↳ stereotypes, racial targeting

8th grade was a turning point in my understanding of race :
· learned about slavery
· learned about white supremacies effects
· learned about racism, mostly towards african american people (mostly systematic racism)

teachers for the most part avoided the topic of race

school is not as diverse as it could be :
- 4% black
- 49% asian
- 30% white
- 15% hispanic
- 3% other
↓
As a result, students here are exposed more and less to certian groups of people

Have always thought of race as what people looked like on the outside & havent questions its truth → if it is real or what races really are.
|
only ever thought of racism towards african americans. I may have forgotten about other people affected by it.

Lesson: Expecting Confirmation Bias and Asking: How Can We Work Against It?

CONNECT: Explain to your students that you will be exploring a particular type of bias that we are all guilty of: confirmation bias. You might say something like: "Confirmation bias is a shortcut that our brain takes to help us make quick decisions. It focuses on information that already matches a pattern that we've seen before and ignores information that may contradict and complicate that pattern. In simple situations, confirmation bias can help us make choices efficiently, but when it comes to complicated issues like the ones we're studying, it can lead us to ignore facts that might help us see more and understand more."

Then, illustrate with a simple example. Ask your students to consider the pattern 2, 4, 8 and then create a series of numbers that follow the same rule. Your students will likely suggest something like 5, 10, 20—a pattern doubling the previous number. Explain that their brains saw a simple pattern and jumped at the simplest rule that confirmed their belief, but that unfortunately the pattern is incorrect. Invite them to try more numbers before revealing that your rule was simply any three numbers in ascending order. Facing History and Ourselves' video "Can You Solve This?" (2020) elegantly illustrates this activity, if you want to refer to it or show it instead. Explain: "It's impossible to escape confirmation bias, which is how our brain filters information and ideas, giving more significance to and remembering more of what we agree with already, and giving less importance to and tending to forget the stuff that challenges our views and beliefs. The best that we can do is to work hard to be aware of confirmation bias and then to apply rigorous questioning of our assumptions so that we can test their validity. Ethical researchers actively ask themselves: 'How am I working to confront confirmation bias?'"

TEACH AND ENGAGE: Engage students in a shared inquiry, asking: "How can we confront and resist confirmation bias in our own research?" As students talk, you can create a shared chart (or have one started that you reveal and add to) so that you end up with a collection of strategies like those in Figure 1.14.

LAUNCH INDEPENDENT WORK TIME: Invite students to work with a partner to make a quick plan for how, specifically, they will work to confront confirmation bias as they read. Will they pause to reflect as they move to a second text, asking themselves how they chose that text and why? Will they pause to think: "Did I get all I could have from the text I just read? Am I inadvertently valuing only the information that supports my views?" Then, send students off to work.

SHARE: At the end of the lesson, ask students to reflect on their research. How did they push back on their assumptions while they read today? What strategies worked for them? Ask them to share with a partner, or to jot down their process in their notebooks.

FIGURE 1.14 Confirmation bias is so automatic that students will likely need a lot of coaching in the use of the approaches suggested here. You might encourage students to discuss with each other which strategies they are using so as to become more aware of them.

Lesson: Looking Out for Filter Bubbles, Echo Chambers, and Search Engine Distortions

CONNECT: One way to engage students is to show them how, when two of you search the same terms, and you're signed into Google on your own computers, you get different results. It's illuminating. Explain: "When we use a search engine that has gathered history on our online interests, the results it gives us are shaped by our choices. Whatever kind of text you tend to choose (in terms of content, authorship, or perspective), the next time you search, you'll be shown more of those same kinds of texts. We end up, then, in danger of being trapped in an echo chamber, where we think we are researching fairly, but we constantly receive input that reinforces the views we already have. Additionally, researcher Safiya Umoja Noble (2018) has found that search engines themselves—independent of users' search histories—often offer up 'erroneous, stereotypical' results in relation to marginalized groups of people."

TEACH AND ENGAGE: Next, you might set kids to an internal inquiry, asking them to think about their major sources of information on social media, and how those might act as a bubble. If, for example, you follow a soccer team, then you'll receive mostly laudatory information about those players and the games, and denigrating information about opposing players or incidents in a game that felt unfair to your team. If you get your information about friends from a subset of social media sources, then your view is shaped only by that information.

LAUNCH INDEPENDENT WORK TIME: Before sending kids off to work, take digital anthropologist Rahaf Harfoush's advice (2018): challenge kids to think about their algorithm diets—what they see/read/watch. Suggest that we have to actively seek people, voices, and sources outside of our bubbles and beyond the results of a quick online search.

As you work through the lessons in this chapter, consider creating an anchor chart, or a place to document new learning, like the chart shown in Figure 1.15. These kinds of charts become records in the room of what's been taught. Kids can use charts as reminders to increase their agency with trying out new work.

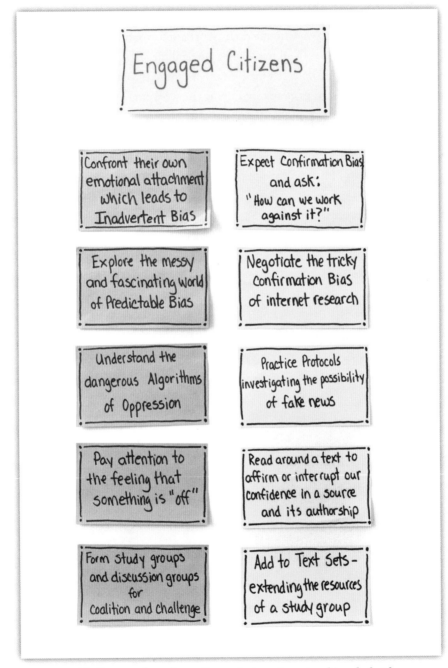

FIGURE 1.15 Create a chart that reflects what you have taught and what has resonated with your students.

Involve Families and Communities

Whenever your curriculum steps into personal matters like bias and identity, it is good practice to reach out to families in advance to inform them what to expect. Families like to hear what you are doing. And when you are stepping into sensitive matters, families also like to know why you are doing it. This information can be shared in your teaching philosophy, spoken to during a curriculum night, included in a monthly newsletter, or sent in a purposeful email. Another option is to make a quick video, perhaps with some of your students, describing the work you are taking on.

In addition, create an online resource, like a family Padlet, that has the latest research on issues affecting young adolescents. You can even include one of the Bias Centers for families to explore on their own. When you are reaching out to families, also give them questions to ask their child, such as: "What stood out to you at school today? What challenged or expanded your thinking? What act of kindness did you observe today? How were you brave today? What will you do differently for tomorrow?"

Send your students home with questions such as these to ask their family: "What is identity? What or who has been the biggest influence on your identity?" Or "How would you define hate speech? How does hate speech affect a community? Have you ever stood up to hate speech?"

Families want to have conversations. Providing questions is one way to help.

Be Ready for Anything

Discussions of identity and bias are seldom predictable. One student's comment might (intentionally or unintentionally) infringe on another's identity. An examination of biases might prompt a difficult realization. A discussion in which there is a clear majority may leave outliers marginalized. Before embarking on this work, consult with your school social worker. Share your plans and get their opinion on how to proceed responsibly with the students in your care, being mindful of their emotional well-being as well as their identities. Never put a child in the position of having to be an entire identity group's representative.

Make sure that you have a culture of mutual respect and support in your classroom. If students tend to insult each other, even jokingly, or they have trouble listening to one another, you'll want to address these classroom culture concerns before beginning any of the work of this chapter. You may need to spend extra time building relationships with students to establish your room as a safe space before you embark on work that asks them to be extraordinarily vulnerable. Consult with colleagues who are familiar with your classroom and discuss honestly whether you've set the right conditions to proceed safely for your students.

Given our fraught political moment, this work can also be potentially difficult for the parents and families of your school community. You're wading directly into the biases that are shaping our national discourse, a daunting prospect when you're doing it with adults at a dinner party, let alone with your students. Fearful parents and families may think that you've overstepped by introducing ideas that they believe should be addressed only at home, or they may feel offended that you are asking kids to question things they learned at home.

You'll find that your best preparation for the work of this chapter is to expect all of these challenges and to get ahead of them through clear, frank, and transparent conversations with your administration, your students, and their parents and families. Fourth-grade teacher Rachel Hsieh's experiences offer valuable guidance on how to handle these hard conversations head-on.

EDUCATOR SPOTLIGHT

Rachel Hsieh is a fourth-grade teacher in rural Oregon where about two thirds of her students are white. Roughly a third have recently immigrated from Latin America, and a handful are students of color who are not recent immigrants. Rachel herself identifies as Chinese American and is one of two lead teachers of color in her entire school. Over the course of the year, Rachel leads the children through discussions distinguishing between equality and fairness, dives into current events, has the students write biographies about "change-makers," and helps them draft letters to the governor about issues that concern them. She considers herself a social justice educator and has been fearless about addressing issues that her students' families might consider controversial.

Rachel is candid about her experiences tackling politically sensitive topics, explaining that she has faced parents and families who actively resist certain topics and even demand that their children be removed from the classroom when they are discussed. She offers the following suggestions:

- Write to the parents and families before a unit. Explain what you are going to study, why, and how multiple perspectives will be addressed.

- Spend a lot of time getting to know the parents and families, and establish relationships.

- Anticipate that students will ask for your opinion and consider what your response will be. Rachel often tells her kids, "You may want to know what I think, but my job is to bring you lots of facts and lots of opinions, and to give you the tools to decide what makes sense to you."

- Do the research! Rachel makes sure that she knows the varying perspectives on her topics and that her texts represent these perspectives.

- Be fully transparent. If a classroom conversation was heated, let the parents and families know before they find out through their kids.

Be patient and respectful. Consider your role as adding to the perspectives of others, rather than changing them.

Practice What You Teach

It is difficult to question one's own assumptions—first, because we are not always aware that we have them, and second, because they form an integral part of how we see and interpret the world. Once we've reflected, we have to do the hard work of constructing new schema. We cannot ask our students to take on this type of self-reflection if we haven't tried it ourselves: to do so would not only be dishonest, it would be an abdication of teacher responsibility. Exploring identity and bias in a classroom is not solely the work of our students—it is a joint journey toward creating mutual understanding. Doing this work ourselves is not simply about anticipating challenges, or even preparing us for the discomfort that children will face as they stare down their own biases, it's really about connection and laying the groundwork for sustained, honest conversations. It may be helpful for teachers to have affinity groups in this work.

Ask yourself questions from the lists that follow as you embark on this work:

Set Your Purpose

- Why am I doing this work with my students? How will it deepen and strengthen our classroom community? Why is this essential to my classroom culture?
- How do I hope to change and grow through this work?
- How will this benefit my students in their daily interactions with peers, parents, and the new folks they meet?
- How will this work help my students to be engaged citizens?
- What do I hope my students will take from this once the year is over?

Identify Yourself

- How do I identify in the world? What identity markers mean the most to my sense of self?
- How might the identity markers that mean so much to me manifest in the classroom with my students? Are they readily observable? Are they hidden?
- What have I shared about myself with my students? What have I kept to myself? If I've kept some aspects of my identity private, what's my rationale? Could we all benefit from my sharing more?
- How do my identities affect me as an engaged citizen?

Explore Student Identities

- What do I know about my students' identities?
- What biases might I have about my students?

- How do these biases affect my approach to my kids?
- How much time have I spent getting to know the students in my room individually? Where have I made the time to do this? How much of a priority is this for me? How can I make it part of my daily work?
- How can my understanding of my students' identities help me to support them as engaged citizens?

Again, we acknowledge the difficulty of taking on this work and answering these questions. It may help to have a colleague with whom you discuss your answers, someone who can challenge you to remain as honest and open about your responses as possible. After all, it is only through candor, however challenging, that we make the necessary changes to become our best selves for the particular students in our care.

CHAPTER

Civic Virtues Addressed in this Chapter

- recognizing the gaps in one's own knowledge
- caring enough to research deeply
- attending to a balance of perspectives
- looking for the complexity within a topic

Planning Your Time

Whether you're planning a one-day response to a shocking proclamation made by a political candidate; a month-long study of a historical event that continues to have reverberations in contemporary society; or an immersion into current social, political, and scientific realities, you'll find that amassing the needed background knowledge for your students to engage with the topic will generally follow in three phases:

1. building initial engagement
2. immersing, learning, and wondering
3. responding, setting plans for future research, and going deeper.

Plan your work so that the second phase—immersing, learning, and wondering—gets the largest chunk of time. Use the ideas in this chapter to curate text sets for this work and to familiarize yourself with the skills in the lessons in this chapter. If time permits, you can follow the complete arc of lessons in this chapter. If not, in the time available, focus on the skill or skills that you think students most need.

ENGAGED CITIZENS BUILD BACKGROUND KNOWLEDGE

s civically engaged teachers, we believe that citizens should be curious about the world and skeptical of simple answers. Responsible citizens are informed; their participation in society is grounded in what they have learned through wide-ranging inquiry. They are the kinds of people who search for information across as many sources as possible. They read more than one newspaper, they watch excerpts from different newscasts, they talk to neighbors and friends with varying opinions. These citizens know that there is no single source perfect enough to provide them with the depth, nuance, and complexity to match reality. As we work with the young citizens-in-training in our rooms, let's consider how we model for them the art of building the background knowledge needed to construct informed opinions.

While this work is important for kids as future citizens, it's also important for students at this moment in their academic lives: when we research kids who are doing particularly well in content classes, a few unifying characteristics pop up again and again. One is that they *already know* something about the subject. Kids who do well in science know something about science. Kids who do well in history know more than is taught in their class text. But that personal knowledge is attainable for all kids if we democratize the habit of building background knowledge rapidly and personally. Learning to do this work will help kids become more expert, quickly, in the subjects they study for school. And it will also become an internalized approach to learning about anything, which will increase the likelihood that our students will move through the world as informed, knowledgeable citizens, able to advocate for themselves and others, able to find out more about subjects that affect them, able to respond to media and news around them.

Our kids have grown up in an age like no other, one in which the world's knowledge is readily accessible to more people than ever before, and, with many students spending months engaged in virtual learning, more people than ever connected through the internet. The answers seemingly are all in our students' pockets or on their desktops, but we need to teach them how to ask the right questions and how to push themselves to look beyond what a search engine has spat out at the top of the page, or what their textbook publishers decided they should know. While our students may be accustomed to googling fact-based queries, they are often apprentices to delving deeper into inquiries to ferret out the nuance in complex issues.

To start with, let's seriously reconsider the role that textbooks (or their digital equivalents) play in this problem. When your kids graduate, they aren't going to find answers in a textbook. There is no textbook that will help you decide how to vote. There is no textbook that will teach you about activist groups that need your support, or groups who wish to curtail your rights, or your position on current issues. There is definitely no textbook that centers on groups whose histories have been marginalized or distorted, that seeks and promotes in-our-own voice authors, or that actively attempts to disrupt corruption, oppression, and privilege.

As Jason Reynolds and Ibram X. Kendi write in *Stamped: Racism, Antiracism, and You* (2020), people don't like to give up power, and the forces represented by large publishing houses that publish textbooks are no exception. There are reasons that textbooks tend to describe the history of the United States as one of individual, mostly white, men of vision and courage. Then there is the problem that novelist Chimamanda Adichie (2009) proposes of the danger of a single story: as a single source, a textbook can delve deeply only into a single perspective. And there is no textbook that can constantly update itself to keep up with our rapidly changing world. As we learned vividly in 2020, as schools closed around the world and teachers and kids pivoted to a drastically changed landscape, no textbook can ever support students in responding to contemporary breaking events that shape their experiences. Instead, we need to let go of the textbook as a valid source and the comforting fiction that everything we need can be summarized in one book. We also need to let go of the idea that text sets that we built a few years ago will be adequate today. Instead, we want to work with colleagues and our students to build a habit of reading as much as possible, all the time.

We need to teach our students not just how to keep their heads above water in the sea of information (and misinformation!) that's available to us—we need to teach them how to dive in and swim in it.

This chapter offers suggestions for helping kids to build background knowledge in response to contemporary news events, as well as at the beginning of longer, sustained units around an issue or content topic.

In this chapter we'll help you to:

- make decisions about the issues, topics, and events that your students need to study
- develop diverse text sets that you can update with contemporary knowledge—and that kids want to read
- teach kids specific strategies to build their own background knowledge
- involve families and communities
- be ready for anything
- practice what you teach.

Make Decisions About the Issues, Topics, and Events That Your Students Need to Study

With the constant churn of the news cycle and the endless reservoir of history to draw from, it can be a daunting task to decide what to devote your precious, limited classroom time to studying. When schools closed and then moved to online learning during COVID-19, many teachers pondered whether to make the pandemic itself the curriculum, with its evolving text sets of sociological and scientific data, of national and international political decisions, of communities and people faring in drastically different ways. Or would it be better to go on with the planned historical curriculum, forging connections when possible to current events?

We strongly believe that what you choose to study with your students should be shaped by your classroom community, the cultures that comprise it, the histories that shaped it, the concerns that are bubbling up within it, the outside forces that it finds itself immersed in. While you read the paper, listen to the news on the radio, or read about a historical event, consider the students in your class and how they would be shaped by what you just learned. Just before the COVID-19 crisis unfolded, we were with Sara Ahmed at Teachers College for her talk "When the World Gives You a Curriculum" (2020). Sara pointed out that in the wake of major news events, some of our students will start their day feeling a little less safe, based on their identity. At IS 289, Marc saw this immediately, as his many Asian students told of fears of how the disease would affect loved ones, and of anxiety about racist responses to the pandemic. Later, in the wake of George Floyd's murder, Brown and Black students, especially young males, expressed anxiety about their safety. Marc needed to make the political and social landscape of the pandemic and of racism an urgent part of his curriculum. As educators, we will devote time with students to historical events that we can learn from, but we can also devote time to current events that unfold around us, that are our students' own curriculum.

Below are some guiding questions to help you determine what might be worth exploring with your students. When determining topics and content to explore with students, ask yourself:

- How are my students experiencing this event, issue, or history?
- Do my students have perceptions about this event, issue, or history that should be challenged and unpacked?
- Will some of my students feel vulnerable or disempowered?
- Is there a way to shift the study so that it is more empowering for students?
- Can learning about this event, issue, or history help my students with their own identities and roles as active citizens concerned about injustice?

When evaluating the qualities of the texts that illuminate this event, issue, or history, ask yourself:

- Are the texts comprehensible for the age and reading levels of my students?
- Are there texts representing diverse perspectives, particularly underrepresented voices?
- Are the texts that represent minority groups written by authors who identify as members of those groups?
- Can I find a range of modalities (print, digital) to engage students?

When determining the importance of a particular event, issue, or history for your students, ask yourself:

- Are my students' lives affected by this topic in deeply relevant ways?
- Will knowledge of this event or issue shed light on some aspect of my students' contemporary reality?
- Will knowledge of this event or issue broaden my students' perspectives and/or inspire them to new insights and activism?

No matter how much time you have to devote to this work directly, the goal is to hook the students by stoking their natural curiosity and hunger for justice, not to drown them in lectures and facts. As you plan your one-day lesson, mini-unit, or full-length unit, you'll want to budget time for the students to immerse themselves in the topic through engaging and accessible texts that focus on compelling narratives.

Develop Diverse Text Sets That You Can Revise for Current Knowledge—and That Kids Want To Read

FIGURE 2.1 Consider these options as you build sets that guarantee greater access for your learners.

When you make the ethical decision to move away from textbooks or text packets you've used for many years, you create a gap in your classroom resources. Suddenly, you're faced with the question, "What will kids read?" We believe strongly in the power of curated, current text sets. These are text sets, initially created by teachers, that kids can add to as their knowledge of a topic grows. The goal is to get into play several copies of multiple texts that seem especially appealing and accessible. We'll begin by looking at how to create sets from predominantly online sources, which will be essential when exploring contemporary topics and issues. Then we'll look at how to get trade books into students' hands for longer, in-depth study of historical events—and to study with critical literacies. You'll want your students to have *both* experiences in your classroom. The immediacy, cost-effectiveness, and limitless

» YOUNG CITIZENS IN ACTION «

Intermediate School 289 in lower Manhattan offers its seventh graders a unique opportunity: to write and produce an opera on a topic that reflects the students' study of the Constitution and Constitutional law. The students decide on the focus, conduct research, write the narrative, compose the music, design the sets, and produce the drama, with support from Marc, who teaches at IS 289, and Gordon Ostrowski, a local theater expert who volunteers his time to help students promote their social justice agenda.

In 2018, in the wake of the Pulse shooting in Orlando and other high-profile acts of oppression and violence against queer and trans young people, the seventh grade decided to take up transgender acceptance. They researched barriers to acceptance, read interviews and studies, listened to transgender people describe their transition and the challenges to acceptance. Then they wrote their opera. Families, students, and community members—many of whom feel differently than the seventh graders about this issue—came to see the seventh grade enact the story of a young person seeking acceptance in a new community.

When the audience of family and community members, as well as the grades 3–5 students in the elementary school below IS 289, came to the opera, most of the audience that came knew in advance the subject matter. (And Marc cautions that if you tackle this kind of work, it's important for your student public-relations group not only to advertise the event but also to hint at the content.) The adult population that came to watch this opera probably had a lot more misgivings than the student population did. But they came and sat in awe not because of the controversial content but because the young adolescents were able to take an informed stance and make their own interpretation public.

The opera's theme of acceptance also became a lens through which the students viewed early US History. As students identified outsiders in history and considered the structures designed to keep them on the outside, they not only found parallels to the oppression that trans people face in our society today but also identified structures in their own lives that have marked them or others as outsiders.

expanse of resources online can be balanced by the quality-controlled, carefully edited books that are published especially for young readers. There is also something profoundly beautiful about seeing kids fall in love with book-length nonfiction. In their unit of study, *Literary Nonfiction*, Audra Robb and Katie Clements showed that, when you give kids access to books like *The 57 Bus* and *Hidden Figures*, they will read long, dense nonfiction.

When you're building text sets, think about not just adding to kids' knowledge but disrupting their thinking as well. In *Disrupting Thinking*, Kylene Beers and Robert E. Probst (2017) suggest that it's not only okay for kids to struggle with texts—it's important: they *need* to read texts that challenge their thinking. That means texts that sit outside their comfort zone, in terms of the points of view and information they encounter. Tricia Ebarvia, cofounder of #DisruptTexts, also reminds us to consider the authorship of texts to ensure that students are reading #OwnVoices texts. The notion of access to noncanonical texts is just as important in nonfiction as it is in fiction.

Creating Online Text Sets in Response to Contemporary Issues and Current Events

The idea of building background knowledge can call to mind images of lectures and of long, required reading lists. Since the kinds of vital issues and topics we engage are multifaceted and complex, aren't we responsible for ensuring that our students understand them as completely as possible before they begin?

In a word, no. Our goal in this work is to teach students how to become better readers of their own world. If we insist on spoon-feeding information—even important information—we are not helping students develop the autonomy that we eventually want them to have as informed citizens. We also run the risk of turning an important issue into something they find boring because we have over-controlled access to knowledge.

Our suggestion to you is that rather than launching a study of a topic with an information "dump" in the form of a lecture or a single text, you instead pique kids' curiosity about a topic. Launch quickly, then give kids the time and resources to immerse themselves in a topic by reading fast and furiously. When we say "read" we mean *devour*. When we say "resources" we mean any combination of print and digital texts that will serve as a starter set for kids so they can synthesize, compare, and layer knowledge rapidly. If this kind of energetic, student-authored research is new to you, we highly recommend Chris Lehman's *Energizing Research Reading and Writing* (2012). It's a fabulous introduction to getting kids interested in research, and to essential research skills.

Our aim here is to teach kids to rapidly figure out the lay of the land, the terrain of a topic. We let go of perfect understanding of any one text (an impossibility anyway) for deeper understanding of the complexity of a topic. This teaches a skill that will serve students well throughout their lives: to learn about something new, you must first dive in and learn its terrain. If you are engaging in a deep unit of study, students will find more information about the parts they are most curious about and invested in when they have the opportunity and resources to narrow their research.

To begin formulating a text set, you'll want to do a little text set mapping to help you plan. It helps ensure that you consider the complexity of an issue, topic, or event and that you find texts that serve a variety of purposes. Figure 2.2A shows facets of the topic to consider as you research. Figure 2.2B shows what a text set map might look like for the issue of *Family separations at the US–Mexico border in 2019–20.*

It is important at this point that we include multiple perspectives on the issue, even if we don't necessarily agree with all of them. In the case of family separations at the border, for example, even if our own sympathies are with the families, we need to include some texts that offer explanations of this event from the executive branch's perspective. We do this because it's crucial that we teach students that

TEXT SET MAPPING

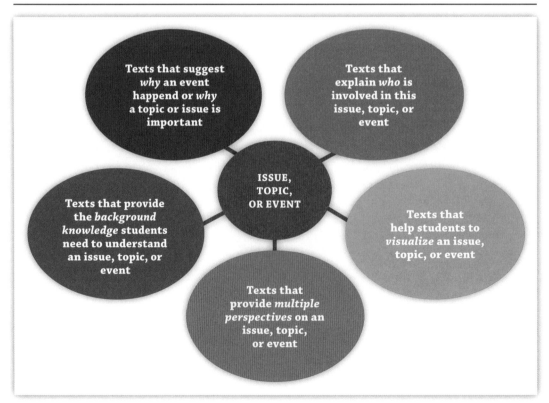

FIGURE 2.2A A "text set map" can help you consider the balance of texts that you are putting in front of your students.

people do things for reasons, and it's important to understand those reasons in order to understand all sides. Understanding others' stances also helps you to fight back more effectively against injustice.

At this point in the research process, we suggest that you avoid including flawed, biased, and distorted news sources in a curated text set—you can add those in later when you are explicitly teaching how to recognize and deal with them. We can layer texts strategically—introducing a curated text set to begin, then gradually adding to that text set as students learn more discerning evaluative skills. Chapter 3 discusses this in greater detail.

Using Accessible Texts and Increasing Access to Challenging Texts

Your search for texts from a wide variety of voices on contentious issues will undoubtedly lead you to some complex texts. In some cases, this might not be a tremendous hurdle: as Alfred Tatum describes in *Teaching Reading to Black Adolescent Males* (2005), high engagement and personal relevance will greatly help students tackle the challenges

Sharing Digital Texts

Options for how to make a digital text set available to students are constantly evolving. As of the writing of this book, we tend to use Padlet™ (www.padlet.com), an intuitive digital archive website that allows us to organize weblinks, PDFs, videos, etc., in a compelling visual format, and GoogleSites or GoogleDrive. Creating a digital archive, instead of simply creating a list of links, makes it easy for students to preview and access the resources you've curated—and because it is so visually compelling, kids are more engaged with sources. Your school or district does need to get a subscription if you want to use these apps often. Good digital archives also set you up well for virtual learning, when needed.

A SAMPLE TEXT SET: FAMILY SEPARATIONS AT THE U.S./MEXICO BORDER IN 2019–20

FIGURE 2.2B A sample "text set map."

EDUCATOR SPOTLIGHT

Taylor Bingle was teaching IB History in a classroom of kids with many home languages, when one of his students came to him with a concern about an assignment. Taylor explains: "Nico came to me overwhelmed and confused. He was visibly tired and worried. His major concern was that there was 'nothing written' on his topic, a military junta in Argentina that began in 1976. I was sure that he was mistaken as there is extensive scholarship online and in our classroom books. However, he explained that it wasn't a lack of content coverage; rather, it was a lack of relevant material to answer his research question, which was asking about the extent to which human rights violations contributed to the downfall of the regime. I remember asking him if he had researched in Spanish, to which he responded, 'Can we do that?' I sort of laughed with him, but deep down I took this as an opportunity to reflect on the importance of encouraging students to research in their native language or in a second language they possess. Even by the end of that class period, his body language changed. He was astonished at the amount of material online in Spanish. This led him to wonder how many books there might be that were written in Spanish about the topic, which led him to visit his grandparents, ex-Argentine patriots (who had fled the junta's repression). I'll never forget how proud he was coming into class one day with a stack of seven or eight books. Old, dusty, and smelly! His confidence had been restored, and even better, this was an example for students who spoke Italian, Hebrew, Catalan, Spanish, German, and French to begin researching their topics in other languages. I remember hearing students reflecting with each other saying things like, 'I didn't know we could research in another language.'"

See the online resources for Nico's essay and, most importantly, his reflection on the final page, describing how his attitude toward research changed when he began to research in his home language.

Websites to Help You Create Balanced Digital Text Sets About Contemporary Events

AllSides (www.allsides.com): site that provides links to trusted news sources from across the political spectrum

The News Literacy Project (https://newslit.org): national education nonprofit that provides nonpartisan programs teaching students how to navigate news in our digital era

CNN 10 (www.cnn.com/cnn10): condensed news digests that succinctly summarize the major news stories of the day. Helpful for getting a quick synopsis of an issue or event

The New York Times Learning Network (www.nytimes.com/section/learning): lesson plans, activities and suggestions for how to bring current events into the classroom

Above the Noise (www.pbslearningmedia.org/collection/above-the-noise-collection): PBS series aimed at young people that explains current-events issues

Teen News Sources: Jr. Scholastic, Upfront, Sports Illustrated (for kids and adult), KidsPost, Teen Vogue, Newsela

of texts that may be above their independent reading levels. Additionally, tackling tough texts with support from you helps students to view reading as an opportunity to forge their own paths in research, not simply to accept a watered-down summarization. However, you never want to assume that kids can read a text or to leave kids floundering at frustration levels. There is still much you can do to increase access to the texts kids want to read. You might:

- offer a text introduction by highlighting some of the big ideas, showing how the text is structured, getting kids started
- read portions of texts aloud to your students
- encourage students to read more accessible texts first, before shifting to more difficult ones
- have students read in partnerships so they have a processing partner to coauthor understanding
- have students read with the assistance of a text-to-speech program
- include video documentaries and interviews as well as a variety of digital texts.

If you are reading current news, you may also consider using websites, such as Newsela (Newsela.com), that take content from other publishers and edit them for varying levels of text complexity. Newsela can be a helpful resource for building text sets and for adjusting the level of those sets to match your students' reading levels; however, sometimes the "text compacting" that happens in making a text easier can lead to oversimplification in ways that can be problematic. Consider carefully before sharing such a text with students; the easier-level texts may underrepresent complexity, limit perspectives, or even include stereotypes.

Look at your starter text set. Ask yourself:

- Will all of my students have access to this subject matter in ways that grab their attention and stimulate their curiosity? Do I need more texts geared to novice readers? Do I need more texts for highly proficient or expert readers?
- Where are there gaps in my set, especially in terms of perspective? Are there perspectives that I haven't considered?
- Have I been fair to sides I might disagree with but that represent the spectrum of people's views?
- Did I provide enough visual support for my students so that they can make abstract subject matter tangible?
- Do my texts provide enough narrative to grab the attention of my readers? Are their hearts going to be as stimulated as their heads?
- Have I made it clear that students can research in multiple languages?
- Do any of these texts involve serious, ugly moments in history or current events that might create emotional labor or even trauma for students who

have been oppressed? If so, what am I going to do to ensure those students' well-being? (If you can't answer the second question, rethink using the texts.)

You'll want your background starter text set to hew towards narrative reporting—photojournalism, documentaries, and in-depth first-person reports. In *Minds Made for Stories*, Tom Newkirk (2014) describes how the human mind is drawn to stories. We make sense of our lives and the world around us through story. Compelling stories are much more likely to grab your readers than a bar graph, or a list of facts. You'll also want to be alert to the potential effects of the texts on your students. As you look across the texts in a set, think about how the texts may intersect with vulnerable students' identities and consider how you'll offer students the choice to write quietly, to *not* discuss in a large group, or to speak quietly with a friend or adult. Consider, as well, if you've included enough texts that offer narratives of strength, of hope, of change, of sustaining forces. Our aim isn't to take an ugly history and make it less ugly—that would be disrespectful of the human suffering of the people involved. But we can include the voices of young citizens and adult leaders, of groups and organizations, who rise up.

Giving Kids a Tool for Using Primary Sources

When viewing primary sources, such as images, sometimes kids are initially engaged, but they need support going deeper in their interactions with visual texts. You may want to guide students on how to use a note-taking tool like this one provided by the Library of Congress (see Figure 2.3). You don't need to copy this exact tool for them! Instead, show it to students as an exemplar and suggest they might set up their notebook in similar ways.

Along with powerful images, you'll want to share articles that are threaded through with narratives. Consider how Liz Goodwin of *The Boston Globe* begins an article titled "'Children are Being Used as a Tool' in Trump's Effort to Stop Border Crossings":

> *McALLEN, Texas*—Every night before bed, Wil, who is 6 years old, says his prayers and then kisses two printed-out photos of his mom and dad that are taped on the wall by his bed goodnight.
>
> A few hours later, he's likely to wander out of his bunk bed and stand outside the door of his foster parents' room, crying and saying his stomach hurts.
>
> His foster parents, Coryn and Silas—who asked to be identified only by their first names to protect the privacy of the immigrant children staying in their Michigan home—try their best to comfort him. You're safe now, they tell him. But Wil's anxiety remains.

"You can't take away that they miss their family," Silas said. "They miss their parents."

US Border Patrol agents separated Wil from his father six months ago, after the pair made the long journey from violence-torn Honduras to the US border in Arizona, attempting to claim asylum there. Within days of arriving in the United States, Wil watched as his father was taken away in handcuffs, joining a long line of other chained men. That, according to his foster parents, was the last time he saw his dad. (2018)

Narratives do more than arouse academic curiosity; they draw you into the story. You may choose to stop your reading of this piece here and invite students to turn and talk, asking them to share how the piece makes them feel, as well as what questions they still have. You might ask them to record these questions in their notebooks and to revisit them as you continue reading the piece, or you might stop there and tell them that the rest of the story is included in their folders.

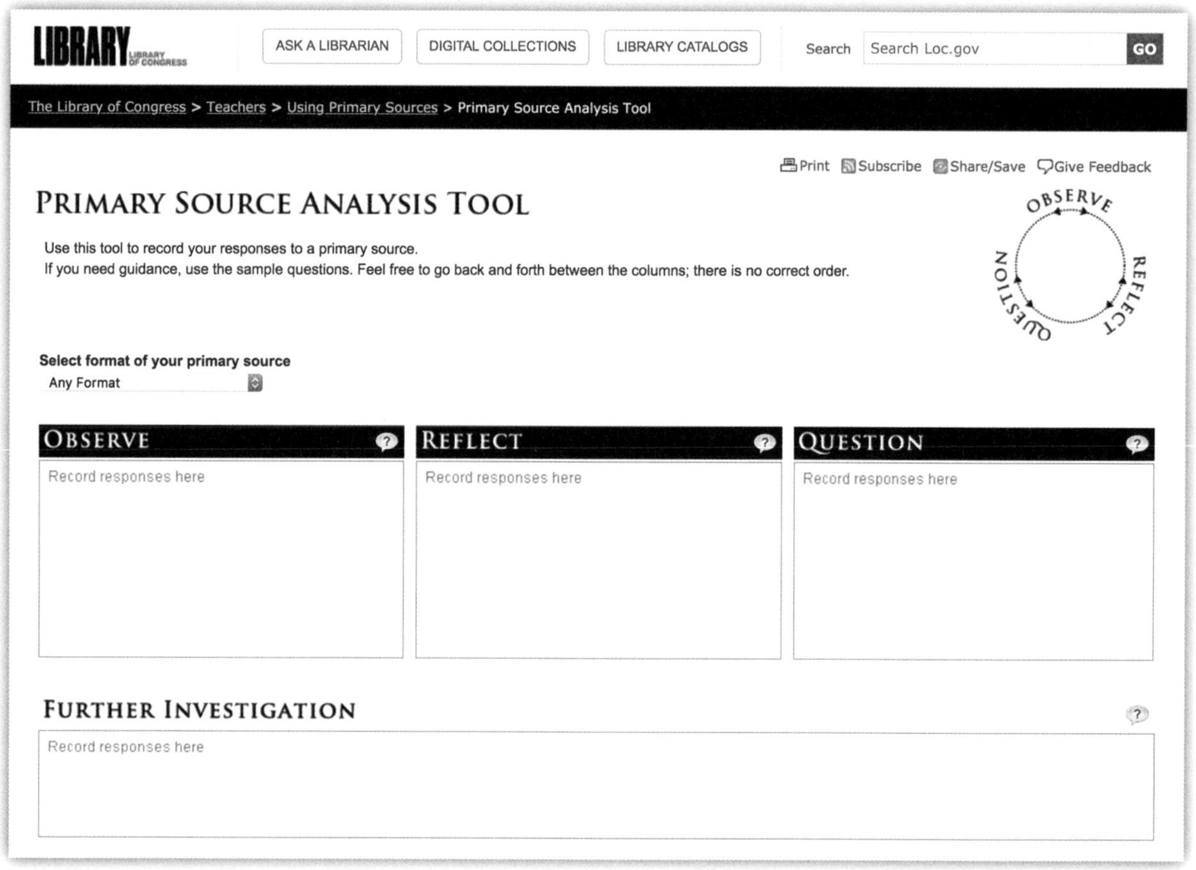

FIGURE 2.3 Graphic organizers like these can inspire students to collect and order their thoughts.

Creating Rich Nonfiction Content Libraries for Extended, In-Depth Units

When studying a historical topic or a complex issue that is at the core of your curriculum and that you would like to return to year after year, consider using some of your book budget to develop a rich subject-specific classroom library. While the internet can certainly provide a lot of information for your students, the experience of spreading out books across your tables and interacting with them directly makes learning tangible for students—they often read more, and read more quickly, when they can dive into engaging books. Publishing geared at teen readers has exploded in the last decade and high-quality books written by accomplished authors abound.

We are also fortunate to live in a time when more and more publications oriented toward adult-level readers are creating high-quality spin-offs for younger audiences. Physical and online subscriptions to journals like *Jr. Scholastic, Scholastic News, Upfront Magazine, Sports Illustrated for Kids, Teen Vogue, PostKids,* and *Latinita,* provide a tremendous range of high-quality journalism that tackles urgent social and political topics significant for kids, from taking a knee, to gun violence, to child labor, to climate change. Whenever possible, we want to surround our students with the physical evidence of our study. A varied and rich classroom library is an important part of this immersion.

The first question that's likely to come to mind about building physical text sets is how to pay for them. One way is to ask for part of the budget for books in your building to be dedicated to creating collections of accessible print texts for your major content studies. Textbook adoptions cost a fortune: suggest that you would like to take the money that would be spent on textbooks and put it into high-quality trade books. You may also consider borrowing texts from the local library. Many libraries offer special teacher library cards that allow you to borrow as many books as you need, for as long as you need. If the thought of carting over a hundred books to your school is too daunting, ask your students to borrow books from the library themselves and to label them with their names on sticky notes in the inside covers. Keep these borrowed texts on your shelves until the end of your unit.

Next, decide what texts to include in the set. Rely on your own experience, to be sure, but don't be hesitant about asking for the input of others as well. Your librarians may be a great help in identifying texts. Additionally, teacher-dedicated bookstores and book wholesalers, such as Bank Street Bookstore and Booksource, can help you find trade books that represent multiple levels and perspectives. We are particular fans of Booksource's online *Advanced Search* (see Figure 2.4), which allows you to search by reading level and interest level in addition to subject.

As with the text sets we mentioned earlier, you'll want to be careful to add in lots of easier texts that offer access to the subject for novice readers. In *What Really Mat-*

ters for Struggling Readers, Richard Allington (2012) reminds us that most kids read nonfiction about two levels below the level they read fiction. Let kids know that no text is too easy when beginning to build background knowledge, and that even books for young children can help us grasp initial concepts, vocabulary, the gist of historical events.

In any of these text sets, print or digital, strive to include texts with multiple viewpoints and by authors of color. Including a variety of perspectives disrupts the scripted historical narrative and curriculum. Alfred Tatum (2005), for instance, has spoken about how often textbooks show only victim narratives for people of color, and he insists that text selection is one of the most ethical choices a teacher can make. For an in-depth and step-by-step exploration of creating text sets and coaching students to synthesize across them, we highly recommend Sunday Cummins's *Nurturing Informed Thinking* (2018).

Giving Kids Time to Read by Containing Our Instruction

When we want to turn kids into readers, we turn to Jason Reynolds, Kwame Alexander, Matt de la Peña, Renee Watson, Jerry Craft, Suzanne Collins: the gorgeous, brilliant, provocative writers who mesmerize young people. We offer kids their books, we provide kids with time to read, and the kids dive in.

Kids need the same resources to become nonfiction readers. They need mesmerizing nonfiction, and they need time to read it and fall in love with it. To build in time to read, limit your instruction to launching kids into texts, and shift parts of your teaching to conferring and small-group work while the class reads. To make sure that kids get a lot of pages and text read, initially leave more-detailed instruction on critical literacies and synthesizing across texts for later, and

FIGURE 2.4 Booksource's *Advanced Search* can be a powerful tool when creating physical text sets.

concentrate on getting kids going; then coach them as they work. If this requires a major shift in your approach, you might find models in great math classrooms, science classrooms, art rooms, and music rooms in your school: teachers in these classrooms expect to limit their teaching so that kids can do math, make music, and so on. They circulate while kids work, coaching, encouraging, adjusting kids' practice. You can do the same. While whole-class teaching or lectures might help us to feel that we've covered content, any information that we may transmit is far less important than giving students opportunities to become engrossed in their learning.

Teach Kids Specific Strategies to Build Their Own Background Knowledge

In addition to letting kids explore the rich texts you've given them on their own, you can teach them specific initial strategies that will help them dive into research, begin to wrap their minds around a topic, and ask critical questions right from the start. Use the lesson starters below to introduce kids to these strategies in all-class minilessons, conferences, and small groups. Then, cocreate a chart with the class like the one in Figure 2.5 to help them hold onto the strategies they learn.

FIGURE 2.5 An expanding anchor chart like this reminds researchers of their growing repertoire of skills.

Lesson: Previewing a Range of Texts

CONNECT: Begin by briefly telling a high-interest story about the subject you've chosen. Describe the ramifications and relevance of the chosen subject. Then, explain: "Whenever you embark on a new study, it's worth it to browse multiple texts in order to build background knowledge. These might include websites, articles, videos, museum sites, book reviews, books, study guides, and films. As we begin learning more about _____, we'll be working with an initial text set. That's just to get you started. As you learn more, you'll be adding to this set and making your own."

TEACH: Demonstrate by showing students a text set. Show how readers expect to build expertise by reading multiple texts on the subject and asking themselves:

- "What are the big events, perspectives, and voices here?"
- "What texts will I want to start with? Which will I want to return to?"

ENGAGE: Invite students to choose a text to begin, and read a bit of it, pausing to compare summaries.

LAUNCH INDEPENDENT WORK TIME: Send kids off to preview texts and begin reading. When things are going well during this independent-work reading time, you'll see students reading, not pausing yet to take notes, but instead gathering a bigger picture of the topic. They will pause to talk to a partner regularly, comparing what they've learned and the texts they've read. They may make both initial reading plans and homework plans with their study group.

Lesson: Reading Fast and Furiously

CONNECT: Students are masters of short-hand: after all, they manage to say volumes with acronyms in text messages. Remind them that the point of their notetaking at this stage in their reading is to jot down a thought quickly, just as they would dash off a text that says a lot in as few words as possible, so that they can continue on with their reading and gathering of information. Explain: "When you are building background knowledge, you want to spend most of your time reading and learning, which means only a little time recording and note-taking. Plan to begin with texts that you find easy to read, and to read large chunks of text before pausing to note-take or talk with someone about what you've read."

TEACH: First, model for your students how you decide between an article that looks dense and complex, and one that seems more straightforward. Be frank and unembarassed about choosing the easier piece, considering your still-limited knowledge of the topic. (See Figure 2.6 for factors you might help students to consider in choosing a text.) Then model for your students how you read a bit in an article and then strike something that grabs your attention. Before jotting your notes on a sticky note in your notebook or in the margin, make a big show of how quickly you're going to do it. You might ask a student to time you as you jot your thought. You might model using a symbol system to record notes efficiently, or you may want to show how acronyms (like those used when kids text) might help you write quickly so you can move on.

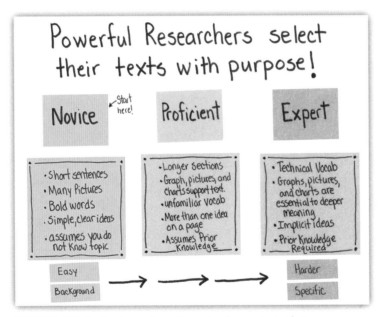

FIGURE 2.6 Students may be reticent to choose texts that appear "easy." A tool like this can encourage them to ramp up the level of text complexity as their expertise grows.

ENGAGE: Read a portion of the same text, then reach a predetermined stopping point. Tell the students that they have fifteen seconds to record their thoughts before you resume reading. Repeat a few times, if necessary, to get students used to this ratio of reading-to-writing time. (And remember, if some kids struggle to write about reading, you can have them say their thinking into a device, recording it either through speech to text or via video). The point here is for kids to spend most of their time reading.

LAUNCH INDEPENDENT WORK TIME: Remind students that their main objective right now is to read a lot, not to write a lot, so they should first choose a text that feels accessible to them, and second, keep any notes short, brief, and purposeful. Students will likely choose more basic, accessible texts at this stage so that they can work through a few in a short period of time. Some students might annotate as they read, using a simplified symbol system to record their reactions to a text, while others might read and write short messages to themselves or speak their ideas into a device. Post a chart like the one shown in Figure 2.7 to give students options if they feel stuck.

FIGURE 2.7 Tools like this can support small group, partner, or individual work as researchers tackle a topic.

Lesson: Noting Texts to Return to and Keeping Track of What You Read and Watch

CONNECT: Compliment kids on how they have been diving into reading, and share that you, too, have been opening texts (if you're working from a Padlet or drive), or grabbing books (if you have lots of print), and reading swiftly. Then share that you want to return to the text you were reading yesterday, but can't find it—and you realize that you haven't been jotting down any references. Suggest that this is one of the biggest challenges nonfiction researchers face: keeping track of what they've read and researched so they can return to it, quote it, and give credit for the words and ideas they use. Explain: "When you are beginning to research a topic, it's worth it to note the texts you read, so that you can return to them, either because you want to read more deeply, or because later texts contradict or challenge the text you are researching now."

TEACH: Invite students into a shared inquiry, asking: "How can we keep track of our sources so that we can return to them later, and reference them in ethical ways? What kind of information might be useful for us, as researchers, to note?"

Then give students a chance to share with each other, and begin a chart or tool to capture these ideas. You might offer some tips: Annotated bibliographies, where the researcher jots a quick note about what this text is useful for, can be helpful for researchers. If kids are using technology, digital tools such as Mendeley reference manager can help them to keep track of their sources.

ENGAGE: Have students choose a system they'll pilot as they research, suggesting that they may need to pause and revisit this system to see how efficient, accurate, and helpful it is.

LAUNCH INDEPENDENT WORK TIME: Send kids off not only to research, but also to keep more careful and helpful notes on their sources. Reminders like those in Figure 2.8A can support students in this work, or you might consider showing students some examples, such as the one in Figure 2.8B. Kids may need to spend a few minutes returning to record reference details for sources they've already read. Then they'll go on with their research, being more careful to develop a system for keeping track of sources. At the end of the period, you may want to invite students to share their systems in a gallery walk, or have research clubs meet to compare their systems.

FIGURE 2.8A–B It is enormously helpful for students to record source information from the very beginning of their research.

Sources

> 1 Title
> 2 Author
> 3 Source - Publisher, web, organization

Title: Issue Overview: Guns in America
Source: tcrwp.padlet.org / TCRWP / Gun Control

Title: After a long gap supreme court poised to break silence on gun rights
Source: nytimes.com

Title: Americas gun violence in charts
Source: bbc.com

Title: Gun Violence Archive
Source: gunviolence archive.org

Title: Switzerland has a stunningly high rate of gun ownership
Source: tcrwp.padlet.org / TCRWP / Gun Control

Title: Nearly 40000 people died from guns in the US, last year, highest in 50 years
Source: nytimes.com

Title: Gun Violence in America
Source: everytown research.org

Title: Gun Violence Statistics
Source: lawcenter.giffords.org

Title: Gun Safety
Source: mikebloomberg.com

Title: Leading causes of child and adolescent deaths
Source: thetrace.org

Title: March for our lives
Source: youtube.com

Title: Gun Control
Source: justfacts.com

Lesson: Asking Critical Questions Right from the Start

CONNECT: Show a snippet of a provocative text that leaves you asking, "What?" or "How did this happen?" or "Wait, this is different from what I read before." For instance, if you had read a bit of *The Lost Colony of Roanoke* by Jean Fritz and Hudson Talbott (2004), or any common classroom text on Roanoke, you would find scholar Lee Miller's work surprising. Miller, who is of Kaw heritage, has written several books on Roanoke. She suggests in *Roanoke: Solving the Mystery of the Lost Colony* (2002) that Roanoke was a cover-up and a rewriting of history, that the settlers were not massacred by hostile Indigenous Peoples, such as the Secotan, but instead were abandoned by their own people. Explain: "Researchers don't wait to ask questions as they read. As they move from one text to the next, or one part of a text to the next part, they ask, 'How does this new information fit in with what we already know? How does this support, or add to what we've read? How does this new information disrupt what we already know? Where do I see signs of dispute?'"

TEACH: For this lesson, it will help if you've chosen a text that prompts critical questioning—a very interesting text, but one that also might represent one side more strongly, in a topic. For instance, if you're reading Lee Miller's *Roanoke: Solving the Mystery of the Lost Colony*, she begins with the voice of the Secotan leader. Then she shifts to the perspective of the leader of the settlers. It is unsettling.

Invite students to share the work with you, as you demonstrate the kinds of reasoned and curious questioning that researchers practice—and you note those questions in your notes. Give students a tip that some questions won't be answerable in your current research: some questions are bigger and will be ones you're curious about for a long time.

ENGAGE: Invite students to go on with a snippet of the same text, inviting them to also think about more critical questions, about representation, about fairness. Have them share the questions that emerge. You might collect their ideas on a chart such as the one shown in Figure 2.9.

LAUNCH INDEPENDENT WORK TIME: Send students off to continue researching, suggesting that they consider where in their "lean notes" (spare notes, the fewest possible so that researchers get a lot of reading done) they want to capture the questions that are raised as they read. Students can continue their research, jotting their critical questions as they read. They'll pause in their research to compare their questions.

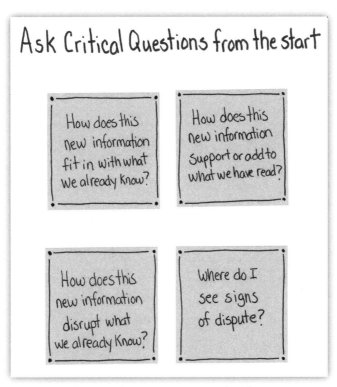

FIGURE 2.9 Kids can sometimes read without really thinking about what they are reading. Critical questions can act as interpretive lenses, shaping kids' reading from the start.

Lesson: Taking Lean Notes

CONNECT: Show a page of notes from your research that has lots of fascinating details and lots of facts. Then note that this page is from only one page of text. Suggest that sometimes we take notes too early, with too much detail. Taking these kinds of exhaustive notes takes the place of getting a lot of reading done. Explain: "When you are immersing yourself in a topic to build background knowledge, you want to take lean notes. For some learners, this means jotting rather messily and then doing a little bit of organizing with captions, annotations, or color to make sense of their notes. For others, sketching and diagramming can be fast and helpful. For all researchers, skimming and flagging before deciding what's worth jotting lets more reading get done."

TEACH: Demonstrate how, instead of taking lots of notes from the get-go, you can flag pages as you read a book, using small sticky notes for any parts you may want to return to. Demonstrate how you can do the same with a video, by noting the time frame. Then show how you might return, and, with a better of idea of what's important and what's not, jot very lean notes after reading more.

ENGAGE: Show a two-page spread of text, or preview a minute or two of a video, and invite students to consider what they might flag. Or show some pages of lean notes and invite students to talk about what other researchers have done to allow themselves time to read while capturing some initial information. You can find examples of lean notes in Figure 2.10 and in the online resources.

LAUNCH INDEPENDENT WORK TIME: Before kids go off to work, have them make plans for how many pages/how much text they'll read, as well as for how long a time they might read and flag before they pause to jot. Encourage them to read for much longer periods of time and more pages. Ask students to share these plans with a partner, making ambitious plans for lots of pages/text. Have them set a time frame for when they'll pause to jot some lean notes and then share those with a partner. Explain that their goal is to try to read for longer periods of time before taking notes or sharing. If there is time, a gallery walk of students' lean notes would be a good final share for the day's work.

FIGURE 2.10 Here, students take lean notes, applying only light organization, and jotting the most important information and concepts they want to return to.

See the online resources for more examples of students' lean notes.

Lean Notes—Who are the Wampanoag?

Source: pilmoth.org

The Wampanoag is a Nation of Native Americans. It is one of many. They have Wampanoag people all over North America.

Wampanoag people don't like to be called "indians" and they like being called Native people.

Wampanoag means people of the First Light.

There was 40,000 Wampanoag people in 7 villages. The villages covered along the east coast. It covered as far as Wessagusset (today called Weymouth). They have been living on this part of turtle Island for over 15,000 years.

4000–5000 Wampanoag live in New England.

The Wampanoag now can not live the same way ancestors did. It is because all of the change has happened. They can still live like the People of First Light. Their beliefs are the same but land has changed.

The Wampanoag provided food for the [...] in it.

#1

Source: Henry Hudson By Ruth

friendly	unfriendly
- Gave each others gifts	- scouting party that Henry Hudson sent was attacked by them and one got killed with two other wounded
- On shore, the Lenelape gathered around Henry Hudson and sang	- Another time the ship was attacked by Indians who fired arrows
- Traded and offered Henry Hudson corn	- Henry Hudson's crew fired back with muskeets and cannans
- Henry Hudson noticed they had weapons like bows and arrows	- John Colman was the crew member that got shot and killed
- They slept under the "Blue Heavens"	- Just got his pillow taken and the theif stole his c[...] Just killed the theif
- came aboard the ship to greet them	

Eastern woodlands Indians by Mir
Pg 22 – 23   Europeans arrive

The European got rich off of the fur from the Indians.

Indians traded fur for European goods.

Brought tools, guns, glassware, beads, and cloth to America.

What happened when the Europeans arrived?

Tribes FOUGHT each other to control lands and the waterways to get fur and trade to the Europeans.

16th century: The time when the Europeans started exploring North America.

1620 – the Europeans brought the Indians deadly diseases.

Lesson: Creating Recursive Notes

CONNECT: Remind students about what they already know about the role of revision in the writing process, and explain that thinking about research can benefit from revision the same way: it allows us to "see anew" and to highlight patterns and connections that we hadn't fully expressed or explored. Explain: "As you begin to know more, it can be helpful to rethink by going back into your notes. Annotating—jotting in the margins—of prior notes, by adding in new thinking, making connections, and questioning, often leads to powerful new insights. Be especially alert to ways that new texts and perspectives lead you to critique earlier texts or revise your thinking—and go back into your notes to capture those critiques and revisions."

TEACH: Show students your own notes. Explain that these notes represent what first grabbed your attention about the topic, as well as your initial thinking on that topic. Explain to students that as you go on in your research, new texts make you rethink prior reading. Then demonstrate how you go back and rethink, paging through your notes and using colored pens to add connections, questions, new insights. Figure 2.11 and the online resources show some examples of students' recursive notes, for reference. You may want to draw arrows across sections, showing how information from one text supports or refutes information from another text. You may want to pose questions for yourself, such as:

- When I revisit this page of notes, what new thinking do I have?
- Where am I seeing any patterns (who is represented, how fair are these texts)?
- What connections am I seeing?
- What critiques of earlier texts or of my own thinking am I making?

ENGAGE: Hand out colored pens and invite the students to spend a minute or two rereading a part of their notes while referring to the previous questions. After students mark up their notes, pass out sticky notes to each student and have them write a quick one-sentence plan that can guide their next steps as researchers and note-takers. Will they reread? Read on? Revisit more notes? Set up new pages differently? All of the above?

LAUNCH INDEPENDENT WORK TIME: Remind the students of the importance of rereading notes with an eye for emergent patterns and how those patterns will lead them to new realizations. You might finish with a gallery walk of annotated notebook pages, as this is a crucial study skill. Also suggest that, knowing they will be annotating, they might leave more white space the next time they take initial notes. Students might reread their notes and mark them with colored pens or jot in the margin.

FIGURE 2.11 Here students create "recursive notes" by taking time to reread and reflect on their research.

See the online resources for more examples of students' recursive notes.

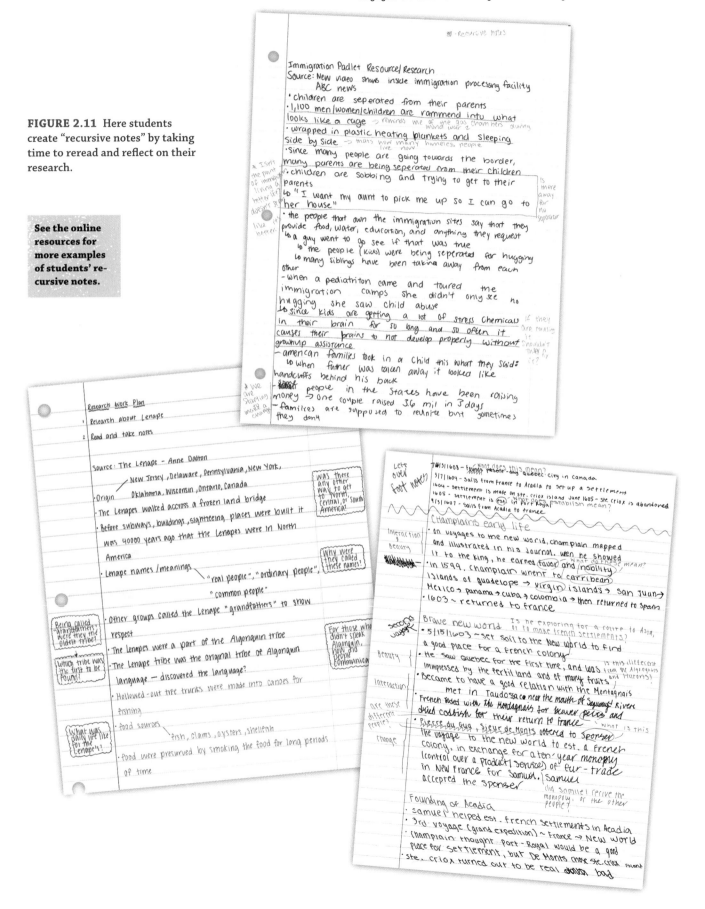

Lesson: Creating New Notebook Pages to Synthesize, Develop, Highlight, and Share Our Thinking

CONNECT: Let kids in on how students who tend to do well academically in challenging classes often take the time to go back in and reorganize their notes. You might share some beautiful notebook pages of famous thinkers, such as DaVinci, Darwin, and Goodall—their notebook pages are easily available on Google images, and they are inspiring. You might share some powerful infographics: go to Google images and search "Infographics Climate Change" or "Infographics Voter Rights." And/or you might share a range of beautiful reading-notebook pages, where students have created serious notes to hold onto and expand what they've learned (we've provided a few in Figure 2.12 and in the online resources).

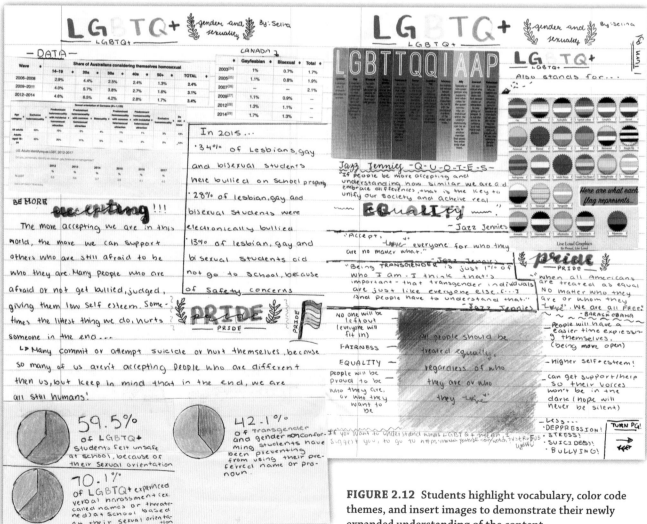

FIGURE 2.12 Students highlight vocabulary, color code themes, and insert images to demonstrate their newly expanded understanding of the content.

Explain: "Researchers, there are other kinds of note-taking you can do besides lean notes. Once you have been researching for a bit, it can be very helpful to pause to take the time to synthesize your thinking into new pages, that can help you organize and clarify what you've learned, and tease out some of the bigger ideas— what's most significant so far. It's almost like you're making a study guide, useful to yourself and others in your study group."

TEACH: Demonstrate how you might look over some of the samples and exemplars and consider what these thinkers have done—how they've used charts and diagrams, compelling visuals, color, and design or infographic elements to organize their learning in compelling ways. Show how you might zoom in on one or two mentor texts for inspiration, and then plan by sketching, or talking through what you want to do. Definitely model how you consider a few of the biggest ideas, moving away from fascinating details to ideas and details that add up to big theories, connections, critiques, or questions.

(continues)

See the online resources for more examples of students' synthesis notes.

ENGAGE: Invite students to study a few of these mentors and exemplars with a partner and talk about what design elements they're drawn to. Have them make a quick plan for the synthesis page(s) they'll make today.

LAUNCH INDEPENDENT WORK TIME: Let students know that you'll be having a gallery walk, and send them off to create synthesis pages. Providing swag (sticky notes, markers, colored pencils, glue sticks, scissors) can help kids to dive into this work, as well.

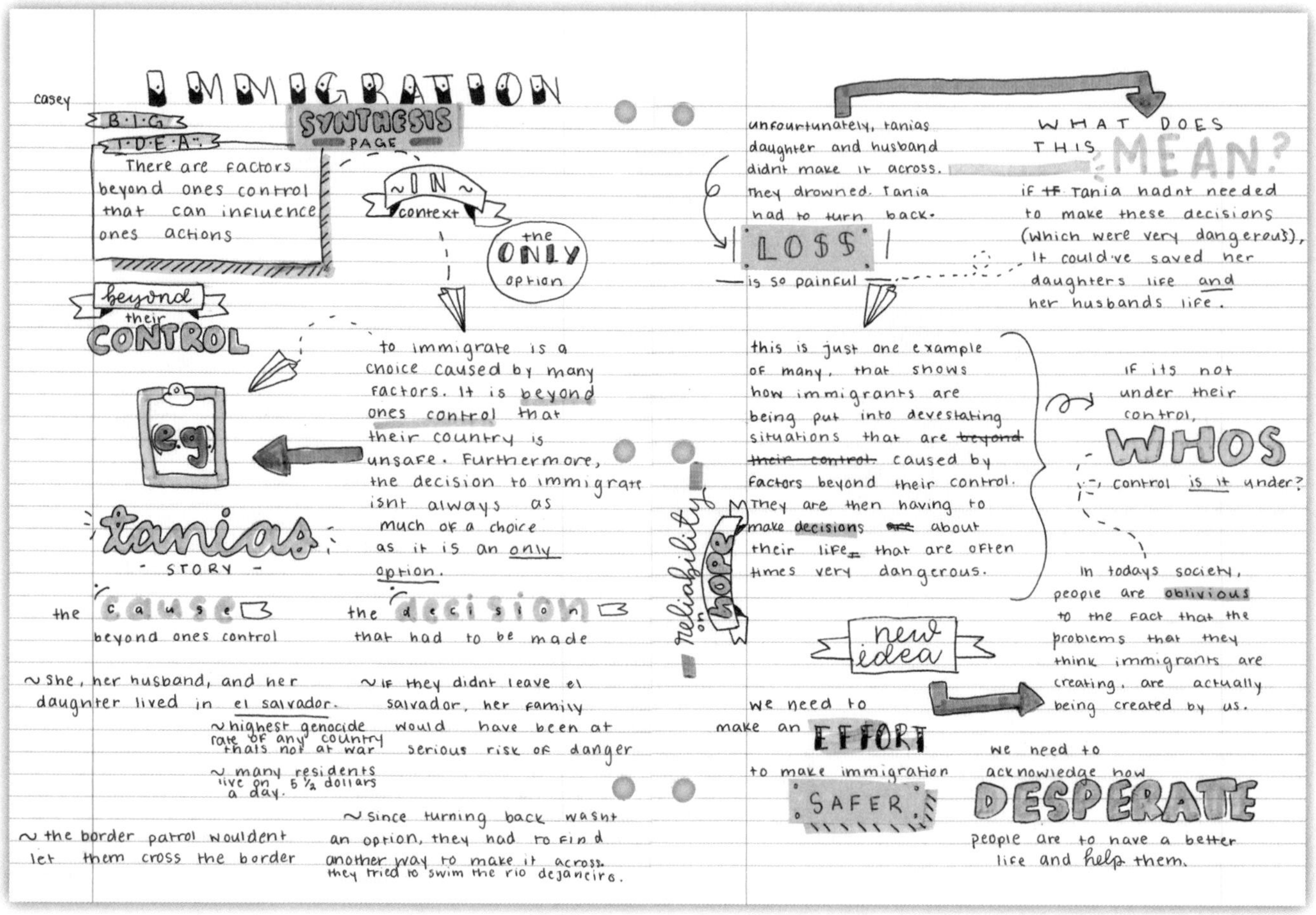

FIGURE 2.12 (*continued*)

Lesson: Talking to a Variety of People About What You're Learning and Thinking

CONNECT: Tell kids about the "water cooler effect," which is known in work-places, such as Google and NASA, as the informal moments when people share knowledge in ways that lead to insight. Explain: "Whenever researchers are learning new things, they talk to lots of people about the ideas and information they are studying. Often, people will end up recommending texts, or wanting to hear more, or asking questions, and these opportunities help deepen their understanding of the complexities of a topic."

TEACH: Demonstrate how you might consider your different opportunities for a "water cooler effect" by mapping some of the people you might talk to about your research. Include any family members who might have different perspectives so that kids' cultures are valued, and the different perspectives inside your community are heard.

ENGAGE: Invite students to do similar mapping. Encourage them to consider their study group and when and how they might talk inside and outside of class, as well as others who might offer ideas, perspectives, interpretations.

LAUNCH INDEPENDENT WORK TIME: Send kids off to work, making sure they reserve some time at the end of the period to meet with their study group to talk over what they've learned so far. For homework, ask students to talk about what they're researching with someone outside of their study group—another student who is researching something different, a family member, a teacher, another adult, a friend. Suggest they return ready to share any insights gained from explaining their research or from this person's response.

Lesson: Building Agency and Independence

CONNECT: Share with students that kids who learn to do particularly well in academic classes often share three attributes: they form study groups, they take their notes seriously, and they take on some related learning of their own outside of school. The previous lessons have addressed the first two. Now, let's consider how students might do a bit more outside of school to further strengthen their learning. Explain: "Learning to take charge of your own learning outside of class—or work—is a huge part of becoming more powerful and independent as a student and later as a citizen. One way to do this work is to assign yourself small extra tasks, such as reading a bit more of a text, finding another source, or talking to someone who might have a different perspective. Another way is to consider contributing to a study group—adding to a text set, creating a page of notes to share, finding out if any study group members want support."

TEACH: Invite students into a shared inquiry, posing these questions: "What do students already do to add to their own learning set? What do they already do to add to a study group? What ideas do they have about contributing to study groups and extending their work outside of class?" Create a chart of some of their ideas. If needed, give students some tips, and add those to the chart.

ENGAGE: Give students an opportunity to reflect with a partner on what they've already done in terms of contributing to a group and, more importantly, what they might do next. Encourage them to lean on their strengths. If they are big readers, they might preview texts. If they love to debate, they can challenge current research. If they are socially alert, they might check in on other study group members to find out how they are doing.

LAUNCH INDEPENDENT WORK TIME: Send kids off to research, this time alerting them that they will be meeting with their study group near the end of the period, so they should actively think about using this time to prepare to contribute to the group.

Involve Families and Communities

The adults who care for our students—their parents, family members, or guardians—want them to achieve. You can help make this process easier by providing resources for outside of school as well as in.

One of the most democratic ways to involve these adults in this work is to create a lending library of texts so that they can help their children learn, and can learn alongside them. It's most helpful if you can create a lending library of books that kids and families can read *before* an upcoming unit of study as well as during a unit. Have a shelf or shelves where there are books to support an upcoming unit. Let kids take them out at the end of the day and bring them back before school. Create a card with suggested books and films that families might want to read and watch together. Send home a card with links to museum sites, websites, and digital articles. Ask parents and community members for help seeking sources in more than one language and from more than one perspective.

Think, as well, about bigger projects that might anchor a study in a topic that is relevant to their family or community. Then, consider ways to involve family and community members in this work. Students can build a tremendous amount of background knowledge by tapping the resources of their local community. See the Young Citizens in Action box on page 70 for an example of what this work might look like.

Be Ready for Anything

Whenever you embark on innovative curriculum, especially curriculum with a high degree of autonomy for students, there will be trouble. Some of this trouble you can predict and prepare for. We suggest that you don't try to avoid trouble—kids learn from mistakes. You can, however, be ready for some predictable trouble and have strategies and coaching tips prepared—for kids and for you.

One trouble that can arise is dealing with anxious families or community members. Sometimes the topics your students are researching will make some community members anxious or angry. It's helpful if kids have a choice of research topics so that there is no one topic that is mandatory for any student. It can be helpful to send a letter home, with links to topic choices so that families can see the available options.

Another trouble can be internal on your part; for example, you might worry that your administration won't have your back if you include contested topics in research options. Bringing your studies and your ethical stances to your principal can be helpful. You might begin by asking, "What if . . ." or "How would it be if

» YOUNG CITIZENS IN ACTION «

In Brownsville, Brooklyn, Akeem Barnes's eighth-grade classes at Riverdale Avenue Middle School developed their background knowledge about community policing by relying heavily on a mediography compiled by their local librarian, oral history from an elder in the community, and first-hand interviews with residents. To develop these close ties to the community, Akeem enlisted the aid of a local activist and community organizer, C. Aaron Hinton. Aaron acted as the class's "fixer," arranging meetings with well-connected residents and, eventually, with the police department itself.

Akeem, Aaron and the students began the research phase of their civic action project with a trip to the Brownsville Heritage Center and local public library. The Heritage House occupies the top floor of the local library and is run by Ms. Marion, an octogenarian of boundless energy who has lived in the community all of her life. The oracle of Brownsville, Ms. Marion carries with her the accumulated knowledge of decades of firsthand experience in the neighborhood. Aaron wanted to make sure that the students would have an opportunity to experience her enthusiastic storytelling, so he arranged for the classes to be split: half the group would be upstairs with Ms. Marion and half would be downstairs performing research. Akeem and Aaron had contacted a local librarian who eagerly assembled a mediography of resources on community policing both in Brownsville and across the country and the students were encouraged to record their notes and thoughts in their social action journals. Even the walk to the Heritage House was designed to further engage the students with their neighborhood, as Aaron had recruited elders from the community to serve as chaperones.

Having gathered information from the local library and from Ms. Marion, the students were now informed enough to enter the next phase of their social action project, which we will return to in greater detail in Chapter 5.

Librarians are a powerful resource as you develop your text sets. Whether the librarians are in school or in the local community, they have the knowledge, access, and time to develop lists of rich texts for your readers. Kids can also act as librarians and curators, previewing texts, categorizing them, rating them. This starter text set was compiled by the local librarian for the Eighth-Grade Riverdale Avenue Civic Action Project.

BOOKS

○ Alexander, Michelle. *The New Jim Crow: Mass Incarceration in the Age of Colorblindness.* 2012.

(continues)

(continued)

ARTICLES

- Center for Constitutional Rights. "Stop and Frisk—the Human Impact: The Stories Behind the Numbers, the Effects on our Communities." July 26, 2012. https://ccrjustice.org/sites/default/files/attach/2015/08/the-human-impact-report.pdf.

- Community Service Society. "New Neighbors and the Over-Policing of Communities of Color." January 6, 2019. https://www.cssny.org/news/entry/New-Neighbors.

- Fayyad, Abdallah. "The Criminalization of Gentrifying Neighborhoods." *The Atlantic.* December 20, 2017. https://www.theatlantic.com/politics/archive/2017/12/the-criminalization-of-gentrifying-neighborhoods/548837.

- Florio, Angelica. "Brownsville and Bed-Stuy Voiced Concerns About Police-Community Relations and Over-Policing." *Bushwick Daily.* March 18, 2019. https://bushwickdaily.com/bushwick/categories/community/5937-brownsville-and-bed-stuy-voiced-concerns-about-police-community-relations-and-over-policing.

- Ishak, Natasha. "Bushwick Named in New Gentrification Report on Over-Policed Communities of Color." Bushwick Daily. January 14, 2019. https://bushwickdaily.com/bushwick/categories/news/5798-bushwick-named-in-new-gentrification-report-on-over-policed-communities-of-color.

AUDIO

- Center for Constitutional Rights. "Stories of Stop and Frisk." August 5, 2015. https://ccrjustice.org/stories-stop-and-frisk.

- Gallishaw, Allahlife. "Oral history interview conducted with Allahlife Gallishaw on 2016 October 27." *Our Streets, Our Stories.* Audio interview conducted on October 27, 2016, by Carmen Lopez in Bedford-Stuyvesant. www.bklynlibrary.org/digitalcollections/item/4b15c712-7dd9-4e92-b332-dc8a23d273e2.

- Osorio, Eric. "Oral history interview with Eric Osorio on 2015 December 15." *Our Streets, Our Stories.* Audio interview conducted on December 15, 2015, by Taina Evans and Naheem Morris at Red Hook Library. www.bklynlibrary.org/digitalcollections/item/85d7dc37-e269-43df-a327-ee5eb1d0c185.

VIDEO

- Race Forward. "How Does It Feel to be Stopped and Frisked?" July 29, 2010. https://youtu.be/UvIBIn5Xp7s.

- Wolff, Spencer, director. *Stop—Challenging NYPD's "Stop and Frisk" Policies.* 2015. www.youtube.com/watch?v=02Hp-KZ9ov4.

we tried . . ." or "Thinking of our students, I'd like to try. . . ." When people feel part of building something new, they are much more receptive than when they are told a finished plan. We highly recommend David Rock's *Quiet Leadership* (2006) for suggestions about building coalition, involving stakeholders, and managing difficult conversations. As Steve Zemelman explains in *From Inquiry to Action* (2016), proactively building relationships with administrators and getting them onboard with the aims of real-world research and action can go a long way in making this a collaborative rather than confrontational process.

You may also have concerns about tech proficiency— you haven't used Padlet, you're unsure how to archive your digital texts, you're not sure about using digital citation tools, and so on. Don't worry, you don't have to be the digital expert—there will be tech experts in your classroom. We have taught units in which we did not learn the software that kids were using, because we had other expertise to offer. Instead, consider the technological strengths that your students bring and invite a few kids to be tech consultants. Entrust these consultants with researching the software you want to use, teaching it to other students, and troubleshooting.

Practice What You Teach

Our lives are so busy with responsibilities to work, family, and friends that it can be difficult to put aside the time to engage in the type of research that we are asking of our students. Think about the last time that you chose a topic of deep personal interest and learned more about it by delving deep into the internet, seeking out videos about it, searching for discussion groups, or perusing the shelves in the library. Perhaps you have a hobby that draws your attention during your free moments. Pablo has a friend, Mike, who is an avid woodworker in his spare time. He has shelves of books devoted to the craft, takes countless notes as he learns new techniques, and is always seeking out the counsel of more-experienced woodworkers. Mike's habits as an engaged researcher are the same we want in our students. Images of his notebooks and workspace would make for ideal exemplars in the classroom. Think about your own life, or the people in your life who embody the type of curiosity you want to see replicated in your classroom, and consider bringing in examples to show your students.

In preparation for the work of this chapter, ask yourself:

- When was the last time you were devoted to a research project?
- What kept you going deeper and deeper to learn more about the topic?
- What habits did you develop to keep track of all that you learned?
- How did you reach out to others to assist you in your learning?
- Did you read across multiple sources of information in your quest for new knowledge?
- Were sources always consistent about the information they presented?
- How did you cope with contradictions between sources?

Seek out opportunities to show your students your own research passion—whether it's a contemporary political issue or a personal project—and your practices. Your example will remind them that this is work that people do in the world beyond the walls of the classroom.

Civic Virtues Addressed in this Chapter

- critically consuming media and texts
- questioning sources to spur further research
- resisting resignation and cynicism

Planning Your Time

Introduce questioning sources of information by devoting significant time, from three days to a week, inside of a unit of study. Begin by teaching ethical research and close, critical reading practices. Then, work with colleagues to carry these practices across the curriculum so that students internalize the act of interrogating texts. When an incident or event occurs, guard against introducing only one text on the event. Even in a short time frame, try to position reading in such a way that students see that critical reading, within and across texts, is a consistent way of engaging with media.

ENGAGED CITIZENS QUESTION THEIR SOURCES OF INFORMATION

As civically engaged teachers of adolescents, it's our responsibility to foster the questioning spirit and sense of justice that our young people bring into the classroom naturally and to channel it toward wrestling with the difficult problems facing our world. Our students are not only ready to do this work, they are hungry for school to offer them a challenge worthy of their attention! Questioning the motives and credibility of sources of information poses just such a challenge. By giving them the tools to consume media intelligently, you are satisfying their growing desire to be a partner at the table rather an object of adult whims.

In tackling this critical-reading work with your students you'll first need to unpack the notion of nonfiction. In our experience in schools, it's not uncommon to hear students say that fiction is not true and nonfiction is true. While this is a clear and simple distinction, it leaves children and adolescents vulnerable to a wide range of misinformation. Instead, teach that nonfiction, even at its best, is someone's perspective on the truth. At its worst, it is a complete fabrication.

We have the difficult job of teaching young people to approach nonfiction cautiously. On one hand, we must teach them that a text will inevitably reflect biases and concerns that may be significant even if they are submerged. On the other hand, we must protect our students from disillusionment: when citizens stop trusting journalism and news, they stop seeking information, stop weighing the news, and stop trying to make a difference. In *"The Daily Show* Effect: Candidate Evaluations, Efficacy, and American Youth,"* Jody Baumgartner and Jonathan Morris find that to a vast extent, US citizens' exposure to journalism is now through soft news—news-as-entertainment shows like *Last Week Tonight,* or *Fox and Friends,* which might differ in their stance but not in their emphasis on soundbite and spectacle. It turns out that this consumption of news as spectacle makes viewers more cynical toward political systems. Ironically, viewers report a sense of greater understanding of politics, but a decreased urge to engage or vote. As Baumgartner and Morris find, "lowered trust can perpetuate a more dysfunctional political system" (2006, 363).

Striking the balance between critical questioning and outright distrust of the media is essential for the health of our democracy as a whole—especially in today's media minefield, where apps that deliver news feeds seek to profit off our "likes" and where foreign governments deliberately abuse such platforms in order to sow social discord.

The antidote is to teach students to read closely, to bring sophisticated reading practices to the texts in front of them, including reading for underlying, implicit ideas; for logical reasoning and logical fallacies; for connotative language, and to interpret embedded numbers, statistics and charts.

We'll begin this chapter by briefly introducing the teaching structures that will best support the close reading required to question sources. Then, we'll give some suggestions for introducing the idea of using multiple texts rather than relying on a single source. Finally, we'll offer lessons for reading critically, weeding out the most problematic of sources, and questioning sources.

In this chapter we'll help you to:

- proceed with care and caution
- utilize teaching methods that support close, critical reading of nonfiction
- make reading across multiple sources the norm
- teach students to read with healthy skepticism
- teach students to be wary of persuasive techniques and logical fallacies
- teach students to weigh sources and their credibility
- involve families and communities
- be ready for anything
- practice what you teach.

Proceed with Care and Caution

In the previous chapter we worked on quickly building our background knowledge about a topic. This process usually has us and our students treating sources largely as repositories of relevant facts. We are in need of the *who, what, when* and *where* of a topic, so we look across sources to get a strong grounding in shared, accepted truths. In this chapter we will focus on how to go deeper into our sources, looking at them not as collections of facts, but rather as *interpretations* of facts. In this shift we'll wade into difficult waters. The texts that will be most problematic, those that will very concretely betray bias in a way that helps our students see how nonfiction is someone's interpretation of the truth, have the potential to be hostile to the identities of the students in our room. You will need to proceed with awareness as to how your students may be emotionally impacted by the bias communicated in the text you choose, whether the time frame is historical or contemporary.

You may want to return to the identity work that you launched earlier in the year. Do the texts that you plan to read together attack, demean, or diminish the identities of your students? For example, below we use newspapers from the late 1890s and early 1900s that address the Chinese Exclusion Act of 1882. During the COVID-19 pandemic, historical anti-Chinese sentiments became even more raw in the classroom, for instance. The papers from the 1880s denigrate Chinese people and promote a policy of barring them from entry into the country. While the ugliness of humanity needs to be explored both in history and the present, especially if it's an inescapable reality, what might appear to be an intellectual exercise for a white teacher could be retraumatizing for a student who has been oppressed because of their race. You'll likely want to:

- consider the words of Jason Reynolds and Ibram X. Kendi in *Stamped: Racism, Anti-Racism and You,* or watch one of their many video interviews as they discuss how important it is to not evade reality when teaching kids, especially kids who suffer oppression due to their race, ethnicity, or religion

- seek out and highlight alternative texts and voices so that the history you teach is not only a history of victim narratives but also one of protest and change

- offer a range and choice of texts, so, for example, some kids might read about the Chinese Exclusion act while others might read about other immigration events of the time period. This gives kids options for negotiating the curriculum.

- preface any all-class reading by explaining your rationale for reading it to students and families; be transparent about curriculum

- acknowledge that it's possible the texts will elicit strong emotions, and offer the students opportunities to express those emotions. Let students know that you have an open-door policy: any student who has issues with the texts you are reading can come to talk to you privately and express their concerns. It's possible that students may feel too intimidated to address their concerns directly, in which case, you might add extra time for free-writing, with the option of giving their writing to you.

- be explicit about racist tendencies that produce certain texts and agendas. Don't attempt to apologize for or whitewash racist or otherwise bigoted texts. Show them for what they are.

As with other sections of this book in which we suggest diving into difficult topics, we always recommend transparency with the parent community and with administrators. You may also want to enlist the aid of mental-health professionals in your school and ask their advice about presenting difficult content and addressing emotional responses appropriately.

Utilize Teaching Methods that Support Close, Critical Reading of Nonfiction

Questioning sources of information is complex and demanding work. Even experienced readers can take the path of least resistance and end up wholly trusting the authority of the words on the page. To combat this tendency, we'll need to create structures in our room in which we can share responsibility for critiquing sources of information.

A read-aloud, shared reading, and partner reading are indispensable teaching methods when working to improve students' ability to question their sources, especially when students may be accustomed to taking the authority of the texts in front of them for granted—and especially those given to them by their teachers. The transition to becoming healthily skeptical is a difficult one. In a read-aloud, you orchestrate a strategic reading of the text, not only reading aloud to make the text more accessible but also inserting critical lenses and discussion prompts. In shared reading, you return to a portion of a text, inviting students to study collectively with you, annotating, interrogating, rereading to figure out not just what the text says but how it works. In partner reading, students read silently for a bit, then compare their understanding and response to the text so far, then go on, unpacking a text in partnership. You can read more about all of these techniques, and how to implement them with grace and purpose, in Lucy Calkins' *The Art of Teaching Reading* (2001).

Collaborative reading practices support students in thoughtful critical reading and set the foundation for the type of reading we hope students will do as adult citizens who create—and debate—meaning with others. Our favorite literacy books on this are Sonja Cherry-Paul and Dana Johansen's *Breathing New Life Into Book Clubs* (2019), Kate Roberts' *A Novel Approach* (2018), Christopher Lehman and Kate Roberts' *Falling in Love with Close Reading* (2014), and Shana Frazin and Katy Wischow's *Unlocking the Power of Classroom Talk* (2020). The same techniques that we use to develop kids' literary conversations—partnerships, analytical prompts, sentence starters and academic language prompts, and mostly, highly engaging and relevant texts—will work with developing kids' talk around nonfiction texts.

Using Prompts to Support Critical Reading

Our work in supporting students as critical readers lies in giving them enough structure to support growth but not so much direction that they lose their sense of autonomy. Well-chosen prompts—when paired with the collaborative reading practices below—can provide that just-enough structure. Students can use analytical prompts such as these to question sources:

Reading Around the Text

- Read about the author. Ask: "Who are they—do they have an area of expertise? Does anything in their bio suggest any agendas?"

- Read for sources. Ask: "Where did the author get their information? Do the sources seem to represent any particular groups or coalitions?"

- Read other perspectives / sources. Ask: "Are there nuggets that appear in most sources or that suggest an underlying truth? Are there highly contested parts or versions?"

Reading for Warrant, or Reasoning

- Read for argument. Ask: "Does the author state an explicit opinion? Does the author try to lead their audience to an opinion? Do they acknowledge other opinions?"

- Read for evidence. Ask: "In what ways does the author support an opinion or claim? Is the evidence convincing, or does it seem slippery?"

- Read for angle. Ask: "What aspect of a big topic is the author spending most of their time on? What do they not mention, or spend little time on?"

Reading for Craft and Structure

- Read for the writer's word choice. Ask: "Does the word choice suggest the sympathies of the author? Are there surprising word choices? Why might the author have made those choices?"

- Read for the writer's techniques. Ask: "What writerly moves is the author using, and what effect do they have on you as a reader?"

- Read for structure. Ask: "How does the author lead me to ideas? How do the parts fit together?"

Reading for Representation and Perspective

- Read for audience. Ask: "Who is the author writing for? Who would benefit from this piece?"

- Read for voice and representation. Ask: "Who is included in this piece? Who is left out, marginalized, or distorted?"
- Read for #OwnVoices perspectives. Ask: "Whose stories are being told here, and whose voices are telling those stories?"
- Read for power and resistance. Ask: "How does this text reinforce existing powers (voices, groups, structures, narratives, points-of-view). How does it resist or disrupt those?"

Using Strategic Read-Alouds

To give students shared, interactive practice with close reading, use a strategic read-aloud, where you read a text aloud and engage students in collective interpretation—thinking, talking, and jotting along the way.

The following shows the components of a strategic read-aloud for a class that is about to read a 1901 newspaper article titled "Chinese Exclusion Convention Comes to a Most Brilliant Close" as part of their study of the Chinese Exclusion Act of 1882, a topic that gives historical context to the Anti-Chinese racism during the outbreak of COVID-19 and the various travel bans and quarantines. Of course, before embarking on this topic, a teacher would have made sure to explain that the newspapers and images they will examine use language and images that are offensive and racist. She might say something like, "We'll be exploring this era to better understand the fear and racism that has shaped our country in the past and continues to shape it today. Before we begin let's think about ways to handle the difficult feelings that may come up when studying this material—individually and collectively." She would then lead a discussion on classroom norms for responding to difficult and inflammatory content. Facing History and Ourselves' website (www.facinghistory.org) provides some very helpful guidance for "contracting," or setting expectations with students. Their process begins with student reflection and then moves into discussing classroom norms that include using "I" statements, listening, working with the teacher to find a way to be heard if the space does not feel safe, and responding to hurtful or oppressive interactions by identifying the comments (rather than the individuals) as problematic.

A read-aloud is generally comprised of the following major elements:

Text Introduction and Rallying Cry: Introduce the text in a way that stirs up interest and rallies kids toward higher-level thinking work. For example, here's what this part of a read-aloud might sound like: "Historians, we've been exploring a dark time in American history, a time when both citizens and government were so afraid of immigrants that they created a law called the 1882 Chinese Exclusion Act. The goal of this law was to ban an entire ethnic group from entering the country. In the wake of COVID-19 in 2020, some fringe groups made the same call, lumping all people of Asian descent together, no matter where they lived or whether they had any more contact with the virus than non-Asians—so this study of how people justify racism matters, in history and now. The article we will read together today was published in 1901 in *The San Francisco Call*. It describes a convention in which people discussed renewing the law."

Analytical Prompt and Reading: Introduce an analytical lens and invite students to listen closely, with this lens in mind, as you read the text aloud. (See Figure 3.1 for an example of how we might plan points to discuss in a text.) Students may jot as they listen. Explain: "When we think of a newspaper article, we usually believe that it will be totally objective, that it will present only the facts of what happened and not the opinions of the writer. We have to be careful, though, because opinions and bias are inevitable, and sources sometimes represent or serve certain interest groups. One way to see these biases is to ask yourself: 'Who do I sympathize with and admire in this text?' Then ask yourself: 'How does the author's word choice set me up to admire and sympathize with some people and positions?' As you listen, keep your ears open to any specific words that catch your attention." Prompts like those in Figure 3.2 can help to move the conversation forward.

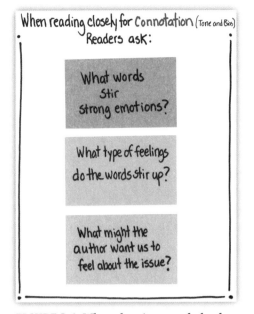

FIGURE 3.1 When planning a read-aloud, record your stopping points, critical lens prompts, and tips in advance.

FIGURE 3.2 Planning your read-aloud so that you're addressing both what you'll say and the content of the kids' conversations can result in deeply analytical experiences.

Turn and Talk: Invite partners to briefly talk with each other to share their thinking about the prompt given before reading. Say: "Now that we've read the title, subtitle, and the caption to the central image, turn and talk to your partner. What words in the title, subtitle and caption suggest that this might not be a totally neutral article?"

Teacher Summation (and Elevation) of Partner Talk: Share a few summaries of the comments you heard during the turn-and-talk. Use this opportunity to tuck in academic language or interpretive insights. Explain: "Historians, I heard many of you say that the article seems overwhelmingly positive about the Chinese Exclusion Convention—about excluding Chinese people. You pointed to words and phrases, such as *most brilliant, strong,* and *eloquent,* and you determined that the writer seems to want us to feel good about the event. When we read news articles, we'll want to pay careful attention to not just *what* events are described but also *how* the events are described and how specific word choice shows not just implicit but explicit bias."

Feedback: Give feedback, perhaps in the form of a tip as the students talk, to help them move their thinking forward. You might say: "I want to compliment you on noticing moments when the author's word choice gives off a feeling, or connotation, about the events he describes. I want to suggest that you can also pay close attention to the techniques the author uses to accomplish this task. How does he use specific craft techniques to emphasize the positive connotations of the convention? Think back to your study of poetry, narrative, and argument writing— what writing moves might the author be using? We can often reread sections with craft in mind to better understand a writer's perspective or purpose."

Repeat this structure throughout your reading, giving students a chance to apply feedback. When you want to offer them a new challenge, give students another analytical lens to continue to raise the level.

Lesson: Using Shared Reading

You can also use analytical reading prompts with shared reading. Unlike read-aloud, in shared reading, students have access to a print or digital copy of an excerpt of the text, which is helpful in engaging students in full-group discussion of close reading strategies, in targeted rereading, and in thoughtful annotation. Usually the text has already been introduced, and shared reading is a rereading process, where students read closely with critical lenses.

A shared reading lesson for our unit on the Chinese Exclusion Act might go like this:

CONNECT: Remind students of a text you've introduced that you'll return to. You might say: "Historians, we're going to go back to a text that we looked at briefly the other day. It's the piece from 1892, in the *Dalles Daily Chronicle,* which is an Oregon newspaper. Today I want to suggest that when you reread, you often notice a lot of details that didn't stick out in a first reading—and that if you reread and annotate at the same time, it can help you go even deeper. Marking up a text helps us notice smaller details, word choice, and other language that we might have skipped over in our first read. Watch as I get started rereading, and this time I'm going to underline and annotate as I read, noticing word choice and craft techniques that stand out. You have a copy of the text, some pens, and some sticky notes: you can begin to annotate what you're struck by as well."

TEACH AND ENGAGE: Demonstrate how you reread, rethink, and annotate, making notes on the page as you go. (See Figure 3.3 for an example of what an annotated piece might look like.) Explain: "I'm going to go back to the titles and subtitles to get started, as often those give a strong indication of the author's stance. Let's see . . . the title of this article is 'A Celestial Horde: Hiding in Sequestered Nooks, Ready for the Break—Only One More River to Cross.' And we know in this article the author suggests that Chinese immigrants are massed in Canada, waiting to cross over into the US. So, for me, what stands out is this use of the word *horde.* That's a word I associate with armies, and invasions like that of Genghis Khan and his horde. And those words *sequestered nooks,* which suggest secrecy, and that phrase *ready for the break,* as if this 'horde' is massing, just waiting to pounce. It all builds a mood of something ominous, which definitely suggests an anti-Chinese bias.

"Did you see how I zoomed in on specific words and phrases that stood out to me in rereading, and I underlined and circled them, and then jotted a note in the margins so that I would hold onto my thinking? Then as I keep reading and annotating, I can see how it all begins to add up."

CONDUCTING A READ-ALOUD

Watch Pablo's sample analytical read-aloud.

http://hein.pub/ CivicallyEngaged Classroom

Engage students in going on with this work of rereading, annotating, and rethinking for bias. Then say: "Let's go on, and as you read, try out this annotating—circle, underline, jot—doing your best to read more deeply, more alert to details and word choice that suggest underlying bias. Then take a look at what you've annotated, and compare with a partner."

LAUNCH INDEPENDENT WORK TIME: Let your students know that it's not just going to be this article that you dove into together that will use language suggestive of bias. Whether reading in print or digitally, students should annotate as they read, alert to word choice that reveals bias. You might also invite students to bring in current news articles that are worthy of this same level of close, critical reading.

FIGURE 3.3 Here you can see a marked-up section of a text that has been annotated in a shared reading experience. Using a document camera or other device, as well as showing student examples when kids are midway through the work, gives them models to help them strengthen their own work.

Using Partnerships and Study Groups/Club Work

Partnerships and study groups/clubs are key to close reading: as kids read the same text, they can compare their interpretations and help each other with comprehension—lifelong study skills. Ensure that the groups remain small: when kids have only a partner or a group of three friends reading the same text, they are more likely to remain focused on their reading and discussion.

Returning to our Chinese Exclusion Act example, a teacher might introduce a choice of a third, longer text to students and have them pair off to read and practice the analytical lenses they've been using in the full-group context. The teacher might say: "Now let's read a longer text with our partners. I've provided a few for you to choose among. As you get ready to read, please make a plan: Consider, first, how much you will read before you stop and, second, whether you'd like to discuss and then note-take, or the other way around. Quick, make your plan. [Pause] As you read, I will be coming around to look at your annotations of this new source and to listen in on your conversations about the material. I'll pay particular attention to how you apply the close reading lenses we've been practicing so I can give you feedback. I'm really interested in what you notice, what you see in these texts. With the news today full of bias as well, it's so important to become skilled at this work."

Make Reading Across Multiple Sources the Norm

Both the news and the history that we read, listen to, and watch rely on language to convey experiences we likely didn't witness, in contexts we've likely never seen, in times when we were likely not present. We're also accessing these events through intermediaries—authors or reporters who are themselves interpreting events, so it goes without saying that we have to be cautious with how we interpret what we read. In the section above we discussed the importance of reading closely and collaboratively in order to weigh our interpretations with those of other trusted people; in this section you'll find some ideas for teaching students the importance of reading around a topic and paying particular attention to how ostensibly objective sources might suggest very different connotations about the very same event.

Newseum's "Today's Front Pages" Feature

https://newseumed.org/curated-stack/archived-todays-front-pages-key-moments-history

Comparing Headlines

One powerful way to highlight how objective sources of information can still dramatically differ in the way they portray events is to compare headlines and front-page photos on the same topic from different news outlets. You might find your own headlines or turn to Newseum's "Today's Front Pages" feature, which shows how papers in different parts of the country and the world might report on the same stories—you can also turn to archived pages. The site is free, but you do need to create a login.

Before the lesson, find the front pages of three different newspapers for the same day, addressing the same topic. Note that including international newspapers will give you a wider range of perspectives.

Begin your work with students with a close read of a single newspaper front page. Lead the students to analyze for word choice in the headline by asking them: "Are there any words in the headline that suggest a feeling or tone, rather than strictly facts? What words in the headline suggest the opinion, or stance, or bias of the editors? How might the image(s) on the page convey a point of view?" At this point, layer on the second front page and ask the students: "How does this one compare to the first? Does this headline seem to have the same tone or something slightly different?" (Figure 3.4 includes additional useful prompts.) You might also say to the students, "These two newspapers deal with the same event, but do they focus on the same parts of that big event? What do these headlines choose to focus on?" Then, you might add in the third text, and ask how it relates to the first two.

FIGURE 3.4 Tools like this will help students refine their comparing and contrasting skills as they juxtapose sources.

This type of exercise will help your readers to be more cautious about the news. They'll see that even a reputable source will take an angle on an event and that those angles will affect their reader in subtle ways. As informed readers, it's our job to be aware of these angles, and to try, whenever possible, to triangulate meaning by reading more than one source about an event or issue.

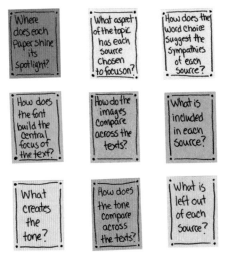
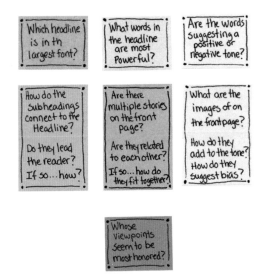

» YOUNG CITIZENS IN ACTION «

In the fall of 2011, Pablo's seventh-grade class at School of the Future was entranced by the Occupy Wall Street protests that had sprung up in Zuccotti Park. The kids had watched the tent city grow on television and wondered what could have motivated so many people to leave the comfort of their homes to camp out in the center of Manhattan with a thousand other strangers. The class read numerous articles about the protests and watched news coverage, which ranged from glowing support, to condescension, to outright accusations of criminality. Confused by conflicting sources of information, the students asked if they could go to the protests themselves and find out firsthand what had motivated people to join them.

With digital cameras, cell phones, and notebooks in hand, Pablo's students paired off and wound their way through Zuccotti Park on a mission to interview as many protestors as possible and record their conversations. Students witnessed the "human microphone" as announcements were spread throughout the park using only the power of the human voice magnified by hundreds of people. They collected stickers, posters, flyers, and other artifacts to analyze back in class. Most importantly, they took videos of the individuals who made up the Occupy movement. The students interviewed a diverse range of subjects—young and old, middle class and homeless—who shared their personal stories.

Over the next two days, the class pored through their artifacts and raw footage and then created mini-documentaries to answer the question, "What caused the Occupy Wall Street Protests?" While internet research and news articles offered these students the background information they needed to grasp the larger context of the Occupy Wall Street protests, it was the direct interviewing of the individuals taking part that allowed students to develop their own interpretation of events. The students learned firsthand the difference between secondary and primary sources.

Reading a Range of News Coverage

Today, we have an array of online tools that can help us to introduce our students to a range of news coverage and help them to practice analytical reading, including:

- **Newsela** (newsela.com) provides news stories daily, to classrooms, at five different reading levels. Newsela is great for getting kids to read about current events every day and for putting more nonfiction into kids' hands. The texts are preselected for kids, with a focus on engagement. When you're using Newsela, you should also be aware that when the reading level is reduced, the complexity of the topic can also be reduced in ways that become problematic, and that the site's comprehension questions promote restating—not critiquing—the author's main point.

- **Newseum** (www.newseumED.org) aims to promote cross-text reading and critical reading of multiple sources. It provides same-day front pages for newspapers around the world and around the country. The levels of the text vary mostly by the intended audience, with the *New York Post* having an easier reading level than the *New York Times*, for example. Newseum also archives front pages for significant days in history.

- **Google News** (www.news.google.com) can also offer contrasting coverage of an issue. Input any event, narrow the date range if you choose, and then see what media from all over the world have to say about it.

- **Allsides** (www.allsides.com) argues that all news carries some bias. They strive to provide sources from across the political spectrum. The texts can be at a high reading level.

- **Google Scholar** (www.scholar.google.com) searches for academic texts on a topic, and it also provides any text that has cited that source since it was written. You can trace the influence, then, of texts and voices.

Another way to practice this work could be to take a newsworthy event and then compare and contrast the ways that international news sources treat the event. For example, when we compared the coverage of Fidel Castro's death in an American newspaper ("Fidel Castro, Cuban Revolutionary Who Defied the US, Dies at 90," *The New York Times,* November 26, 2016) and a French newspaper ("Mort de Fidel Castro," *Le Monde Diplomatique,* November 26, 2016), the portrayals of Castro varied greatly: while the *Times* called Castro "the fiery apostle of revolution," *Le Monde* painted him as David to North America's Goliath.

Teach Students to Read with Healthy Skepticism

At the beginning of this chapter we noted the danger of instilling a sense of cynical detachment; that is the opposite of civic engagement. We are not in the business of creating cynics here. We don't want our students to throw up their hands in frustration and simply wave off all nonfiction and journalism as suspect or corrupt. Rather, we want our students to have a highly tuned radar for bias so that they are cautious with their media consumption. The lesson starters below offer suggestions for how to walk that line so that our students approach their reading with an appropriate wariness rather than a crippling distrust.

Lesson: Weighing and Evaluating Evidence within a Text

CONNECT: When we read Op-eds we should be careful to evaluate the evidence they use to see if their points are well supported. Explain: "Critical readers not only read around texts and compare sources—they also reread an author's evidence closely, weighing and evaluating the strength of that evidence and the reasoning the author uses to unpack the evidence, rather than simply accepting the statements of the author. We can practice this skill by reading Op-eds—essays (not news stories) in newspapers that express opinions of their writers."

TEACH: Return to a text you introduced in read-aloud, or choose a related text. Your text might be related to your unit of study or, if you are simply looking for a strong text that will help you to model evaluating evidence, you might consider using an excerpt from Jason Reynolds and Ibram X. Kendi's *Stamped* (2020), or an excerpt from Jay Z and Molly Crabapple's *New York Times* video, "A History of the War on Drugs" (2016). Model for students how you analyze multiple points in the text to identify those that are strongly supported and those that are less strongly supported. The goal here is to show kids that it's not only that some texts overall are more strongly supported: some *ideas* within a text are also more strongly supported. A continuum like the one shown in Figure 3.5 may help the students rank how well an idea is supported within a text.

ENGAGE: Going on with the same text, invite students to weigh and evaluate evidence for a second point, or turn to a second text and suggest that students evaluate the evidence of part of that text.

LAUNCH INDEPENDENT WORK TIME: If you are focusing on a shared text that you have introduced in the read-aloud, you might let kids continue with parts of this text, perhaps with different partnerships evaluating different points and then coming together in small groups to compare their analyses. If kids are researching in study groups, they could go off to their own research and apply this work to the text they choose to read and/or reread.

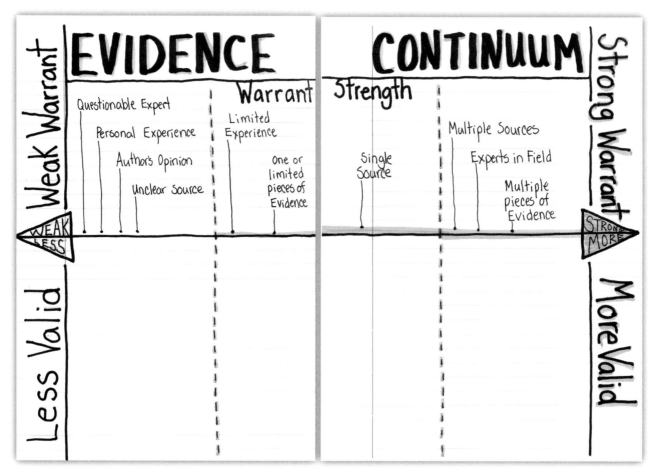

FIGURE 3.5 A "Fairness Continuum" can help researchers track the range of their sources.

Lesson: Interpreting Numbers, Statistics, and Embedded Charts with Careful, Cautious Attentiveness

CONNECT: Let kids know that often our brains are seduced by numbers, statistics, and elaborate charts. Often we find them authoritative and even slightly intimidating, and so we sort of skip over them when we encounter them in a text, assuming that they are valid, and the author's interpretation of the data they present is valid. Other times they seem self-explanatory, and we take for granted that they are fair and accurate. Explain: "Often, when readers encounter statistics, numbers, and complicated charts in a text, they assume that the author will explain these accurately and fairly. Yet sometimes these numbers are represented in ways that distort their meaning. Critical readers, then, attend carefully to embedded numbers, statistics, and charts, paying attention to things like scale, representation, and author interpretation."

TEACH: Show a few news articles that include dramatic numbers. Choose one article, and show students how you analyze the numbers, statistics, or charts as you read—not only thinking aloud as you determine what the information is trying to convey but also considering whether the information is trustworthy or whether it has been distorted.

ENGAGE: Working in pairs or groups of three, ask students to consider the use of data in another article. Provide thinking prompts like those in Figure 3.6 to help students as they work.

LAUNCH INDEPENDENT WORK TIME: Have your students return to their research with this lens as a tool in their toolkit, encouraging them to pause when they get to embedded math-related arguments and to read extra-critically.

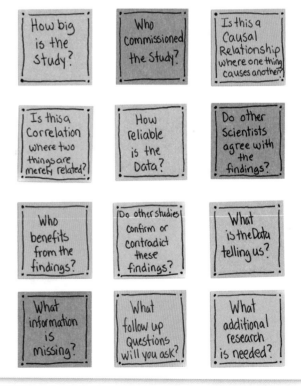

FIGURE 3.6 Students often see numbers and statistics and assume that they represent a hard truth. Use these questions to help them read the numbers critically.

Teach Students to Be Wary of Persuasive Techniques and Logical Fallacies

From the country's first snake oil huckster handing out pamphlets, to Madison Avenue advertising agencies, to modern-day internet ads targeted to our tastes, we've been immersed in a consumer culture that thrives on persuasion, on the selling of something that we may neither want nor need. We can teach our students to recognize when they're being sold on something and to differentiate between reasoned, rational argumentation in which valid points are supported with evidence, and manipulative emotional appeals designed to tug on our basest feelings.

See the online resources for printable descriptions of common logical fallacies.

The experience that students have with modern media primes them for thoughtful work analyzing common persuasive techniques. Some of the most pervasive persuasive techniques have their roots in propaganda, so we will begin with those techniques first named by the Institute for Propaganda Analysis in their seminal work, *The Fine Art of Propaganda* (1971). We suggest that you build centers in which partners work with a series of cards that include some of the most common persuasive techniques and logical fallacies that are often used deliberately, and sometimes slipped into inadvertently, in implicit and explicit arguments.

Centers: Persuasive Techniques and Logical Fallacies

1. Unpack your techniques and fallacies cards and review them with a partner.

2. Choose a video text to analyze.

   a. *The Simpsons*: "The Bear Patrol and Lisa's Tiger-Repelling Rock"

   b. Direct TV Commercial: "Don't Attend Your Own Funeral" (2014)

   c. The O'Reilly Factor: "The Bill O'Reilly and Geraldo Rivero Bust Up" (2007)

   d. Campaign Ad: Dale Peterson (running for Alabama Agriculture Commissioner) (2010)

   e. Café Scene from *Inception* (2010)

   f. *Sesame Street*: "Ernie Has a Banana in His Ear"

3. Read closely, and reread critically, alert to possible persuasive techniques and logical fallacies. Jot down the ones you notice, and then compare with your partner, talking about how these were used in the text.

Lesson: Questioning Representation and Marginalization from the Start

CONNECT: Show students a political cartoon or propaganda poster, such as a WWII poster that overtly demonizes or heroizes, an image of Rosie the Riveter, or German propaganda posters from WWII. Remind students that no text is neutral—but that some texts are more obvious and some are more subtle in how they affirm stereotypes or demonize groups or individuals. Explain: "Researchers also actively question representation in the texts they read. They notice who is included and who is marginalized, distorted, or invisible. When we realize who is seen and who is not, we can seek out texts and sources that include underrepresented voices."

TEACH: Demonstrate how you read a bit of the text, noticing how people and events are described and asking: "How does this text make me feel about this event/person/perspective? How does it accomplish this task?" Also ask, "Who is marginalized, distorted, or invisible?"

ENGAGE: Invite students to try this work out in a new part of that same text or in a parallel text. Coach them to ask these same questions.

LAUNCH INDEPENDENT WORK TIME: Send students back to their text sets, suggesting they apply these lenses to texts they've already read and to the ones they'll read next. Ask students to revisit texts they have read before with this new lens, rethinking how fair and representative those texts are and perhaps annotating or coding these to note representation. From there, encourage them to continue researching, remaining alert to representation as they read.

Teach Students to Weigh Sources and Their Credibility

In the previous chapter we discussed how to create initial text sets to help your students develop background knowledge around contested issues. As your students delve deeper into these issues, you'll want to include texts that are flawed, or biased. For years, we shunned these texts, offering only well-researched, thoughtful texts in our text sets. Of course, we want most of the texts in a text set to be trustworthy, but the problem with not including flawed texts in the work of school is that then we don't prepare kids for what they'll encounter outside of school. Our media landscape these days is littered with untrustworthy news sources. We have a duty to teach our kids how to consume the media around them responsibly and to be wary of the information that streams through their news feeds and inboxes. So now we're strategic about layering in texts that are overtly biased or distorted in their presentation of information so that students can practice critical interpretation skills. We can't leave the hard work for kids to encounter outside of school and only do the work inside that is safe and easy. Our young citizens must be ready to sniff out texts that are satirical, manipulative, or distorted—or are outright fabrications.

Of course, we have to be very careful about how we add in these troubling texts. If we add them to our curated set from the beginning, students are very likely to assume that they are perfectly fine as sources for two reasons: 1) the students aren't very trained in evaluating their sources yet, and 2) the texts come from you, their trusted teacher! Instead of sneaking them in from the beginning, we advise that you explicitly teach a lesson on sniffing out flawed, biased, and untrustworthy texts (see "Investigating the Possibility of Untrustworthy News" on page 97) and then inform the students that you added new texts to their sets today, a certain number of which are deeply flawed. You might say something like: "Students, today I've added five new sources to your text sets, two of which are of dubious quality. While you research today, be on guard that you don't cite from one of these inadequate texts! We'll discuss the offending texts at the end, during our class share." This way your students will have ample warning, and you'll be able to coach them into critical reading habits.

If you are teaching a longer unit and have ample time to dig into media literacy, you may want to devote some class time to unpacking the phrase *fake news*. In a quick but illuminating video entitled, "A Brief History of 'Fake News,'" the BBC refers to the phrase as a catch-all that includes everything from misinformation to conspiracy theories to political spin. The term has also been used as a way to dismiss information that one simply disagrees with. We suggest that you avoid using the phrase *fake news,* instead focusing, as the video suggests, on teaching your students how to differentiate "facts, opinion, speculation and outright fiction" (BBC 2018). The lessons that follow offer some suggestions on how to do this.

Figure 3.7 shows a chart created by Claire Wardle at First Draft Media, which can serve as a helpful tool in identifying different types of mis- and disinformation. Once you've introduced these and invited students to be extra alert to signs of these types of disinformation, it's also worth it to teach students to pay attention to when something just feels murky or off.

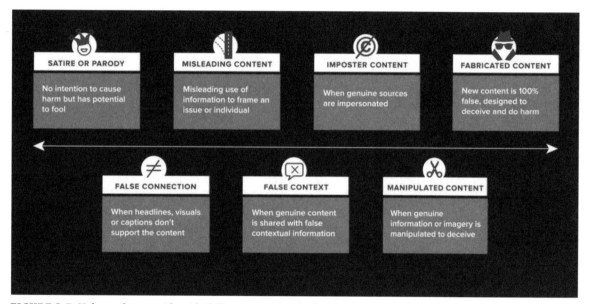

FIGURE 3.7 Help students to identify different ways in which information can be intentionally or unintentionally misleading.

See the online resources for a printable version of this list.

Sites to Help You Teach Students How Misinformation Is Created and Spread

Operation Infektion—illuminating and troubling *New York Times* documentary on how Russia manipulates our public opinion through the sowing of misinformation and has been doing it for decades.

www.nytimes.com/2018/11/12/opinion/russia-meddling -disinformation-fake-news-elections.html

Factitious—game developed by American University that tests students' ability to spot fake news.

http://factitious.augamestudio.com

Bad News—simple game developed by researchers at the University of Cambridge that simulates the spread of fake news.

https://getbadnews.com/#intro

Media Literacy Booster Pack—feature from the Newseum that provides lesson plans, activities, and resources for teaching topics, such as differentiating fact and opinion, identifying fake news, detecting propaganda, and recognizing bias.

https://newseumed.org/edcollection/media-literacy-booster-pack

The Center for Information Technology and Society (CITS) at UC Santa Barbara—an explanation of how untrustworthy news is spread.

www.cits.ucsb.edu/fake-news/spread

News Literacy Project—organization that provides activities, quizzes, and lessons to promote news literacy and that offers professional development for teachers interested in infusing more media literacy in their curricula.

https://newslit.org

Lesson: Investigating the Possibility of Untrustworthy News

CONNECT: Show students a journalist's "triangle" (see Figure 3.8) that introduces the concepts of *Who, What, Where, When, Why,* and *How.* Then, introduce a news report, print or digital, that follows this format. (See Figure 3.8.) Explain: "Just as journalists often use the 5Ws and an H to be sure to include important information for their audience, so readers can use these same lenses to question whether a piece of journalism seems trustworthy. When any of these elements seem murky, it might be that the news is distorted or untrustworthy."

TEACH AND ENGAGE: If you want a light touch to introduce this work, you can turn to the parodic article, "Litany of Lies" (ClickHole 2014), and demonstrate how the text doesn't refer to the school or district, or give any information that would help a reader confirm the story. Then, move on to a problematic text on a high-interest topic. You can find the biggest fake news stories of 2018, for instance, at www.buzzfeednews .com/article/craigsilverman/facebook-fake -news-hits-2018.

Show how you apply the protocol of the 5Ws and an H to reconsider murky or missing information. You might demonstrate using one or two of the Ws, asking kids to do the rest, or you might reread the text, with students noticing any of the 5Ws and an H that seem unclear.

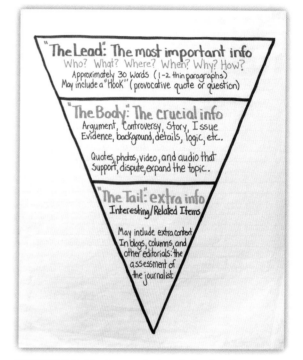

FIGURE 3.8 The inverted triangle for drafting news reports—the parts journalists include—can also be lenses that help readers question the fullness and clarity of journalistic reporting.

LAUNCH INDEPENDENT WORK TIME: Suggest that students review their texts and apply this same protocol to their research as needed. You may want to deliberately introduce a few untrustworthy texts into the students' text sets and caution students to look out for them as they read. Most importantly, suggest that they carry this critical lens with them to all of their consumption of media.

Lesson: Reading Around a Text

CONNECT: Suggest that when readers are suspicious, they can turn to outside sources to affirm their suspicions or confirm a source. Explain: "The world of internet research is full of flawed sources. Often, when we get a feeling that something might be off about a text, or it seems important to confirm something in a text, we can turn to outside sources, especially ones that engage in public fact-checking."

TEACH: Return to a text that you and the class have already noted as something that might not be trustworthy. Demonstrate how to go back into the text in question and pull out some key search terms, such as the event, character names, place, and/or author, and combine those with the name of a reputable news source to get another reporting of the event. Here you may note that, while no news source is perfect, there are a few that regularly win prestigious awards for excellence in journalism, such as the *New York Times*, the *Washington Post*, the *Los Angeles Times*, the *Boston Globe,* and the *Wall Street Journal*. These sources are often a good starting point for verifying information.

ENGAGE: Invite students to try checking the text in question, using another source. Either pull one up yourself and invite students to notice inconsistencies in what was reported, and/or invite students to combine search terms with a different source and notice how the event was reported. Then extend this work by suggesting that you can also research authors in order to investigate the groups and agendas they may be affiliated with.

LAUNCH INDEPENDENT WORK TIME: Suggest that as students go off to research, they consider finding another source on a particular moment or event. Remind them that they can also investigate authors and their public agendas. As they do so, encourage them to be alert to journalistic sources that fact-check and revise publicly and that are recognized by established organizations for strong journalism.

Lesson: Considering the Effects of Master Narratives

CONNECT: If you're introducing your students to the concept of master narratives, you might want to begin by watching the jarring Schoolhouse Rock's *Elbow Room*, with its overt celebration of a master narrative of Manifest Destiny. Then explain: "A master narrative gives an account of events that shows a dominant group's perspective, often justifying that group's dominance. It does not reflect the perspective of those who are not in power. For instance, the master narrative of Manifest Destiny— the belief that it was destiny that settlers expand westward—justified (in the settlers' minds) the genocide of Indigenous Peoples. Master narratives of the superiority of some and the inferiority of others not only constitute a perceived justification for oppression but also rewrite history to favor some groups and erase others. Master narratives can be less dramatic, and less obvious, but their impact can be significant because they are so ingrained in society that they are not questioned."

TEACH: Chances are, if you open any US history textbook to the chapter on the Pilgrims or the Founding Fathers, you'll get a strong sense of the master narrative that a small group of idealistic white men founded this country and made it what it is today. If you have any of these kinds of textbooks in your closet, get one out: now is the moment to find an excerpt to share. (One example is a feature in a US history textbook, *The Pilgrims Before the Mayflower,* extolling the virtues of the Pilgrims and titled "They Never Gave Up.") You might demonstrate finding one master narrative in a text and leave others for students to find.

ENGAGE: If you stay with the same text, you can invite students to suggest other possible master narratives. Or you can move to a second text. Chart some of the master narratives that emerge. We've found a particularly compelling text to be JayZ and Molly Crabapple's video documentary *A History of the War on Drugs* (2016), which explicitly dismantles racist master narratives propagated deliberately in the War on Drugs.

LAUNCH INDEPENDENT WORK TIME: When kids go off to work, you might suggest that they read, alert to some of the master narratives that emerged in the minilesson (if you studied a content-related text). Or, suggest that their partnership or study group revisit their research briefly, charting some of the master narratives that emerge. Then they can read on, alert to the presence of these master narratives.

Lesson: Center Counternarratives

CONNECT: If US history textbooks mostly align with a master narrative that this nation was honorably founded on the ideals of a few enlightened white men from the British colonies, then the Broadway hit *Hamilton* subverts that master narrative at almost every level: people of color are cast in most of the roles, women fight on the battlefield alongside men, and two of the most important characters (Hamilton and Lafayette) are celebrated as immigrants. You might play a video of the cast's 2016 performance at the Tony awards, asking kids to ponder what this show suggests about who has peopled and made America "great." Explain: "In history, popular culture, and literature, there are not only master narratives but also counternarratives, which show the perspectives of those who have been oppressed by the master narrative. By seeking out and studying counternarratives, we can gather a fuller understanding of an event, movement, or time period."

TEACH AND ENGAGE: Here is where you want to emphasize and highlight voices who have been underrepresented and voices who offer counternarratives that suggest possibility, especially to kids in your class. You might turn to teen activists such as the Parkland kids, whose speeches and activism have disrupted a master narrative of teens as children and victims, or to any of the Climate Warriors, such as Autumn Peltier, who have led the world in activism. Or you might return to your content, bringing out the counternarratives that are often submerged there.

Some texts that can be helpful in offering explicit counternarratives:

- *Stamped: Racism, Anti-Racism, and You,* by Jason Reynolds and Ibram X. Kendi (2020)
- *An Indigenous Peoples' History of the United States for Young People,* by Debbie Reese, Jean Mendoza, and Roxanne Dunbar-Ortiz (2019)
- *A Queer History of the United States for Young People*, by Michael Bronski and Richie Chevat (2019)
- *A Young People's History of the United States* by Rebecca Stefoff and Howard Zinn (2009)
- *An African American and Latinx History of the United States,* by Paul Ortiz (2018)
- *Home of the Brave: 15 Immigrants who Shaped U.S. History,* by Brooke Khan and Iratxe López de Munáin. (2019)
- *American Trailblazers: 50 Remarkable People who Shaped U.S. History,* by Lisa Trusiani (2019)
- *Vice* Magazine, including "Vice Profiles".

LAUNCH INDEPENDENT WORK TIME: At this point you can send kids off to actively seek counternarratives that relate to the research they've done so far, or you can send them off to go on with their research, alert to the possibility of counternarratives.

Involve Families and Communities

One of the most immediate ways to involve families and communities in helping to raise children who question sources and seek alternative voices is to actively seek the perspectives of family members and community members. Invite students often to interview family members for their perspectives on the topics students are studying and the texts they are reading. Ask family and community members to suggest voices and texts that will deepen and broaden students' perspectives.

No single teacher can ever know as many texts and histories and voices as those that will be known and celebrated by our students' families and communities. This will be especially true when we teach multiliterate students. Then our own language barriers may prevent us from accessing texts that our students can access. Ask for help from families, colleagues, and students.

When you have curriculum night, or parent–teacher conferences, it can also be helpful to share ideas for magazine subscriptions and magazines that are found at the local library or online. Giving kids access to *Latinitas* or *Teen Ink* or *Sesi* can help kids to find themselves in print communities and to develop a personal reading life and sense of identity they bring to their school selves.

Be Ready for Anything

Expect this work to be difficult for your students as they're unlikely to have had much experience directly critiquing sources of information. At this point in their academic lives, your students have largely expected that the texts given to them are simply "true," and the idea that people will have varying angles on what's true is complex and disconcerting. Students will need lots of practice with analyzing sources. Try to introduce sources in pairs, so that through comparison and contrast students can see where texts overlap and differ, then introduce a third text and ask which one does it align with more and why. Getting into the practice of triangulating meaning from multiple sources is a key habit for critical readers and engaged citizens.

In a similar vein, you may find that students find it difficult to hear bias during your strategic read alouds because they are unaccustomed to questioning sources. You may want to begin your first read through a text with emotional language rather than academic language in your prompt. For example, instead of "listen for bias," you may start by asking, "How does this text make you feel?" Priming the students with social and emotional prompts generally leads to greater success when you follow up with a thorough, academic, second read.

As with much of this book, there is a risk of conflict when pointing out the bias or slant of different news publications or political advertisements. You'll want to make sure that you frame your work as universally as possible. Show that publications and political campaigns across the political spectrum use the same techniques to sway their audiences.

Practice What You Teach

It's easy to look at a news story that has been debunked and wonder how anyone could have fallen for it, but the truth is that no one is immune to propaganda. The questions below might help you recall anecdotes to help you remember what it feels like to learn the lessons this chapter teaches and, perhaps, to share your own experiences with your students, to let them know that their own learning curves in this work are to be expected.

- When were you surprised by disparate coverage of an event?
- When have you realized that one of your trusted sources of media actually had biased coverage of an event?
- When were you duped, or confused by a source?
- When have you inadvertently "liked" or shared a post in your social media account that you later realized was disinformation, or untrustworthy?
- When have you seen studies, charts, infographics that paint a persuasive picture, but are actually flawed?
- When have you seen egregious examples of propaganda techniques in advertising, either for products or political campaigns?

We have all had lapses in our news literacy and acknowledging it can help us—and our students—realize the importance of vigilant reading. As civically engaged educators, we can learn from our own mistakes and even help our students to learn from them as well.

Civic Virtues Addressed in this Chapter

- finding one's voice through writing
- engaging with urgent social issues
- revising one's thinking
- becoming a radical listener

Planning Your Time

We have included a few different curricular options inside this chapter. We've used the identity essays that launch the chapter as a fast-paced, one-week unit before moving into text-based argument essays or literary essays. We've also used them as a longer, three-week unit in which kids draft a couple of essays and then bring one to publication. In that second model, you can spend more time with some different generating strategies, and writers can collect for longer. In the same way, the study of mentor texts for content, structure, style, register, and craft can be a quick one-day study, or it can be something you return to across the writing process, rereading with specific lenses. The same is true of flash-debating and listening to counterclaims. That can be a rapid, ten-minute activity at any time in the process of research and writing, or it can be a full period, with kids rehearsing, debating, considering counterclaims, and preparing rebuttals.

FOUR

ENGAGED CITIZENS COME TO NUANCED AND RECEPTIVE STANCES

When we were kids, we never dreamed of the kind of content-area writing revolution that is happening now. Writers like Jared Diamond, Naomi Klein, Atul Gawande, and Siddhartha Mukherjee have made history, science, and journalism fascinating and relevant to millions of citizens. There is a huge schism, though, between the kind of writing that kids do for school and the kind of writing that matters in the world. It's almost as if school hasn't caught up, which is what worries researchers such as Jamila Lyiscott in *Black Appetite, White Food* (2019), or Tony Wagner in *The Global Achievement Gap* (2014), or Mitchel Resnick in *Lifelong Kindergarten* (2017), or Eduardo Briceño in his 2020 TED talk "How to Get Better at the Things You Care About." The world needs young people who have spent time in school honing their creative capacities, exploring their unique voices, trying out different registers and modalities, and seeking the modes in which they are most compelling and authentic. In many classrooms, however, time is spent trying to get all the kids to write and speak in one register, in a single modality.

Instead, we can value kids' voices and give them opportunities to grow as writers by valuing more than one register or modality in writing. We can help more kids access writing as a learnable skill that enhances their voice and we can show them how their voices can be powerful. Look at the Scholastic Art and Writing Awards, and you can see how they relentlessly embrace and reward hybrid essay tones and structures. Look at the explosion of nonfiction graphic novels, of YA literary nonfiction like Susan Cain's *Quiet Power* (2017) and Mark Kurlansky's *World Without Fish* (2011), and Jason Reynolds and Ibram X. Kendi's *Stamped: Racism, Anti-racism, and You* (2020), and you see the shift—the deliberate shift of tone and style—to engage a wider audience. The publishing world has shifted. But school hasn't shifted.

Today, as in the last few decades, school is driven by five-paragraph essays and AP or IB writing assessments that have changed little over decades. The texts kids write about have changed (a little), there has been a tiny bit of opening up of choice, but essentially these tasks and assessments value the kind of writing someone would have done at Yale or the Sorbonne a hundred years ago. It's a kind of intellectual analytical writing that values structure over almost all else, that rewards careful layering of text evidence and attention to transitions, and that severely limits voice, probing criticism, or passionate attachments. And that's a problem, because all over the world, adult professionals are having to relearn writing as a result of that training.

One of the reasons that scientists gathered to reimagine K–12 science standards, which became the Next Generation Science Standards, was because, as they state, it doesn't do any good to do great science if no one believes it or cares about it. You can read more about this crisis in *A Framework for K–12 Science Education* (2012), put out by the National Research Council. It's fascinating and sobering reading about the need for content writers to become more lively, engaging, humane writers. The climate-change crisis—the very real, 97-percent-of-all-climate-scientists-agree-on crisis—is what stimulated the change in the standards to focus so much on compelling argumentation. At the highest levels, there has been a change in what science writers are being asked to do. Alan Alda is giving workshops to scientists on how to speak and write in ways that get people to listen. Mary's partner, Rich Hallett, a federal research scientist who specializes in urban ecology, talks about struggling to change his writing style because he and his peers are now being told *not* to write in the passive voice or the third person that they painstakingly learned, because that style comes across as archaic and passionless. At universities, classes for graduates and undergraduates as well as seminars for faculty now include classes on how to make your writing more compelling, and those classes are for scientists and historians and economists.

With this in mind, it becomes clear that part of being an engaged citizen is the ability to write in a way that not only presents facts but also conveys one's own passionate concerns. There is a fine line between the personal essay and argumentation, just as in the published nonfiction works that make changes in our world today. While we'll stay in the realm of essay, the role of story will be crucial. We'll explore personal identity stories, then look at the role of story in argument writing. Instead of letting school be a place where students learn that their stories don't matter, we can make kids the curriculum, showing them that their lives and experiences *are* worth writing about, not only in personal narrative but also in essay. Additionally, this chapter will address the hardest and perhaps most overlooked part of working with individuals' perspectives: listening to opposing views in ways that let us consider them rationally and empathetically, and being willing to revise our own thinking.

In this chapter we'll help you to:

- consider the identities of the kids in your classroom
- help students to identify and name their own perspectives in powerful writing
- let kids write in their own voices
- teach kids to be radical listeners as they develop arguments
- involve families and communities
- be ready for anything
- practice what you teach.

Before You Begin: Consider the Identities of the Kids in Your Classroom

Often, and at times unbeknownst to us, kids' identities are wrapped up in parts of an argument. It's important to recognize that some kids may experience arguments more as emotional labor than as intellectual play. We worked for a time in Seattle, for instance, when a lot of former child-soldiers were relocated to the city. Studying and talking about the fate of child soldiers didn't feel at all the same to some of these kids as it might to others. We've worked in refugee camps and in detention centers, where conditions of chaos and uncertainty are a crucible. We've worked with kids and teachers who have crossed borders, who have suffered bombings and violence, some of it from American raids. And we've encountered hidden violence in what felt like calm suburbs and fragility where we did not expect it.

The truth is, we can't hide kids from the world. It's not our job to keep the news from them or to censor the topics they want to explore. But we can do our best to expect that a topic raised in class may be far more personal than academic to kids, even if we don't know or fully understand that personal connection. We can read their silence as hesitation and self-protection rather than as indifference or lack of caring.

There are a few things that we can do, as teachers, that can help sustain kids and protect them from the curriculum becoming overwhelming emotional labor. One is to find out as much as possible about our kids and their histories. We can engage kids in personal narrative writing in writing workshop, we can strive to meet kids' families, we can seek to learn about their communities. Finding out where kids live, where they go to worship, where they work, and where they are from is part of teaching kids. Perhaps the best book about this work is Gloria Ladson-Billings' *The Dreamkeepers: Successful Teachers of African American Children* (2009), which describes how urgently African American students need to be known and implies how urgently *all* students need to be known. Ladson-Billings shows that effective teachers find out about their kids and adapt their teaching so that it is relevant and sensitive to the students in front of them. We wish conditions had changed for more kids in this country since this book's publication, but they haven't, and Ladson-Billings' work is just as relevant today as the first day she published. Alfred Tatum's *Teaching Reading to Black Adolescent Males: Closing the Achievement Gap* (2005) also speaks to the texts we choose to put in front of kids—and how they need to teach kids how to live their lives. Brené Brown's *Daring Greatly: How the Courage to Be Vulnerable Transforms the Way We Live, Love, Parent, and Lead* (2012) shows the interconnectedness of vulnerability and courage, and encourages us to be the first to be willing to be vulnerable, to change others.

Another way to help kids negotiate the curriculum is to offer as much choice as possible. Totally free reign of research topics can turn into a surf-the-internet unit rather than a serious research or writing unit, but it's very helpful to have a negotiated range of research topics and text sets that students can choose from. Pablo invites kids to rate and suggest relevant topics related to the curriculum. Marc organizes starter text-sets, and gives kids time to browse them. Mary has worked with teachers around moving from an overarching class topic to related subtopics, striving for a range of representation and relevancy. We suggest a mix of all of these, since anytime you increase choice, you not only increase engagement, you also give kids more ability to negotiate the curriculum.

Another way to help kids with the emotional labor of the curriculum is to give space for free-writing and reflection. Marc gives his kids time every Friday in his social studies class to "write long" about what they are thinking and feeling about the curriculum that week. When we say "write long" we mean giving the students a set amount of time to write freely in their notebooks with minimal guidance from us. Kids write about what they are rethinking and what they've learned. But they also write about when they felt personally connected to something in the curriculum, or when they found something they studied hard and upsetting. Writing helps us through trouble.

Students can write long in a separate notebook (which can be paper or digital, according to the preference of individual students). Students who write every week will have up to thirty-six entries by the end of the year that articulate their beliefs and thinking process on issues that are important to them. As educators, if we want our students to do this type of thinking, then we must provide time and space for them to do it well. Dim the lights. Play some soft music. In the beginning, highlight some writing that is brave and strong. Then move on to teaching students some writing strategies about introducing different kinds of evidence to support their ideas. Teach them the power of elaboration to show an idea matters. Encourage them to try different styles and voices. Give them time to reread their writing for clarity of ideas and to listen to their writer's voice as they write about topics that matter to them. Let them spread out across the room finding their own space for comfort to do their best writing. The audience for this writing is themselves and their research or writing partner if they choose to share.

It's also worth thinking with kids about mirrors and windows in your content curricula, not just in their encounters with fiction. Dr. Rudine Sims Bishop, in her essay, "Mirrors, Windows, and Sliding Glass Doors" (1990), talks about the need for kids to see themselves in the texts they encounter in school. This matters for nonfiction as much as for fiction. It's one reason that textbooks are so problematic: the representation of people of color in US textbooks continues to be overwhelmingly partial, and the narratives are all-too-often victim narratives. Look at your texts and curricula, asking yourself, "How will some of my students experience this text, this film, this representation?" You can also ask, "Who will feel empowered, and who may feel disempowered, in this classroom experience?"

Finally, we highly recommend the "Culturally Responsive Curriculum Scorecard" from the Metropolitan Center for Research on Equity and the Transformation of Schools at NYU (The NYU Metro Center). In collaboration with the Education Justice Research and Organizing Collaborative (EJ-ROC), the NYU Metro Center helps teachers assess their curriculum for equity, focusing on inclusivity, representation, and bias. It's a powerful and sobering tool to help us figure out how to make our curriculum more culturally responsive. When we met with members of EJ-ROC, they were clear that no single unit of study is going to meet all the criteria on the scorecard. But it's illuminating to consider your curriculum overall, noting how some students may feel more visible and empowered inside of it than others. They also provide concrete suggestions for improving equity by working on the criteria of the scorecard.

The process of composing, exploring, and revising our perspectives leave kids and adults alike more-nuanced, complex thinkers and better listeners.

Metropolitan Center for Research on Equity and the Transformation of Schools at NYU's Culturally Responsive Curriculum

https://research
.steinhardt.nyu.edu
/scmsAdmin/media
/users/atn293/ejroc
/CRE-Rubric-2018
-190211.pdf

Help Students to Identify and Name Their Own Perspectives in Powerful Writing

Let's start on a small, intimate scale, with personal arguments–identity essays. Mary first began this work in a tiny NYC middle school, Manhattan Institute of Technology, with Heather Freyman, sixth-grade teacher extraordinaire, who invited her students to think deeply about the issues that affected their lives that they found

Here are some texts that we've found enormously helpful with the hard and beautiful work of coaching writers—from fitting conferring into your busy class schedule, to figuring out what to say to writers, to incorporating methods into your conferences.

- **Penny Kittle's** *Write Beside Them* **(2008)** is a crucial text for supporting your conferring with adolescent writers.
- **Katherine Bomer's** *The Journey is Everything* **(2017)** illuminates the history of journey of thought essays and shows the power of mentor texts.
- **Lucy Calkins's** *Teaching Writing* **(2020)** has a beautiful section on intimacy, where she talks about the close connection that you form when you listen to young writers.
- **Carl Anderson's** *A Teacher's Guide to Writing Conferences* **(2018)** is an essential guide for writing teachers on the humane art of conferring.
- **Roy Peter Clarke's** *Writing Tools: 55 Essential Strategies for Every Writer* **(2008)** makes the art of revision and editing magical.

confusing or painful, and to consider writing to think through those issues. Since then, Heather has moved to IS 289. At 289, master ELA teachers Christina DiZebba and Jennifer Brogan also teach students to write intimate, courageous pieces. It's worth considering why kids and teachers have found this work so moving.

Kids wanted to write about why people were racist, about how they were beginning to realize they didn't think the same way as their parents about some issues, about why they found it so hard to stand up to bullies, about why their neighborhood felt different from other neighborhoods, about the pressure to fit in, about their need to code-switch from family to school to friend groups, about resisting homophobia. Rather than begin with a plan to prove a claim, students began with a desire for illumination, a drive to better understand the issue and their own perspective. Over the course of their work on this piece, the students thought through these issues that had felt messy and difficult at first and found their own clear beliefs. The results are heartfelt arguments unique to each writer, arguments that not only can persuade others but also, perhaps more importantly, can crystalize each writer's sense of purpose. Figure 4.1A–B shows two of these pieces:

You'll find more student examples in the online resources.

Who Do We Say "Good Morning" To

When I was little, I always thought the world was safe for everyone and I always thought that my parents were right about everything. And I want to still think that, but I can't really. I don't think the world is safe for everyone, or that even in this city everyone is warm or dry or even has enough to eat. I don't know what to do about that and it makes me unhappy. Usually when I am unhappy I ask my parents what to do, but this time I can't, because now I think maybe we don't think the same way about everything.

Two years ago, on a cold and wet December day, my mom and I were going into a music store. The rain whistled down the street sideways, blowing into your eyes and stinging your face. It went right through the Patagonia fleece jacket I was wearing and blew around inside it, making me cold to the bones. My mom and I held hands so we wouldn't get blown away. Broken umbrellas flew down the street like bats.

Just outside the store a homeless man was lying by the doorway. He had made a kind of nest beside the door, with an old blanket and some boxes. But the wind had torn the boxes to pieces and the rain had made the blanket soggy, and he looked very cold. His face was full of lines that looked like the lines on my mom's face when she is really tired or sick. But his face was dirty, and my mom's face is never dirty.

The man held out a cup for some money. His hand was shaking and his eyes were red and puffy. I could hardly bear to look at him. I wanted to give him some money but I didn't have any. So I pulled on my mom's hand and asked her if we could give him some money. But she said no, that the man should get a job.

We walked into the store and we didn't give the man anything. We left the man shivering out in the street. And I still think about it. I don't think it would be so easy for that man to get a job. His clothes were ripped and he smelled and he was old. And I think too, about how we didn't even say anything to him, as if he wasn't worth talking to. And the whole thing just doesn't feel right to me.

Next time, I'm going to try to at least say "Good morning." I'm going to try to show that I know this is a person too.

Savaria

FIGURE 4.1A Savaria makes a plea for change not in the world, but in herself. Her essay is a journey of thought, bringing the reader into her growing realizations about how she doesn't always feel the same way about the world as her parents do.

Stop Using Hate Names, Please

"Faggot!" I hear Greg call Taylor this, just joking, hitting him as he runs down the hall. "That's faggy," Warren says this morning, without emphasis, just another casual insult. "Fag," more meanly, he says again later, to the quiet Chinese boy who sits in the front and never says anything.

I wish that for the rest of my life I would never ever ever hear that word again. I wish I wouldn't hear kids say it so hatefully, or say it as if it doesn't even matter. Why is it that some kids feel like they can just throw hate around?

I have two dads. Their names are Jake and Bill. I call them both Dad. They both came to China when I was a baby and they brought me home to New York City. My other parents had given me away because I was a girl, and in China they could only have one child, and they didn't want one who was a girl. They wanted to try again to have a boy. So they gave me away. Some Chinese boys tell me I should be glad they just didn't leave me to die.

My Dads are gay. My dads are kind. My dads play basketball and soccer. My dads gave me my first bike and they taught me how to ride it. All they want in the whole world is for me to be happy. When I hear kids say 'fag,' with that mean voice, I feel it like a knife is cutting into my Dads, slicing them apart right in front of me.

Names hurt. Names tell what we are afraid of. Names tell who we want to hurt. Names tell who we think just doesn't even count. Names make me afraid. My Dads tell the story sometimes, of Matthew Shepard, the college student who was beat up and killed by some kids who didn't like 'fags.' They chained him to a fence and they beat him and beat him until he died. And then they left him there and they went home.

Please stop saying 'fag' and 'faggot.'

Eliza

FIGURE 4.1B Eliza makes an impassioned plea for others in her world to think and act differently.

The clarity and voice in these pieces might make it hard to believe that students did not begin writing them with a finely honed argument or personal conviction in mind. They didn't—in fact, the act of writing led them to develop, revise, and further develop their thinking. Here are some lessons for guiding students as they write.

Lesson: Beginning with Mentors

CONNECT: Students—especially those who have previously been taught to write arguments with a predetermined goal or perspective in mind—benefit from seeing what deeply personal arguments can look like. Share with students that you are inviting them to try a particularly personal and illuminating kind of writing—personal and persuasive essays that are journeys of thought. Explain that while a lot of essays in school aim to prove a claim in the world using reasons and evidence, many essays set out to explore an idea, theory, or question *before* the writers are sure of their thinking—they use writing to figure out what they think. Then explain: "To begin to think about journey-of-thought essays, it can be helpful to study some mentor texts. Thinking especially about how writers develop their ideas, ask yourself: What are some of the parts of these essays?"

TEACH: Demonstrate how, as you study one mentor text, such as Savaria's essay, you consider that it can be helpful to think about the parts named in Figure 4.2. Then show how you look at the first paragraph, asking yourself: "What possible part is this? Is it an anecdote? Does it provide some context? Or is it more of a thesis?" Then label the very beginning of the text. See examples of this kind of work in Figure 4.3.

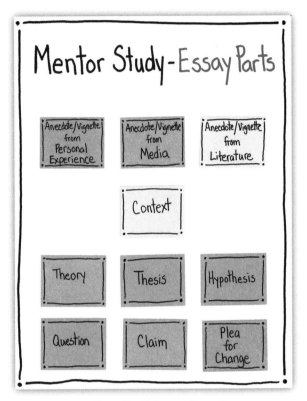

FIGURE 4.2 A chart that helps students deconstruct possible parts of essays. Often students really appreciate lenses for studying mentor texts, especially for structure, for which they have little language.

ENGAGE: Using the same mentor text, hand out one copy each to partners, as well as a marker and sticky notes. Invite partners to study the rest of the text as you read it aloud, marking and labeling the text to identify its structure.

LAUNCH INDEPENDENT WORK TIME: Give students time to work in partnerships, using sticky notes and markers to mark up one or two other mentor texts in terms of structure. At the end of class, give partners a chance to meet with another partnership, inviting them to share the essays they liked, in terms of both content and structure.

Scholastic Art and Writing Awards

www.artandwriting
.org/explore/online
-galleries

Marking up two or three mentors for structure, or parts, helps kids to see that these essays can be written in parts and there is no one way to order the parts. That kind of puzzle is intriguing to kids—the choice of structure provides choice over how their essay might go. Meanwhile, as students study a few mentor texts, they also get an idea of the kinds of things that other kids have written about, and that often helps them to consider meaningful topics. We really like the sample personal and critical essays at Scholastic Art and Writing Awards, where you can choose student exemplars for different grade levels.

HELPING STUDENTS ENVISION THEIR PERSONAL ESSAYS

Watch Mary's sample lesson for using a mentor text's craft moves to consider what students might try in their own essays.

http://hein.pub/
CivicallyEngaged
Classroom

FIGURE 4.3 Marking up texts for writerly moves, or techniques, helps kids see more in mentor texts. They can also move these sticky notes to places in their own writing where they want to try these techniques.

Lesson: Finding Ideas to Write About

CONNECT: Share with students that in these kinds of essays, our aim is to focus less on a claim than on an idea. That is, kids start with an idea they would love to achieve more clarity on, … which is what Katherine Bomer, in *The Journey is Everything* (2017), and Tom Romano, in *Crafting Authentic Voice* (2004), describe as writing to investigate or ponder. Explain: "When writers are looking for ideas they may want to write about, it can be helpful to explore topic ideas together. Often, in the process of finding topics, writers come to realize that issues they thought they suffered alone are issues that others are also experiencing. One strategy that can help writers find ideas and stories in their own lives is to cocreate an issue wall of the issues they care about."

FIGURE 4.4A It is empowering to see students reflect on issues that are important to them.

TEACH: Hang a large piece of chart paper—or create a GoogleSite, Jamboard, or other digital site—and suggest that you collect the issues, or troubles, that have come up in the stories kids have been reading, in the ones they've been writing, and in their own lives (see Figure 4.4A–B). Starting with fiction stories makes it easier

FIGURE 4.4B By providing a space for the issues to be posted, you honor the impact that the issues have in your students' lives.

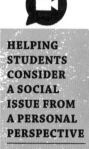

HELPING STUDENTS CONSIDER A SOCIAL ISSUE FROM A PERSONAL PERSPECTIVE

Watch Mary's sample lesson for using an issue wall to spark student writing.

http://hein.pub/
CivicallyEngaged
Classroom

for kids to be brave, and you can model how you think and begin to jot—scrawling as on a graffiti wall—issues and struggles, such as loneliness, fitting in, peer pressure, competition, and so on. Your modeling matters. Talk about how, when you were young, you struggled with fitting in, or with pressure or loneliness, and scrawl those. Add an issue you now care about—perhaps dealing with sexism or bullying.

ENGAGE: After a moment, suggest that kids talk quietly to a partner and add to their notebooks other ideas of issues that matter to them; then collect those so you have a master wall. It often ends up looking something like the examples in Figure 4.4A–B.

LAUNCH INDEPENDENT WORK TIME: Next, demonstrate how you might circle or jot in your notebook the issues that you have personal experience with; then begin to collect moments when you experienced those issues, and draft short anecdotes or vignettes. Essentially, there are two kinds of entries—narrative anecdotes about moments when you've experienced an issue, and reflections in which you think about why you care about this issue so much, sharing context and explanations. You'll find that kids begin jotting almost immediately. There is something cathartic about seeing that issues you felt alone in are often shared. Some kids write privately, sitting in corners. Others are immediately open about what they're worried about. It is helpful if you have set up writing partnerships with kids who trust each other. This is a better time to go for friendship partners than partnerships that aim to match kids by considering academic performance or skills. Kids need to feel like they can talk with their partner—that's more important, right now, than getting writing advice.

Next, give kids two or three days to collect in their notebooks anecdotes and vignettes about one or two or three issues they care about.

One of Eliza's notebook entries, for instance, that ultimately led to her essay topic, is shown in Figure 4.5. You can see that Eliza has deeply felt emotions and ethical concerns about racism and homophobia. Over the next few days she collected more entries, using generating strategies to come up with ideas and issues, writing about where she has seen these issues in media and the news, and drafting anecdotes about when she experienced them personally. That's the work your students will do, whether they are writing about their problems with a sibling, their worries about body image, or their questions about why people find it hard to accept differences.

> I'm going to write the words I wish no-one in school would use anymore. Here's one - FAG. I wish kids would stop saying it. Warren says it in the hallway and Taylor says it in class and Greg says it all the time. I don't think they even know that it is a word full of hate. I wonder if I told them about people I love who are gay if kids who say things like 'fag' could learn to accept them, or just not use hate-words about them?
>
> Here's another word I don't want to hear anymore - Chink. Once I heard some kids in the cafeteria look at the table where I was sitting with my friends and say to some kids 'oh, that's where all the Chinks sit!'
>
> I want to write about names that hurt. I just don't know how to do it yet.

FIGURE 4.5 Kids who write often in their notebook end up finding topics they didn't even realize were possible to write about in school. Whether print or digital, a notebook can be a place where writers wonder, wander, and discover.

Lesson: Drafting in Parts and Playing with Preliminary Structure

CONNECT: Once your kids have some pages of notebook entries, you can spend one period having them commit to their topic and begin to draft parts. It's probably helpful to return to your exemplars, the ones where you boxed out and annotated the parts, so that students can remind themselves of some of the parts of these kinds of essays—and how different writers play with structure. Explain: "Writers often find it helpful to draft parts of their essays, beginning with the parts for which they have the most to say, and then moving to other parts. Getting parts of your essay drafted helps you to develop what you are thinking and want to say, bit by bit, and then allows you to play with structure by moving parts around."

TEACH: Demonstrate how you develop a system for moving out of your notebook and beginning to draft in parts. If you are working digitally, it helps to start a new file, and show how you'll print your parts, probably on different pieces of paper, so that you can move them around. If you are writing with a pen, you might write only on the front of different pieces of paper, so you can do the same work of drafting some parts and then playing with structure.

ENGAGE: Have partners make a writing plan, deciding whether, in this case, they draft better on paper or on a device, and what parts they might start with.

LAUNCH INDEPENDENT WORK TIME: Send kids off to draft their anecdotes as well as their more reflective parts. You may need two class periods for this work. Encourage kids to return to their notebooks to experiment, or to write long about why they care about this topic or when they first began to care. For a lot of kids, talking out their essay—rehearsing it in the air—is really helpful. For some kids, you might do some rapid transcription so they capture their thinking, and/or help them use devices and apps with speech recognition. Don't worry about the thesis/plea for change yet. Get your kids to draft their anecdotes and vignettes, and their contextual explanations, and help them begin to put these into a possible order.

HELPING STUDENTS CONNECT THEIR OWN STORIES TO SOCIAL ISSUES

Watch Mary's sample lesson that helps students identify stories from their own lives and connect them to social issues in their essays and narratives.

http://hein.pub/ CivicallyEngaged Classroom

Lesson: Returning to Mentors to Strengthen Revision

CONNECT: Once your kids have some preliminary drafts on paper, celebrate their drafts and remind them of what Roy Peter Clark (2010) calls drafts—"your ticket to the revision party"! Suggest: "Once writers have a draft, that's when they can begin to play with their writing, trying out different moves to make their voices powerful. One way to investigate writerly moves is to return to mentor texts, asking: 'What are some moves, or techniques that this writer tried, that I can try, too?'"

TEACH: Demonstrate how you look over the possible mentor texts, choosing one that speaks to you in terms of its content and/or style, and invite students to choose their own personal mentor text. Kids don't have to just study essays—they can revise their narrative parts by studying narrative excerpts as well. A note: As always, you'll have to make decisions about mentors based on the age of your kids. We tend towards edgy writing, so you'll want to preview texts for yourself. If you're unsure, Scholastic is pretty much always safe, and their reviewers choose some great pieces. We love some of the writing found in:

- Scholastic's *The Best Teen Writing* (of 2016, 2017, 2018, etc.)
- *Nevertheless We Persisted: 48 Voices of Defiance, Strength, and Courage,* edited by In This Together Media (2018)
- *Hope Nation: YA Authors Share Personal Moments of Inspiration,* edited by Rose Brock (2018)
- *We are Here to Stay: Voices of Undocumented Young Adults,* by Susan Kuklin (2019)
- *Cornered: 14 Stories of Bullying and Defiance,* edited by Rhoda Belleza (2012)
- *(Don't) Call me Crazy: 33 Voices Start the Conversation about Mental Health,* edited by Kelly Jensen (2018)

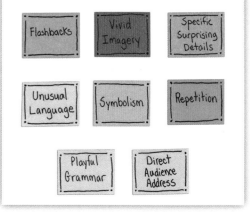

FIGURE 4.6 Providing students with several revision strategies will increase the likelihood that their work changes meaningfully in between drafts.

ENGAGE: Give kids the opportunity to choose their own mentor texts, and give them some lenses for their study. You might, for example, give students sticky notes to label powerful uses of lenses, such as those named in Figure 4.6.

LAUNCH INDEPENDENT WORK TIME: Then dive into an inquiry, inviting kids to ask: "What writerly moves have these writers made that I might try too?" Let kids move their sticky notes that name particular craft elements from the mentor texts to the parts of their own text where they want to try those moves. Then, invite them to try out the moves in their own pieces of writing. (See Figure 4.7.) In this way, inquiry work becomes specific, personal, and practical, and kids will emerge with craft moves they can try in their drafts. Kids can also make personal writing checklists from the mentor texts they study. Having kids keep their mentor texts, checklists, and drafts in their notebooks helps them develop a tool kit for future writing.

FIGURE 4.7 Often kids write more when they sit near other writers. We found this to also be true virtually. Kids at a "breakout room" often get a lot of writing done.

Lesson: Trying Out Sequences and Structures— and Transitioning Between Parts

CONNECT: Let kids know that now that they have spent some time revising parts of their essay, it's time to consider their final choices about how to organize or structure their essays. Suggest: "Writers often return to mentor texts one last time to see how other authors have arranged their writing, and then they try out different sequences and structures for their own piece, making decisions about how they most want to develop their thinking for their audience."

TEACH: Demonstrate how you return to mentor texts to see how other authors arranged their vignettes, contexts, and thesis sections. Note that often, students put their thesis, or plea, or claim, at the end of their essay rather than at the beginning. That's a common structure for published essayists, and it's often a more powerful emotional and intellectual journey for the reader. And you can show that some pieces have another structure: an idea, followed by examples or by reasons and examples. The main thing is not that students choose the "right" structure—there isn't one!—but that your writers develop the belief that they have ideas worth exploring and that their writing can advance their own thinking and the thinking of others.

ENGAGE: Suggest that partners try out at least two different structures, moving the parts of their essay around, thinking about what they want to lead with and what they want to end with. Invite partners to talk to a partner briefly about how they think they might like to begin—with an idea, or a story, for instance.

LAUNCH INDEPENDENT WORK TIME: As you send kids off to play with structure and organize their parts into a final essay, you may need to do some work with sophisticated transitional phrases in here, offering students a word bank of phrases, such as those shown in Figure 4.8. One thing that will stand out in this work—even for writers who are more emergent in their language skills or whose narrative and expository craft is in its early stages—is that when they care deeply about their topic, their writing becomes more powerful. Part of the power of Eliza's and Savaria's words lies in the techniques they studied and tried out. There is logical—and poetic—structure in their essays, there are embedded anecdotes to engage the emotions as well as the intellect, there are clear and moving pleas for change. They use all their writerly craft. But mostly, the power of their arguments lies in how they aren't abstract arguments, they are based on lived experience.

These kids aren't messing around. They take their writing seriously, using it to promote change in themselves or their community. Your students can as well.

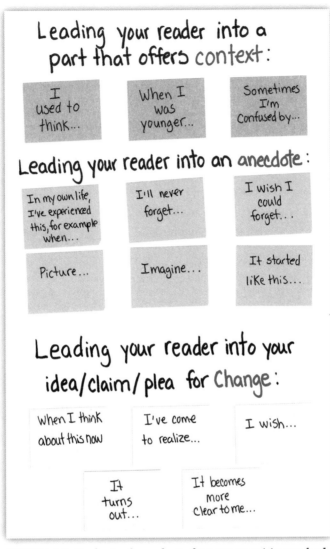

FIGURE 4.8 Students often rely on the same transitions to lead their readers in sequence through their essays. Push them to match the transition with the purpose of the text.

Ensuring All Voices Can Be Heard

We want all our kids to become powerful writers and for their voices to be heard. But what do we do when the physical act of writing—of getting our thoughts from our head onto the page or the keyboard—is a barrier for kids? Colleen Cruz's *The Unstoppable Writing Teacher* (2015), a powerhouse text on believing in and providing access for seemingly reluctant or disengaged writers, is a great place to start. In the book, Colleen provides multiple pathways for getting kids' voices out there. The Universal Design for Learning website is another strong resource for providing multiple pathways for student writers.

Another utterly gorgeous resource is Carla España and Luz Yadira Herrera's *En Comunidad: Lessons for Centering the Voices of Bilingual Latinx Students* (2020), which provides advice, professional research, and deeply personal stories about honoring the language practices of students and their families.

Some immediate tips you can put into play include:

The Universal Design for Learning Guidelines

http://udlguidelines.cast.org

- **Let kids use speech-to-text software.** Kids don't have to physically type or write anymore: they can dictate, and then go back into their text to revise.

- **Transcribe.** Typing is not high cognitive demand, but it can get in the way of kids' voices being heard. If software and apps feel onerous to a student writer, you can help by listening to the student and transcribing. Your ability to paragraph and spell can also immediately raise the level of kids' first-draft writing. It's not cheating, it's helping. Then support kids in learning speech-to-text software and finding helpers as needed. Clarify repeatedly that handwriting and typing are not the same thing as writing: writing is the act of developing and sharing our thinking. Feynman wrote his last books long after he couldn't write physically, and he's only one of many famous writers who had helpers in the physical act.

- **Let kids decide whether to write on paper or with a device.** Changing the surface you are writing on and the implement you write with can help a lot of writers make the physical act of writing easier. Avoid making these decisions for 'the class,' and instead let kids try different processes, so each comes to their own personal method of increasing fluency.

- **Coach your kids in "talking in essay."** Oral rehearsal is key to fluency, and it allows you, your students, and their partners to rehearse and revise before actually writing. It also lets you listen for which kids say more than they write so that you can attend to helping those kids get more of their words on the page.

- **Honor kids' home languages and language practices.** There is no rule that says kids can only write in English. Strengthen your students' multiliteracies. Encourage them to write in more than one language, to tell their stories in multiple languages, and to delve into their family and cultural narrative practices.

- **Consider alternate expressions.** Might kids make an audio podcast instead of publishing an essay? Might they make a video or other digital presentation?

- **Involve family members** in supporting kids as writers in a range of ways—from providing learning apps, to transcribing, to listening, to cheerleading.

Let Kids Write in Their Own Voices

Once when we found ourselves at a literacy conference with author Matt de la Peña as a fellow speaker, we ended up talking about the kind of writing that kids do for school, and how little that whole writing process, let alone the product, is like the writing that writers do in the world. Since then, we and Matt have termed this "writing for school." Also since then, we've spent time listening to Jason Reynolds, when he, too, was a conference speaker. According to Jason, the writing he did for school not only didn't help him as a writer—his classroom experiences actively taught him that he wasn't a writer. His high school English classes discouraged him, nearly annihilated his voice, and filled him with self-doubt. It's not okay that school empowers only the young people who already fit one narrow idea of what it looks and sounds like to be a writer. When we think of the great writing geniuses of our kids' generation—Jason Reynolds, Ibi Zoboi, Elizabeth Acevedo, Kwame Alexander—writers who inspire kids to read and to think, a lot of their writing as well as their voice doesn't fit the ideal promoted by AP and IB assessments, or the Common Core rubrics that insist on a formal style.

The poisonous effects of "writing for school" ripple out in many directions: kids lose their connection with writing and, quite likely, school itself; they may learn not to trust their own ears and voices as the language that moves them might not be valued in school; they may find their voices and perspectives discounted in the classroom. These effects make it clear that if we want students to compose their own principled and ethical stances as they strengthen their own civic engagement, we need to break the pattern of "writing for school." As educators, we must examine our own mindsets and assumptions: how have we let our ideas about what writing should be get in the way of our ability to see, value, and strengthen the particular gifts, histories, and voices that all of our students bring?

Let's take a look at four simple ways in which we can value our students' voices over "writing for school."

Studying the Most Engaging and Influential Writing in Your Content Area

Instead of studying texbook-ish, writing-for-school examples, study writers who make you want to read more about the topic. To find great writers in the genre you are teaching, whom your kids can study, don't worry about matching up content—just turn to writers in that *discipline*. For older students, study Ibram X. Kendi and Ta-Nehisi Coates in the social sciences; study Brian Greene and Naomi Klein in the sciences. For younger kids, study Tiffany Jewel and Jason Reynolds in the social sciences; study Charles Fishman and Mark Kurlansky in the sciences. Take small excerpts that kids will find interesting and ask

Some Engaging Mentor Texts, Loosely Ordered from Easiest to Hardest

- "Introduction: Being a Brief Outline of the Problem," in *World Without Fish*, by Mark Kurlansky

- "Introduction," in *The Big Thirst: The Secret Life and Turbulent Future of Water*, by Charles Fishman

- "The Jacket," in *Fist Stick Knife Gun: A Personal History of Violence*, by Geoffrey Canada

- "What in the Name of High School Football?" by Hank Hill

- "Introduction," in *Why Are All the Black Kids Sitting Together in the Cafeteria?: and Other Conversations about Race*, by Beverly Tatum

- "Introduction," in *Stamped: Racism, Antiracism, and You*, by Jason Reynolds and Ibram X. Kendi

- "Home is Where the Hatred Is," in *Stamped: Racism, Antiracism, and You*, by Jason Reynolds and Ibram X. Kendi

- "The Follower Factory," by Nicholas Confessore, Gabriel J.X. Dance, Richard Harris, and Mark Hansen

- "Thresholds of Violence: How School Shootings Catch On," by Malcolm Gladwell

- "Snow Fall: The Avalanche at Tunnel Creek," by John Branch

kids that same inquiry question: "What writerly moves does this writer make that I can try too?" We've also found the *New York Times* digital reporting and the reporting in *Vice* and *Sports Illustrated* to be compelling contemporary journalism.

Here's what Ibram Kendi says in his introduction to *Stamped: Racism, Antiracism, and You*, Jason Reynolds and Kendi's YA remix of Kendi's *Stamped from the Beginning*:

> I wish I had learned this history at your age. But there were no books telling the complete story of racist ideas. Some books told parts of the story. I hardly wanted to read them, though. Most were so boring, written in ways I could not relate to. But not Jason's books . . . Jason is a great writer in the purest sense. A great writer snatches the human ear, makes your head bob up and down. It is hard to stop when the beat is on. A great writer makes my head bob from side to side. It is hard to stop when the book is open. (2020, x)

Kendi doesn't, we might note, talk about Jason's topic sentences or his logical transitions. What matters about Jason's nonfiction, highly crafted argument writing is that it is gripping—he makes you want to read more.

Look for those same qualities in the kinds of writing you show kids. Show them the most courageous, compelling, engaging writing you can find. Will they immediately write just like that? Maybe. Maybe not. But will they be more likely to want to write, and will they surprise you, and might they be more willing to try out writing voices that are more authentically theirs? Probably so. We include some student exemplars, written in the shadow of great mentor texts, in the online resources.

See the online resources for student exemplars.

Letting Kids Write in the First Person

Another thing that we can learn from these writers, and writers like Malcolm Gladwell (*What the Dog Saw*) or David Foster Wallace (*Consider the Lobster*) or Beverly Tatum, is that using the first-person voice can be compelling. In her opening essay of the 1997 edition of *Why Are All the Black Kids Sitting Together in the Cafeteria*, Tatum begins:

> If you were to ask my ten year old son, David, to describe himself, he would tell you many things: that he is smart, that he likes to play computer games, that he has an older brother. Near the top of his list, he would likely mention that he is tall for his age. He would probably not mention that he is Black, though he certainly knows that he is . . . imagine David at fifteen, six-foot-two, wearing the adolescent attire of the day, passing adults he doesn't know on the sidewalk. Do the women hold their purses a little tighter, maybe even cross the street to avoid him? Does he hear the sound of the

automatic door locks on cars as he passes by? Is he being followed by the security guards at the local mall? As he stopped in town with his new bicycle, does a police officer hassle him, asking where he got it, implying that it might be stolen? Do strangers assume he plays basketball? Each of these experiences conveys a racial message. At ten, race is not an issue for David . . . but it will be." (1997, x)

Tatum's thesis, that racism is a system of advantage based on race and all that is required to maintain it is business as usual, is carefully built across her book. Tatum is unafraid to be personal. Her description of her own son makes her argument more searing. Kendi, Reynolds, and Gladwell use the *I* voice in their writing as well. They do it to better reach readers.

Even though powerful published writers use the *I* voice deliberately and to great effect, we think back to our early days of teaching, and how we "let" kids begin their writing in the first person and then "transform it" by changing their pronouns to *one,* or *the reader,* or any third- person voice, and we shudder a bit at how triumphantly we expunged student voice from their writing. Kingsley Amis, who bore the British title (really) of "Defender of the King's English," in his foreword to *The King's English: a Guide to Modern Usage* (1999), laments how teachers, especially English teachers, can fall into the role of what he calls "petty linguistic tyrants." We cringe at how we may have fallen into that category and encourage you to break free.

Letting Kids Play with Register and Linguistic Choice

One of the greatest ways to escape the expungement of student voice that happens in essay writing, especially in content classes, is to give students opportunities to play with register and linguistic choice—the degree of formality in writing. Register involves decisions about whether you include or don't include popular references and how you make language choices deliberately, including your choice of "English," such as using Black English. In *Linguistic Justice: Black Language, Literacy, Identity, and Pedagogy* (2020), April Baker-Bell describes how some students come to feel ashamed of the way they speak English in school. We need to celebrate and amplify kids' voices and ways of speaking. Embracing register is one way. Author and spoken-word artist Jamila Lyiscott makes register a central point in her discussions of equity. If you're not already familiar with her work, we encourage you to watch either "Jamila Lyiscott is Fighting for Racial Justice in US Classrooms," from Now This (2019) or her 2020 TED Talk, "3 Ways to Speak English," or both, in which Lyiscott demonstrates vividly how she reaches different audiences when she shifts her register.

"Jamila Lyiscott is Fighting for Racial Justice in U.S. Classrooms"

https://nowthisnews .com/videos/news /jamila-lyiscott-is -fighting-for-racial -justice-in-us -classrooms

"3 Ways to Speak English"

www.ted.com/talks /jamila_lyiscott_3 _ways_to_speak _english

A great example of shift in register is the difference between a snippet from Kendi's *Stamped from the Beginning*, written for adults, and his and Jason Reynolds' remix of this historical study, *Stamped: Racism, Antiracism, and You*, written for adolescents:

From Ibram X. Kendi's *Stamped from the Beginning:*

> THE MOST NOTORIOUS victim of what was to be called "massive resistance" to desegregation was fourteen-year-old Emmett Till on August 28, 1955. For hissing at a Mississippi White woman, hooligans beat Till so ruthlessly that his face was unrecognizable during his open casket funeral in his native Chicago. The gruesome pictures were shown around the enraged Black world. On March 12, 1956, nineteen US senators and seventy-seven House representatives signed a southern manifesto opposing the Brown v. Board of Education decision for planting "hatred and suspicion where there has been heretofore friendship and understanding." The Klan fielded new members, and elite segregationists founded White citizens councils. Southern schools ensured that their textbooks gave students "bedtime" stories, as historian C. Vann Woodward called them, that read like *Gone With The Wind*. (2016, 365)

From Jason Reynolds and Ibram X. Kendi's *Stamped: Racism, Antiracism, and You:*

> I mean, why weren't there any White kids integrating into Black schools? The assumption was that Black kids weren't as intelligent because they weren't around White kids, as if the mere presence of White kids would make Black kids better. Not. True. A good school is a good school, whether there are White people there or not. Oh, and of course people were pissed about this.
>
> People were pissed about them both.
>
> And pissed people do pissed things.
>
> A year later, a fourteen-year-old boy named Emmett Till was brutally murdered in Money, Mississippi, for supposedly "hissing" at a white woman. They beat Till so ruthlessly that his face was unrecognizable during his open casket funeral in his native Chicago. The gruesome pictures were shown around the enraged Black world, at the request of his mother. And though supremacists in power continued to blame *Brown v. Board of Education* for the problems, young Emmett's death lit a fire under the civil rights movement, led by a young, charismatic preacher from Atlanta. (2020, 159)

Varying the Audiences That Kids Are Writing For

We should not be kids' primary audiences. They need to write for their peers and their community, for their families and friends, as well as for groups in the world. Writing for a range of audiences and with a legitimate purpose gives them experience in perspective-taking, in adjusting their register, and, most importantly, in taking their place in the world as an engaged citizen.

In Figures 4.9–4.11, you can see an eighth grader adjusting his register for different audiences, as he begins a letter about the condition of child soldiers, to different, specific, targeted audiences.

You can see Gio changing his examples, style, and word choice as he addresses different audiences. And some kids may choose what seems a more radical register change. What matters is that they understand that it's not that one style is better, or more valid; rather, there are a lot of different voices in the world, and they all matter.

> We've included a second example of a student writing about the same topic in the online resources—a high school student writing an essay for a psychology class, a letter to his head of school, and an article for his school magazine; all three are about punitive response to addiction.

Dear United Nations Secretary General Ban Ki-Moon,

You are surely aware that around the world, children have been forced into taking up arms, to fight across villages, towns, jungles, and deserts. Research has shown that worldwide there may be as many as 300,000 child soldiers fighting right now-that's 300,000 children under the age of 18 who have been forced to carry guns, kill, maim (Save the Children, Human Rights Watch). These children are fighting in the Middle East, in Africa, and in South America. Most of these children are children of loss and violence. They have witnessed massacres, lost their families, and been abandoned to war.

 In your position, knowing that child soldiers are mostly forcibly recruited, you can help shape the decision to give child soldiers amnesty. These children should be given amnesty, because overwhelmingly, they did not choose to become child soldiers-they are victims of war. They should also be given amnesty because they were shaped by war. Blame war, don't blame these children.

FIGURE 4.9 Gio, knowing he is addressing the Secretary General of the United Nations, addresses his tone to acknowledge his audience's expertise.

Dear Classmates,

Stop worrying about your grades. Stop giving a **** if you win or lose your soccer game. Work hard. Play hard. But there are things in the world more important than whether we get a B plus or an A minus. Kids are dying of hunger. Kids are sold into sexual slavery. Our parents want to protect us from this kind of information. They want us to care more about soccer than child slavery. There is something seriously ****ed up about that.

No-one is keeping millions of kids safe around the world. When you see pictures of girls the age of your fifth grade sister sold into sexual slavery, your stomach will turn over. But there's another kind of kid you might not give a damn about at first. The kid who has killed other people. The kid who looks tough, and unfeeling, and like he doesn't want any help from anyone. This is the child soldier. The thing is, these kids are being judged in court cases and immigration cases. That means someone decides, for a thirteen year old who saw his family killed when he was ten, who was given a gun and told to shoot it, whether he deserves a chance at freedom. I'm going to argue that we should give a damn about these kids, who are our age, and that we should do what we can to plea for them.

FIGURE 4.10 Here Gio addresses his classmates, and his word choice and syntax are deliberately more informal.

Dear Parents and Schoolboard,

Recently our class did a study of child soldiers. The organization *Invisible Children* came and presented. We read memoirs and news articles. We listened to interviews. We read journalism and studies. It was really painful. Kids cried in class, as you know.

We know that parents complained. You think that we shouldn't be exposed to this kind of violence. It's important to know that we don't agree. People die all over the screen in *Star Wars* and Marvel, and you never say we shouldn't go to the movies. The thing is, the violence we're studying in class now matters. It's the world we are going to live in. We live in a world of school shootings. We live in a world where kids are sold. We live in a world where kids are forced to become soldiers. You can't wish this world away.

FIGURE 4.11 When he addresses the school board, Gio not only changes his tone, or register, he changes his examples.

Teach Kids to Be Radical Listeners

This is the area where we—Mary, Pablo, and Marc—would most change what we did in our earliest work with teaching research essays. We realize now that we did not teach argument writing or ethical processes for arguing to learn. We taught *persuasive* writing: kids chose their "side" on the first day of their research, and they researched only that side. As George Hillocks explains, in persuasive writing, we allow ourselves to include only the evidence and sources that support our views, and we feel free to use emotional and rhetorical devices to persuade and sometimes even manipulate our audience. Persuasion is the stuff of advertising, of propaganda. But *argument*, according to Hillocks, "is at the heart of critical thinking and academic discourse" (2011, xvii). It involves evidence-based reasoning, logical claims, warrants. Even more importantly, though, it involves thoughtful acknowledgment of complexity and counterclaim. In argument writing, students research a *topic*—not a side—exploring multiple sides before coming to a considered opinion.

We're not going to focus here on the initial work of developing claims, reasoning, and evidence—the most frequently taught elements of argument. We have included some flash-debate protocols in the online resources, which give opportunities for students to rehearse logical arguments and for you to provide coaching. Instead, we want to focus here on what we've come to consider the parts of this process that are most crucial for developing ethical citizens—listening, revising our thinking, responding to rational counterarguments, and acknowledging complexity and conditionality. This work is important for an engaged citizenry. It's also good for kids. When kids learn to listen, they become more nuanced. When they learn to listen, they see each other and the world in more empathetic ways. And others respond to them differently as well. Both *Quiet Leadership* by David Rock (2006) and *Thanks for the Feedback,* by Douglas Stone and Sheila Heen (2014), emphasize how, when someone feels listened to, they are more likely to listen to your points. Nilofer Merchant says, "To change someone's mind, stop talking and listen" (2018). Interestingly, listening makes us more compelling. This is very useful information for young people—and for all of us!—to grasp.

> **See the online resources for a protocol for in-class flash debates.**

To teach kids to value listening as part of the process of research and argumentation, you have to create a paradigm in which kids are not learning to argue, or arguing to win, but instead, are *arguing to learn.* If you and your class enter into argumentation with the idea that *everyone* will learn from those whose positions differ, then your students will be willing to accept different points of view more gracefully—and perhaps even change their own. Launch your work, then, by explaining that the mark of a sophisticated thinker is the willingness to revise their thinking.

This is different from the urge to dominate, to win. Your students will instead strive to teach and to learn.

There are some central questions you can teach students to pose as they strive to become ethical researchers and arguers. To be ethical means you don't hide from conflict and you don't override complexity, but, instead, you seek out diverse points of view and honestly try to understand what informs those viewpoints. Some questions to aid in this work include those shown in Figure 4.12.

As we strive to help students become better listeners, we do not ask them to empathize with every viewpoint they encounter. Some arguments are ones where you can't settle on a middle ground. In her article, "There's Nothing Virtuous about Finding Common Ground," Tayari Jones warns against implicitly asking, "What is halfway between moral and immoral?" reminding us that "justice seldom dwells in the middle" (2018). (With thanks to our colleague Kelly Boland Hohne for introducing us to Tayari Jones's work.)

When we listen to Emma Gonzalez speak about school shootings and gun control, or Naomi Wadler speak about unpublicized violence against young Black women, or Autumn Peltier speak about protecting water for her community, it's clear that these young people do not want to give an inch on achieving safe schools or more security for Black women or clean water. They're not looking to meet in the middle.

We're not, then, going to require our students to listen deeply to Holocaust deniers or white supremacists. However, students can practice listening to alternative points of view and even to points of view that diverge *inside of* coalition teams: disagreements not about whether racism is bad or good but about which ways to combat racism are the most powerful; disagreements not about whether we should explore green energy but about the most effective ways to promote green energy or protect the climate. These interior debates are far more nuanced than simply labeling one side good and another bad. They also involve careful listening.

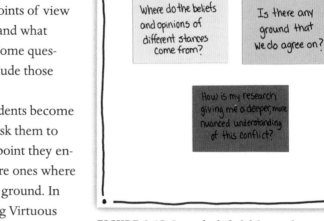

FIGURE 4.12 It can be helpful for students to pose critical questions, of themselves and others, to help them develop their arguments and hear others'.

Emma Gonzalez Speaks at the March for Our Lives

www.youtube.com /watch?v=u46H zTGVQhg

Naomi Wadler Speaks at the March for Our Lives

www.youtube.com /watch?v=EqKy 7TXKO8c

Autumn Peltier Addresses the United Nations

www.youtube.com /watch?v=zg60sr 38oic

Listening, we've found, can mean listening actively as you read, and listening actively to others as you debate and argue. Here are some protocols to strengthen students' listening skills and openness.

Engaging in Low-Stakes Social Arguments

One way to help young people understand that listening is an important part of compelling argumentation is to engage them in practicing small, low-stakes social arguments about causes that are dear to their hearts; for instance, asking their parents for a dog or for a later curfew, or to be able to drive the family car, or asking friends to change in some way. Eduardo Briceño, in his TED Talk, "How to Get Better at the Things You Care About"(2016), explains that it's only when the stakes for failure are low that we are can learn. When you give kids the opportunity to practice personal, low-stakes arguments, and they try them out at home or on their friends, taking time to work on addressing counterarguments gracefully, you teach kids to listen to opposing viewpoints and to respond to them respectfully. This is a significant life skill. Often kids report back that they "didn't get the dog," but that over time, the dynamics in their relationships changed, and they feel more listened to. What has really happened is that they are now more listened to because they are better listeners.

Starting with Hypotheses Rather Than Claims

In the last few years we've done a lot of work collaborating with both science teachers and working scientists on argumentation, especially related to the climate crisis. One thing that scientists have suggested to us is that working scientists don't start with a claim—they start with a hypothesis, even when they are publishing peer-reviewed journal articles about their research. They pose a hypothesis and then show how they have tested out that hypothesis. They're careful to show when their suppositions played out strongly, and when their evidence was less compelling or more opaque. They often explore the boundaries or conditions under which their hypothesis seems most true. These are helpful protocols in any discipline, and you can guide your kids to begin, in any argument process, with a hypothesis. The same principle works in ELA or Social Studies classes, when kids begin with a hypothesis ("It seems likely that . . .") and then test out their idea through the act of writing and/or research.

Developing Rituals for Complimenting Your Opponents' Best Points

Whenever your students are about to engage in a debate or a debate-like discussion, let them know that, after the exchange, they will be telling their opponents which points they found most compelling, and why. When students know that they will need to describe their opponents' best point, they begin to take note when their opponent speaks. When they also practice complimenting, they learn to recognize and respond to the nuances of opposing viewpoints.

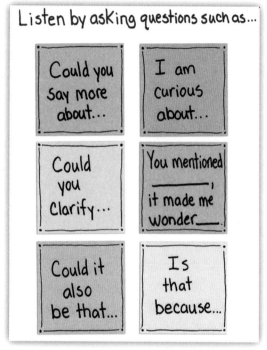

FIGURE 4.13 For a lot of kids (and adults), listening is hard. Giving kids some sentence starters can infuse a language of listening into your classroom discourse.

Questioning as a Way of Listening

Teach students graceful questioning, the kind of questioning that you can only do if you have been listening carefully. Suggest that they jot notes as they listen, and prepare to probe more deeply, not to override but to understand better. Some helpful sentence starters might include those shown in Figure 4.13.

Considering Counterclaims with Thought-Partners

Giving kids time to work together to consider counter claims and to develop their own responses increases students' openness to complexity. First, it helps kids to recognize that there *are* counterclaims and to consider their validity. Second, it helps them see that many topics are complex and there are rational aspects to opposing sides. Third, it helps kids develop rational and responsive refutations to counterclaims so that instead of simply restating their positions, they respond to the points brought up by the other side.

Considering Conditionality

Encourage students to ask themselves, "Under what conditions does my argument most hold true?" Putting constraints on a position can make it stronger, a significant lesson for young argument writers.

Listening for Fallacies

In Chapter 3, we offered some logical-fallacy cards, to help students analyze the texts they are reading for flaws in logic and for manipulative rhetorical techniques. They can do the same work with the arguments they are developing—that is, listening for some of the most predictable logical fallacies and working both to make their arguments more ethical and to call out less-than-logical techniques.

Listening for Bias of All Kinds

As Kendi and Reynolds explain in *Stamped* (2020), bias is inevitable and inescapable. We're all biased, all the time. But we can listen for and reflect on bias that seeps into our arguments. Some questions that can help students tackle this work include those shown in Figure 4.14.

Involve Families and Communities

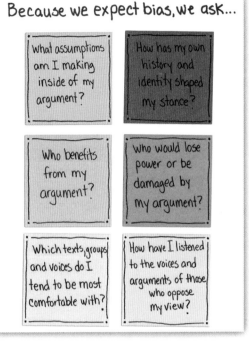

There are two really big ways that you can involve families and communities. The first is to involve family as sources of support for writers. It's really helpful for kids to talk about their writing—to talk often about their ideas for writing, to explain their thinking, to informally rehearse their writing. Much of the work of writing happens before putting pen to page or fingers to keyboard. Mary wrote an article called "Parents as Writing Partners" (2014), that may

FIGURE 4.14 Critical language is also new for many students. You can support kids' critical thinking by giving them some lenses for questioning.

be helpful. Essentially, we believe that you should reach out to parents and families, and communicate with them about how they can help their children by giving them opportunities to talk through their writing.

Some parents and families will worry about their own skills with writing or reading in English. First, it's important to reassure parents that you care about students' multiliteracies, and that you want to develop their writing skills in all their languages. It's also helpful for families to know that students can research in languages other than English; in fact, researching in more than one language will not only deepen their knowledge, it will also broaden their perspectives. So, invite families to support multilanguage research.

Then turn to your community for celebrations and publishing events. Our dear colleague, Cornelius Minor, taught us in our work in Seattle to go to the local laundromats and bodegas, as well as the coffee shops and bookstores and libraries, asking, "Could we display kids' work here?" Almost always the answering question back is, "Will that bring their families in?" Publish kids' essays in anthologies and display them locally. Invite parents and families to sit on panels and in debate audiences.

And reach out to other communities as well by sending kids' writing from your community to other communities. In the terrible days after 9/11, Linda Rief, author of *Seeking Diversity* (1992), organized her students in New Hampshire to send favorite books and personal narratives to the students at IS 289, which had been moved from its location across the street from the World Trade Center. It was a beautiful gesture. Mary invited students from PS 59 and IS 126 to send their argument essays to kids in Jordan, who sent their own pieces back. There was a lot learned about border crossings and water conservation that seemed so new, and then a lot about pressure and dealing with siblings that seemed so familiar. The main thing is, turn to your communities for real audiences.

Be Ready for Anything

Whenever we tackle profoundly personal writing with kids, or "let" them dive into edgy, contemporary topics, we worry about a thousand things. What if one of the kids reveals something that I need to report as a mandated reporter? What if a student reveals something about a parent that feels tricky to share in class or in the publishing celebration? What if the topics the kids choose make some parents or family members anxious or even hostile?

The truth is, these things can happen; in fact, we've faced all of these scenarios. Mary remembers a writing workshop where kids turned over the pages of their writers' notebooks that they wanted to keep "private," which meant that the teachers didn't read them. Then one student, it turned out, had written her thoughts about suicide. That's when we realized that it's important to clarify that a writer's notebook is not a diary and that a teacher is a mandated reporter. "If you write about something that shows you are in danger, I have to report that, because part of my job is to care for you," is now something we say.

Mary also remembers when she and her husband were separating and their son, Jackson, wrote about it in writing workshop—and what it felt like to see those pieces not just in the teacher's hands but on the wall when kids published. It was heart-wrenching. On the other hand, it also moved Jackson's teachers to form a counselor- and peer-led support group for kids whose parents were separating or divorcing or arguing, and for kids who were afraid that their parents were. In the end, almost 60 percent of the kids wanted to be in the group.

Real writing with students is hard and messy and surprising. There are great moments of beauty and pain. We're not sure, if you took away the risk, that the work would be as meaningful to the young writers in our classes. Talk with colleagues, with parents whom you trust, and with friends, so that the level of risk in your classroom feels healthy for you—that cliff edge that gets your heart pumping, but not the uncontrolled slide.

Practice What You Teach

The biggest advice we can give you here is—write! Write alone and in secret, form a writing group with colleagues or friends, write with your kids. Take a writing course or sign up for a writing workshop. All of that prepares you for writing in front of your kids. Your kids need you to be a mentor writer for them. That doesn't mean that they need you to be an expert, highly proficient writer. In fact, when the demonstration writing that teachers do is way above what kids can do, it's often not helpful for kids. So you only have to write a bit better than your seventh graders, or your ninth graders. And really, kids are so interested in the issues you struggled with as a teen and the outrage you feel about injustice in the world that they are not judging your writing—they are interested in you and your ideas.

If you want to become more confident as a writer or about the demonstration writing you do in class, do the same work your kids do—mirror write from mentor texts. Find some articles or essays you admire, and try writing with that same structure and craft and with your own content. Mirror writing raises the level of writing in powerful ways.

Here is a tip: Write your essay before the unit begins. Start with a very rough and basic draft. Revise your draft a few times, focusing on the specific writing strategies you will teach your students. Then, when you are "writing" in front of your students you can also talk about the thinking that is going into your writing. Sometimes we plan out what we will talk about, right? Writing should be no different.

"The Power of Vulnerability"

www.ted.com/talks/brene_brown_the_power_of_vulnerability

The other way to practice what we teach is to be willing to be open and vulnerable about the content we model. When you're making an issue wall, for instance, consider sharing some of the issues that haunted you when you were a teen. Share things that you struggle with now. Brené Brown's work on vulnerability (*Daring Greatly*) shows how powerful vulnerability can be, especially in a leader. It's contagious. When we are open, kids and colleagues open up. You can watch Brené Brown's 2010 TED Talk, "The Power of Vulnerability."

Civic Virtues Addressed in this Chapter

- identifying social causes
- building coalitions
- informing oneself about local government
- advocating for social change

Planning Your Time

When considering a unit of study that includes some form of social activism, you'll want to think carefully about the scale of the action that you're embarking on. Are you expecting your kids to write a letter to a leader about an issue of concern that has emerged from a reading you've done together as a class? Perhaps you could successfully tackle that work in a week, or two. If you are already certain of the issue, have a distinct audience in mind, and have identified a desired product, you could move through the writing process relatively quickly. On the other hand, are you expecting your kids to investigate themselves and their communities to identify issues worth tackling? Are you hoping for them to partner with outside organizations to reach a larger audience and potentially affect change on a scale beyond the school building? Is the product you and your students want to create complex and multimodal? You may want to budget three weeks to six weeks, which is about how long kids can usually sustain intensity on a topic. Regardless of scale, you'll want to consider isolating the issue, determining an audience, and determining a product when considering the length of time you'll devote to your activism unit.

ENGAGED CITIZENS
RISE UP

n Chapter 2 we introduced you to Akeem Barnes' eighth-grade class in Brownsville. In this chapter, we'll start with a return to his work with Aaron Hinton, using it as a more-detailed case study for involving students in social activism.

Akeem's eighth graders had earned a reputation as the most difficult grade in the building, a label that often led them to being denied field trip opportunities and other enrichment. "Oh no, you can't take them anywhere. They're out of control." "Send the permission slips home late so you don't have to take all of them." The advice from teachers and administrators alike was often to engage with these students less, to deny them opportunities for learning. By this point in these students' lives, the institution of school had found it easier to control and contain than to liberate. Akeem and Aaron had to work to resist the institution's implicit message that Black students wouldn't be able to handle greater freedom. They asked themselves, "What if we give more opportunities to step up rather than fewer? What if we trusted them more rather than less? What could these young revolutionaries accomplish?"

Professional activists—those who devote their lives to fighting for a cause, those who question and challenge the status quo—are people stirred by passion and moral clarity. Any teacher who has made the mistake of telling her class that they are going to be held late for lunch because a few students didn't complete their work will tell you that a current of activist passion flows through every classroom. "That's not fair!" is the instinctual call to arms for countless young people. Those of us who have taught fifth and sixth grade have all exchanged anecdotes about the transformation of our classes from the beginning to the end of the year. "Yes ma'am," and "Is this good?" become "Why?" and "That's not what you said yesterday." Our students are naturally changing from following the teacher's lead to questioning all that the teacher does. Couple these natural tendencies with a school environment that leans authoritarian and you've got a recipe for disruptive activism! As educators, we've witnessed student walk-outs, sit-ins, and strikes; the middle school teacher probably sees these more often than most. Who hasn't had a student refuse to do work? That's a strike! Who hasn't had a student grab the hall pass and storm into the hall when denied a chance to go to the bathroom? That's a walk-out! In many ways, school by its very nature is a repressive system and students, particularly those in the middle school years, will find ways to protect themselves from what they see as an assault on their individuality and autonomy. As civically engaged classroom teachers, our challenge is to harness this instinctive activism rather than fight it.

Kids often recenter when they have the opportunity to pour their energies into work they believe in. In Michael Chabon's novel, *The Adventures of Kavalier and Clay*, two escapist boys in Brooklyn dream of becoming comic book writers. Chabon calls these dreams "caterpillar" dreams—dreams of miraculous release and transformation (2012, 481). His characters are transformed—through dreams, through work, through luck. Kids have caterpillar dreams as well. It's one reason that Harry Potter is so popular—it manifests that adolescent urge to transcend the ordinariness of our lives, to be meaningful.

At El Puente Academy for Peace and Justice, a Human Rights high school in Brooklyn, for example, the school has long intertwined students' studies with community needs. Students at El Puente have done neighborhood polls about immunization, tackling the low rate of vaccination in the community. They have studied asthma rates in the wake of an incinerator being built in the neighborhood (Capellaro 2005). The school does serious work with human rights. That kind of curricular work, where students are invited to tackle meaningful community projects, is a natural extension of the project-based curriculum lauded by Mitchel Resnick at his MIT Media Lab. When kids work not to complete a worksheet or to get a better grade on a task, but in fulfillment of their own project design and to meet the needs of their community, they gain a sense of strength and control in their own lives. There's a long history that supports the ways that communities of color, in particular, have always cared about and worked on behalf of the advancement of the collective. El Puente's work and Aaron and Akeem's work at their school build upon this tradition and the belief that the purpose of education is much more than academics—it's about liberation. All students benefit from this teaching mindset, but students like those in Akeem's classes have an especially pressing need for educators who understand this legacy: without it, school becomes another means of oppression.

At this point, if you've tried out some of the work we describe in this book, your students have explored their identities, developed their critical research skills, and composed ethical stances. Now is the time for them to join these intellectual skills with their natural rebelliousness and/or idealism and to identify causes to apply themselves to. They are ready for activism, one of the defining habits of the engaged citizen and the first right enshrined in the Bill of Rights.

When you think about the activism that is possible in your classroom, think expansively. Activism can range from creating pieces of writing, to designing artwork or social action projects, to participating in a protest—whatever suits the cause that most excites your students. Here are some of the things that we've seen kids investigate and work to create change around: developing awareness of racism and its effects, educating their community about E-waste, setting up and working to sustain recycling programs, investigating water quality and access to water, shifting their community from plastic to metal water bottles, researching electrical use and kinds of bulbs in the school; advocating for access to contemporary teen literature, and protesting funding and attention for male versus female sports teams.

While the example that we thread through this chapter shows Akeem and Aaron's class coalescing around a single cause and radically mobilizing to address that cause, not all classroom activism needs to look the same. You might find that it is more difficult for your students to identify injustices because they live in relative comfort and ease, but this doesn't absolve them from responsibility to seek out the wrong in the world and address it. In fact, this comfort *obligates* them to take part. Living with injustice on a daily basis as Aaron and Akeem's predominantly Black students do is a product of systemic inequities; if you find that your students do not suffer from the same inequities, it may be a time to explore why not. Challenge your students to acknowledge their privileges and to question what can be done to ensure that those privileges are extended to more people.

In this chapter we'll help you to:

- show students what's possible
- plan for classroom-based social action
- identify an issue that is important to your students
- consider audience and modalities
- teach students about local government and where power resides
- develop social networks that extend into the surrounding community
- make a plan that plays to students' strengths
- create a social action headquarters
- involve families and communities
- be ready for anything
- practice what you teach.

Show Students What's Possible

As with almost anything we teach, stories are a powerful way to begin. Students may not know what is possible until they've read, seen, and heard the stories of people who have shaped the world through their sacrifices and work. A quick search of young activists and youth movements through history yields a number of powerful case studies to inspire your students. You could study Frederick Douglass, who fought for his freedom at age sixteen, or Sarah Parker Remond, who was a member of the Salem Female Anti-Slavery Society and gave her first abolitionist speech at age sixteen. You could introduce students to the Factory Girls Association, some of whom were as young as ten, who fought in the 1830s for higher wages for mill workers.

There are other examples of activism by young people that you could share. The newsies of the 1890s, later featured in the Disney musical of the same name, mobilized disenfranchised paper boys to strike in protest of rising newspaper costs. The teenagers of the lake internment dissidents of the 1940s protested Japanese detention during World War II and were jailed for their efforts. The White Rose group of young German dissidents resisted Hitler, spread anti-Nazi propaganda, and were executed for their efforts. The four thousand school children of The Children's March of Birmingham in 1963 walked out of school in support of the Civil Rights Movement. The Student Nonviolent Coordinating Committee (SNCC) of the 1960s organized student-led sit-ins at segregated lunch counters and mobilized Black voters in the South. The Black Panther Party of the sixties and seventies fought against corrupt policing and for social programs in Black communities.

We can trace this activist current all the way through Justice for Trayvon Martin in 2013, the Standing Rock Youth of 2016, the March for Our Lives in 2018, and the Climate Strike of 2019. Studying these movements through the nineteenth, twentieth, and twenty-first centuries may inspire your students to see the potential for change that they carry in their own hearts, minds, and hands.

See the online resources for teen activists in history.

See the online resources for contemporary teen activists.

Plan for Classroom-Based Social Action

Engaging in social activism with your students requires a willingness to support their initiatives and to release control. You'll determine a course of action *with* students rather than *for* students. This means going into a unit with only a few parameters set and then allowing it to develop and grow along with your young people. When students have a say in determining the issue, when they decide on the appropriate action to address the issue, and when they help choose the audience for their work, the work becomes *theirs*.

» YOUNG CITIZENS IN ACTION «

In Atlanta, Georgia, in the spring of 2020, a group of eighth graders read novels by Jason Reynolds, Angie Thomas, Ibi Zobi, Jerry Craft, and other contemporary authors who address urgent social issues and injustices. One group of eighth-grade girls read Angie Thomas' *The Hate U Give* (2017) and Nic Stone's *Dear Martin* (2017). The books resonated with their fears, their anger at how unsafe it is to be a Black man in this country, and their universal concerns with erasure. They decided they had to speak up about police violence and the danger to Black men. They set out to research the history of that violence. To make their concerns visible to the community, to bear witness, they transformed the hallways of their school into a living memorial to victims of police violence (see Figure 5.1). Sonja Cherry-Paul (who coauthored the unit with Heather Burns and Mary) was in the school as a staff developer, and said of these students, "Their anger was awe-inspiring."

FIGURE 5.1 Eighth graders in Lawrenceville, Georgia, lay out the images for their time line of victims of police brutality. They have already decided they need more space.

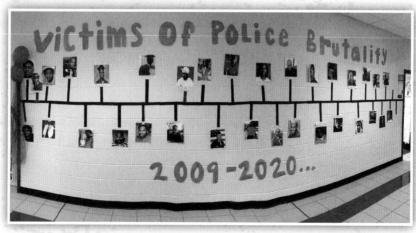

Begin with a time line that lays out a clear start and end to your activism unit. Sometimes you have only a little time, as did the eighth graders in Georgia. They did this work in a week, full of energy, outrage, and vision. Sadly, the research on victims of police brutality was easily available, current, and prevalent. Other times your students will need more time for research and project-building, and you'll carve out significant time in the curriculum. Akeem and Aaron divided the six weeks they had set aside for this project into four phases:

1. considering ourselves and our concerns for the community

2. researching to understand the issue

3. planning and implementing a response to the issue

4. delivering the response.

Once you have the general parameters of the work in mind, develop an arc of how your unit may go. You can see the arc for Akeem Barnes and Aaron Hinton's Brownsville Action Project in Figure 5.2.

You'll notice that this is not a complete unit plan; it's a general idea of the direction that the unit will take. The bulleted lists at each stage of the work aren't checklist items but questions—ideas that Akeem and Aaron *might* use *if* they align with what the kids gravitate to. Having this arc in mind gave them enough structure to know where to steer when necessary, but not so much structure that it overrode the students' genuine interests.

You'll also want to consider what you will assess during such a unit; after all, your students, their parents and families, and administrators will all expect that some form of academic work is taking place and that the work is assigned a grade for the students' transcripts. And, in addition to the skills of engaged citizenship that are central to this work, you'll also be working on students' literacy and/or content area skills, and you'll want to track their growth in those areas. To address these needs for assessment, Akeem developed a rubric that included scores for a social action journal, a social action project, participation and citizenship, neighborhood inquiry, and final reflection. While the parameters for elements such as the social action journal or the neighborhood inquiry could be more defined by Akeem, the social action project itself was left deliberately open-ended because Akeem did not ultimately know what form his class action would take, or even what specific contribution a particular student would end up making to the project. See Chapter 6 for additional guidance about creating and using rubrics effectively.

You'll find a sample rubric for Akeem's project in the online resources.

PLANNING A CIVIC ACTION UNIT WITH RIVERDALE AVENUE MIDDLE SCHOOL

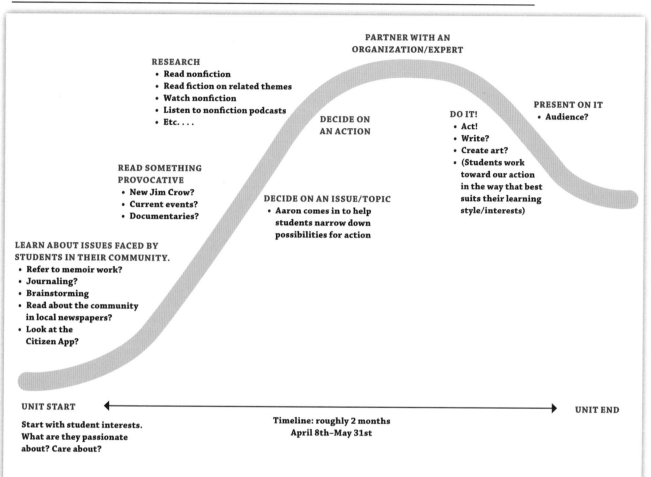

FIGURE 5.2 This plan shows the general form of the unit and how it might fit within a specific time line, but it does not spell out exactly how long each phase will take. Any plan for this type of unit should allow for some flexibility.

Identify an Issue That Is Important to Your Students

The final choice of the issue to be addressed will be up to your students. The better you know your students and the community surrounding the school, the more helpful you can be to your students when it is time for them to make their choice. When we go into this type of unit with some ideas as to the topics that we might tackle, we are better positioned to steer the students toward the issues that are most actionable and where their efforts can have the most traction. As you plan your unit, consider both your students and the connections you have in the community.

Planning Questions

RESEARCHING OUR STUDENTS' INTERESTS

o What issues are students talking about inside and outside of school?

o What previous subjects most excited them?

o What topics come up again and again in their writing?

o What aspects of students' home lives and communities outside of school could be important here?

o What cultures are represented in the class, and what concerns are particularly relevant to those cultures?

o What has been happening in the community recently that feels particularly urgent to young people?

o Engage them in interviews and ask them directly about the issues they're concerned about.

RESEARCHING OUR COMMUNITY ASSETS

o What are the local civic institutions that engage in local issues?

o Who are the local government officials?

o What issues are important to those public officials? What issues did they campaign on?

o How might we reach out to parents and families who are active in local issues and local government?

o How can staff reach out to local community organizations and leaders?

o What talents, hobbies, and interests exist in your family and staff networks?

Once you've researched your students and the community, make a list of potential topics you might address together. Figure 5.3 shows Akeem and Aaron's list.

Taking stock of possible issues and community partnerships will help you to develop a sense of where to guide the students as you open up the decision-making process to them. That said, no one set of issues and community partners applies to every classroom. Students might also be concerned about school shootings, teen suicide, bullying, local curfews, or school policies that infringe on students' rights. They might care about green-energy use, school recycling, e-waste, food waste, gender inequities. The only mandatory common denominator is that the issues directly affect and matter to them.

Now, you're faced with another major decision: Will the class work together on a common cause, or will students identify causes to work on in partnerships or small groups? Both approaches can lead to powerful work and have their distinct advantages and disadvantages. With a common cause, you'll more easily be able to narrow a focus, provide text sets, films, speakers, and outside-of-class experiences that relate to your cause and inform your action; however, you'll likely have some

Possible Issues in Brownsville	Possible Community Partners
criminal justice/mass incarceration	◆ Rikers Island Education Project ◆ Juvenile Prison on Pitkin Avenue ◆ Brownsville Heritage House ◆ Students First New York ◆ Coalition of Young Professionals ◆ Brownsville Partnership
gangs and neighborhood safety	◆ New Yorkers for Parks (Access to parks/open spaces) ◆ Brownsville Community Justice Center ◆ Community Solutions ◆ Brownsville Recreation Center ◆ Brownsville In, Violence Out (BIVO)
homelessness/poverty	◆ Salvation Army
affordable housing/gentrification	◆ Community Board #16
access to affordable, high-quality food	◆ Brownsville Community Culinary Center
police/community relationships	◆ 73rd Precinct Council ◆ Christian Covington (Police relationships) ◆ C. Aaron Hinton (Community organizing)

FIGURE 5.3 Akeem and Aaron support students in finding local resources in the community.

students who are less interested in the issue and may disengage from the work. On the other hand, small-group causes lead to higher autonomy and engagement—but they can be more difficult to support when it comes to providing resources and planning actions that are larger in scope. If your vision for the unit is to create a large action that involves connecting with community groups, we recommend the focus provided by a common topic. If you instead see your actions as smaller in scale—as an *introduction* to activism—small-group projects might be the best course.

Now that you've researched potential resources in your community, it's time to turn more of the decision-making over to your students. Below we chart several

Options for Determining Issues for Social Activism

○ Revisit identity work (identity maps, poetry, journaling) and have the students ask themselves: "What issues are living in my writing and reading? What's unfair in the world around me that I want to speak up about?"

○ Develop a list, give it back to students, and ask them to rank the issues they are most interested in tackling.

○ Create a survey and tally student responses to determine issues of particular interest.

○ Explore current events, especially those discussed in local papers and blogs.

○ Return to readings, either fiction or nonfiction that grabbed student interest earlier in the year, and mine them for social, political issues of local concern.

○ Invite students to work as journalists for a few days, observing and reporting on possible investigative topics or on social action projects in the school and community.

ways to identify topics while maximizing student interest and helping students to consider the community partnerships that can support their upcoming work.

No matter what tools or structures we use in selecting a topic, the most important thing is that we invest in a dialogue with our students, listening intently to their responses. We must guard against trying to steer students into topics we care about simply because they are meaningful to us. Kids have quirky, deeply personal interests, and this is a chance for them to follow those interests. Instead of leading kids out of topics they very much want to pursue, work with them on feasibility. Help them consider the resources available and whether they'll be able to rally other students to a common cause. Through this process we teach our students that their experiences matter, and we create curriculum that is more relevant and powerful than what is provided for us.

As the work progresses, make sure to make writing a regular part of every class session. Students should be recording their thoughts, reactions, and experiences as they go through your unit. This will serve as a reservoir of ideas to draw from when they approach the final project at the unit's end, but it will also help them maintain a deliberate and purposeful mindset throughout, keeping the issue that they have chosen at the forefront of the work. Without consistent writing, the unit can become too loose and students may lose the thread of what you're trying to accomplish together.

Consider Audience and Modalities

As you consider modes of activism, consider the audience for your students' work. You'll want to make sure that the work the students do is not for you, or for their grades, but for a real cause in the world. If the kids are to understand the vital role they play in society, they'll need to be heard by someone outside of their immediate circle. It's often helpful for kids to consider their potential audience *before* they start their projects so that they can work with this audience in mind, choosing their modality, examples, and register in order to be as compelling as possible. Help kids consider: do they want to present to the school board? Stage a sit-in at a public meeting? Present and publish a petition? Call a town hall meeting? Bring in outside speakers? Publish online? Write letters? Host a symposium or debate? Create an event? Publish a TED Talk? Often strong argument essays can be turned into speeches or debates, and research projects can be turned into TED Talks. Other times kids may want to create something dramatic or artistic. Whatever the modality and audience, having a sense of these as early as possible in the project will not only help the students articulate themselves more clearly but also give the project the purpose necessary to spur sustained focus over the project's life span.

Set the stakes high. When Marc's students create their opera, they really do create an opera, not just a quick skit. The entire grade mobilizes, with students collaborating in roles such as project managers, set designers, composers, writers, and performers (see Figure 5.4). And, every year, the students raise their voices to educate their community, including their own parents and families.

As kids think about their audience and modalities, it often becomes clear that local audiences are the most reachable and the most effectively influenced. In this chapter, therefore, we focus most on helping students identify local issues and local forms of activism. While we often consider national issues and campaigns the most important because of their prominence in the news, some of the most impactful movements begin locally, where finding like-minded individuals and organizations committed to common causes, and identifying the locus of power, are most possible. By helping your students to look at issues in the communities surrounding the school, you'll enable them to see democracy as more than the presidential election with its bluster and pandering, but also as complex networks of citizens working to change their small corner of the country.

Akeem and Aaron chose to pursue a single class topic, but they wanted to make sure that their topic reflected the interests of as many students in the class as possible. To that end, they created a survey with a number of topics on it and had the students note the issues that most impacted, or interested, them. Both teachers took time to follow up individually with students to discuss their responses to the survey. After tallying the results, the majority of the class was interested in exploring the relationship between the community and the police officers assigned to protect it. Many had shared anecdotes about having been detained by police, or having been intimidated by police, particularly when traveling in groups with classmates. Through a combination of a survey created with firsthand knowledge of the community (both Akeem and Aaron grew up in the area) and one-on-one and small-

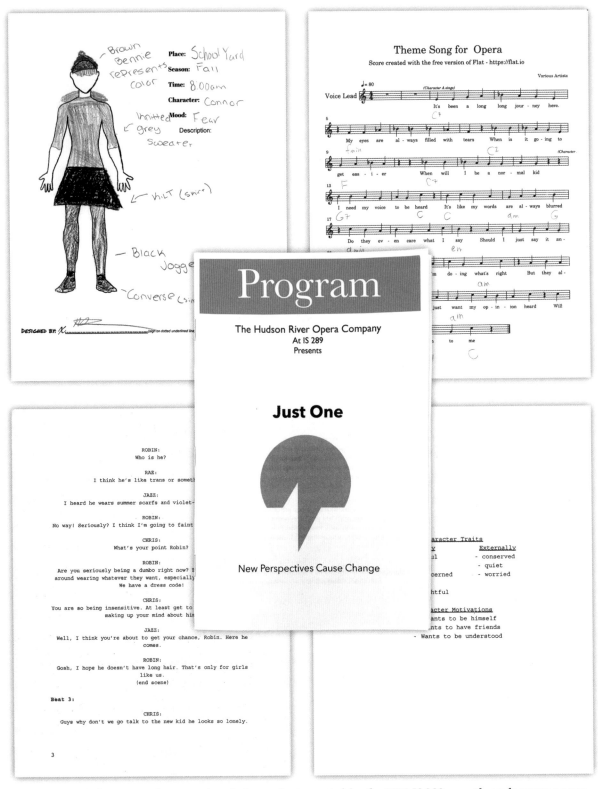

FIGURE 5.4 A glimpse at a few examples of what students created for the 2019 IS 289 seventh-grade opera: a page from the score, a peek at the script, costume design notes for the opera's transgender protagonist.

group discussions with students, they were able to pinpoint a relevant topic that would be of interest as well as begin to collect possible anecdotes that might inform the nature of their activism.

Because the topic they chose was rooted locally, the next step was to see whether their topic resonated with the community. Aaron and the student Survey Committee designed a questionnaire about police–community relationships that collected demographic information and gauged public opinion about relationships with the local precinct and knowledge of the precinct's outreach efforts (see Figure 5.5). Akeem and Aaron divided the class into smaller groups, each one chaperoned by a different adult. Supplied with questionnaires and a simple script, the kids went out to collect information from community members. As we mentioned in Chapter 2, after going out during the school day, knocking on neighbors' doors in the evenings and interviewing family members at home, the students compiled two hundred surveys about their topic and found that 44 percent of those interviewed

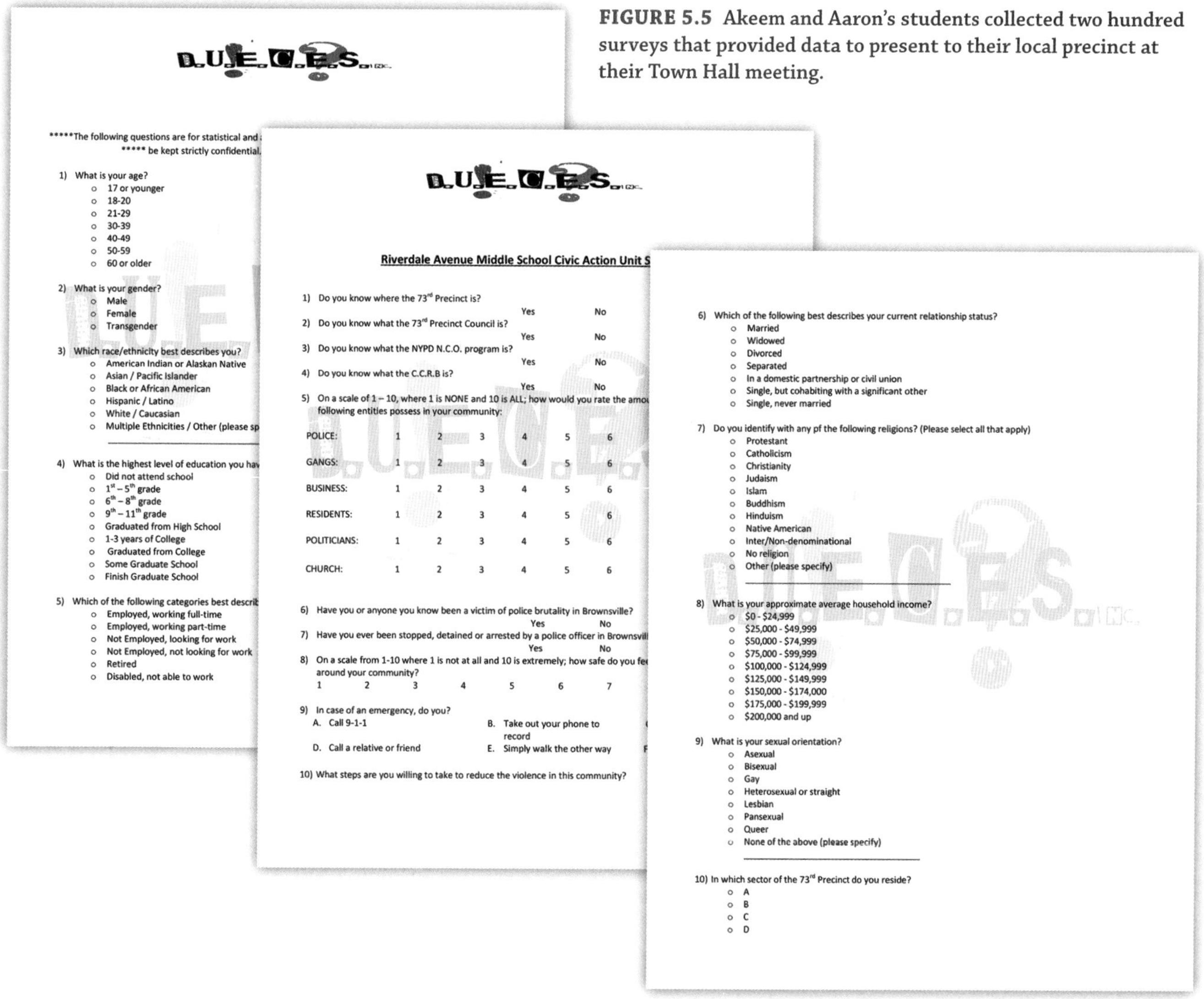
*****The following questions are for statistical and
***** be kept strictly confidential.

1) What is your age?
- 17 or younger
- 18-20
- 21-29
- 30-39
- 40-49
- 50-59
- 60 or older

2) What is your gender?
- Male
- Female
- Transgender

3) Which race/ethnicity best describes you?
- American Indian or Alaskan Native
- Asian / Pacific Islander
- Black or African American
- Hispanic / Latino
- White / Caucasian
- Multiple Ethnicities / Other (please sp

4) What is the highest level of education you hav
- Did not attend school
- 1st – 5th grade
- 6th – 8th grade
- 9th – 11th grade
- Graduated from High School
- 1-3 years of College
- Graduated from College
- Some Graduate School
- Finish Graduate School

5) Which of the following categories best describ
- Employed, working full-time
- Employed, working part-time
- Not Employed, looking for work
- Not Employed, not looking for work
- Retired
- Disabled, not able to work

Riverdale Avenue Middle School Civic Action Unit S

1) Do you know where the 73rd Precinct is? Yes No
2) Do you know what the 73rd Precinct Council is? Yes No
3) Do you know what the NYPD N.C.O. program is? Yes No
4) Do you know what the C.C.R.B is? Yes No
5) On a scale of 1 – 10, where 1 is NONE and 10 is ALL; how would you rate the amou following entities possess in your community:

POLICE:	1	2	3	4	5	6
GANGS:	1	2	3	4	5	6
BUSINESS:	1	2	3	4	5	6
RESIDENTS:	1	2	3	4	5	6
POLITICIANS:	1	2	3	4	5	6
CHURCH:	1	2	3	4	5	6

6) Have you or anyone you know been a victim of police brutality in Brownsville? Yes No
7) Have you ever been stopped, detained or arrested by a police officer in Brownsvill Yes No
8) On a scale from 1-10 where 1 is not at all and 10 is extremely; how safe do you fe around your community?
1 2 3 4 5 6 7
9) In case of an emergency, do you?
A. Call 9-1-1 B. Take out your phone to record
D. Call a relative or friend E. Simply walk the other way
10) What steps are you willing to take to reduce the violence in this community?

6) Which of the following best describes your current relationship status?
- Married
- Widowed
- Divorced
- Separated
- In a domestic partnership or civil union
- Single, but cohabiting with a significant other
- Single, never married

7) Do you identify with any pf the following religions? (Please select all that apply)
- Protestant
- Catholicism
- Christianity
- Judaism
- Islam
- Buddhism
- Hinduism
- Native American
- Inter/Non-denominational
- No religion
- Other (please specify)

8) What is your approximate average household income?
- $0 - $24,999
- $25,000 - $49,999
- $50,000 - $74,999
- $75,000 - $99,999
- $100,000 - $124,999
- $125,000 - $149,999
- $150,000 - $174,000
- $175,000 - $199,999
- $200,000 and up

9) What is your sexual orientation?
- Asexual
- Bisexual
- Gay
- Heterosexual or straight
- Lesbian
- Pansexual
- Queer
- None of the above (please specify)

10) In which sector of the 73rd Precinct do you reside?
- A
- B
- C
- D

FIGURE 5.5 Akeem and Aaron's students collected two hundred surveys that provided data to present to their local precinct at their Town Hall meeting.

had had a negative interaction with a police officer and that 69 percent did not know about the existence of a Citizen Complaint Review Board (CCRB) where they could voice their concerns about police interactions.

Immediately going out into the community and seeing for themselves that the issue they had chosen was deeply relevant helped the students build momentum for their project. They agreed that there needed to be a way to inform more people about their rights and that they needed to confront the police about how they had made so many people feel. After brainstorming possible ideas for publishing their findings, the classes determined, with Aaron's guidance, that hosting a "town hall" meeting at the school with officers, community members, and representatives of the CCRB in attendance could be a way to show their work and research as well as to foster dialogue between groups. The town hall would feature panelists from the 73rd precinct, the CCRB, and the community, as well as students who would facilitate the conversation.

Teach Students About Local Government and Where Power Resides

One of the hard but also beautiful parts of American politics is how differently things are run in different locales. If you teach in a small town, you may have a Town Council, a Planning Board, and a School Board, as well as local Police, EMT, and so on. All of these may be groups to involve—and it can be illuminating to map out on one of your classroom walls what powers each group has, and how decisions are made. In a bigger city there may be a City Council, and many subgroups responsible for different kinds of decision-making, from Parks to Education to City Housing.

In New York City, for instance, the New York City Housing Authority (NYCHA) is responsible for making decisions about which trees to plant and how to maintain them, and which housing sites get city trees. Meanwhile, NYC Parks makes decisions about street trees, and local housing collectives can plant trees as well. This decision-making often results in a lot of inequity since the neighborhoods that are green will suffer less than urban heat islands.

Often, once your students have figured out some of the questions they have and issues they care about, it's worth it to map what groups are involved in decision-making, and figure out who has the power to make local, short-term decisions. Often, groups will have an education mandate and will be open to involving young people.

While mapping these government institutions out physically, using your walls and desks, is a great start to orienting students as to where the levers of power reside in your locale, there really is no substitute for direct participation. Find out when public hearings are being held and plan a field trip. Reach out to parents and families for permission to bring some students to evening gatherings to discuss com-

» YOUNG CITIZENS IN ACTION «

So far in this chapter, we've discussed structures to help you launch your students into action. At times, however, a mix of serendipity and student curiosity—and a touch of teacher influence—may end up creating the perfect conditions for classroom-based activism. In the winter of 2012, Pablo was doing a close-reading lesson using the classic science fiction story, "The Ones Who Walk Away from Omelas," by Ursula K. Le Guin (1975). The students parsed out the social commentary of the piece and wrestled with the idea of a civilization whose utopic beauty was dependent on the misery of a child locked away in a dismal room. In the story, no one can help this child since it would cause the entire society to crumble. Pablo's students debated about whether to help the child or to be among those alluded to in the title who simply left the society without looking back. The following day Pablo was struck by an investigative journalism piece in the *New York Times* called "Invisible Child," with the subhead, "Girl in the shadows: Dasani's homeless life." The piece chronicled the experiences of a child just a year younger than his students, and its opening paragraph described living conditions that eerily paralleled those of the child locked away in an Omelas basement. It begins: "She wakes to the sound of breathing. The smaller children lie tangled beside her, their chests rising and falling under winter coats and wool blankets. A few feet away, their mother and father sleep near the mop bucket they use as a toilet. Two other children share a mattress by the rotting wall where the mice live, opposite the baby, whose crib is warmed by a hair dryer perched on a milk crate" (Elliott 2013). Pablo brought the piece in for the students to read in relation to the science fiction story, and together they discussed the parallels and how much New York City was like Omelas. One astute student even pointed out an infographic in the piece that showed the location of Dasani's shelter on a block where homes were selling for millions of dollars. Struck by the injustice, the students began to ask about homelessness in the community around the school, which eventually led to a partnership with a soup kitchen and a local housing organization called Urban Pathways. Students then organized a day of service at the soup kitchen and a food drive for Urban Pathways, all of which were born out of two close reading lessons of powerful texts.

munity issues. Even if only a subset of your students can participate, the excitement and engagement of a core group can have a contagious effect that helps mobilize the rest of your class. Aaron spent several evenings taking students to police-precinct council meetings and community board meetings. At these events, Akeem and Aaron's students could see and participate in decisions that affected them directly. Aaron could also point out which people lead which committees and could introduce students to those who represented their interests. The students were surprised to see that these meetings were primarily attended by senior citizens who had somewhat conservative views on how to handle some of the community's problems. Participating in these meetings also allowed the students to raise the profile of their own town hall gathering. They addressed elected officials directly to ask them to participate, and they got the word out to other engaged citizens.

Develop Social Networks That Extend into the Surrounding Community

Activism requires that you and your students look beyond the four walls of the classroom for accomplices to help you in your work. Once the class has identified an issue, reach out to local organizations or individuals in the community who are

When Searching for Community Partners

1. Before you reach out to potential partners, work with your students to clearly define your issue and the project you are planning to address the issue. Try to distill the project into a half-page summary that you can present to potential partners.

2. Consider all of the ways in which you might find partners—not only through social media or internet searches but also through personal contacts and connections, including friends, colleagues, and administrators. Canvas your parents and families to find out if they might be helpful partners or if they might know someone who would be. Consider attending a community board meeting or city council meeting, and pay attention to who is the noisiest and the most aligned with your students' work: ask them to participate, or to suggest someone else who might help. Contact your local ACLU, your teachers union, your YMCA, any local youth groups, and find out which groups are most active in your community.

3. Work with students to research potential partners carefully. Have a clear idea of potential partners' missions and how helping you can fulfill both their mission and yours. Create a list of connections and how they might serve your class goals. Post the list in your room for your—and the students'—reference.

4. After making a list, help students forge introductions and make contacts. Some students have tremendous social capital and will easily reach out to adults. Others will need support writing emails, setting up phone calls and meetings. Help students rehearse these conversations.

doing similar work and who could potentially partner with your students. In Akeem and Aaron's project, Aaron connected the class to the district's Neighborhood Coordinating Officers (NCOs) who came into the school on multiple occasions to present the police perspective on law enforcement around the school, as well as to listen to the students' complaints and answer their questions.

On another occasion, Aaron brought Sergeant Harper from the seventy-third precinct, who introduced a virtual reality program that allowed students to step into the perspective of a police officer and experience the decisions that officers make regularly. Reaching out to partner with organizations outside of the school put the students in touch with adults who were really listening to their concerns and taking the time to thoughtfully address those concerns. It showed the students that the work they were doing was authentic, valued, and meaningful.

Make a Plan that Plays to Students' Strengths

Because activism can take so many forms, this work offers a perfect opportunity to differentiate the type of product you are expecting from your students. We all know that the hardest challenges are best tackled when they are broken into their component parts and those whose skills are best suited to particular types of problems are assigned to work on them. The work in your classroom can be similar. Once a challenge is determined by the class, you can create an action plan in which students contribute to the project according to their particular interests and skills.

In order to pull off their town hall, Akeem decided to break the class into smaller subcommittees, each with a different contribution to the event. Each subcommittee had a clear "job description" and students were required to apply for each job with a brief explanation as to why they were particularly well suited to the committee. You can see the names of the committees along with job descriptions in Figure 5.6.

If you choose to create a committee system in your room, consider:

- Who are the students in my room?
- What are their talents and interests?
- What can each student contribute so that they feel successful and proud of their role in the project?
- Which partnerships will build on each other's strengths?
- Who has yet to shine this year, and how can their role in this bring out their best?
- How will you provide each committee with a to-do list that helps them stay on track and organized?

Survey Committee	Publicity Committee	Public Speaking Committee
♦ Finish a survey to learn more about the concerns of the community. ♦ Go out with a teacher to administer the survey. **Skills needed:** – *Ability to ask thoughtful questions* – *Outgoing personality* – *Willingness to engage unfamiliar people in conversation (with teacher present)* – *Confident yet respectful in presentation*	♦ Design a flyer for our event that captures the attention of people walking by, while also informing them what it's about. ♦ Write/design an email invitation to go out to possible guests and speakers. ♦ Communicate with newspaper, TV, and blog reporters about our event. ♦ Write press releases, as needed. **Skills needed:** – *Keen attention to detail* – *Someone who is good at checking and rechecking their work and isn't afraid of doing several drafts* – *Skill with visual art, such as drawing, painting, or digital art* – *Skill with Photoshop or other software a plus*	♦ Write speeches that communicate student concerns about police–community relationships. ♦ Deliver speeches at Town Hall in front of police representatives, elected officials, and press. **Skills needed:** – *Ability to write clearly and persuasively about student issues* – *Willingness to interview peers to gather stories that are relevant to the issue of police–community relations* – *Willingness to revise writing as needed in order to make it polished and professional* – *Poise in front of a large audience*

FIGURE 5.6 Akeem and Aaron differentiated their instruction by creating meaningful committees where students could contribute to the common cause in ways that matched their skills and passions.

- What deadlines will you have for each committee to make sure they are using their time efficiently?
- What is the work?
- What are the jobs involved with the committee work?
- How many students can each committee accommodate?
- Can a student become the overall project manager?
- How and when will the committees communicate?
- What materials will the committees need in order to be successful?

You might decide to create a role specifically for a student, or a group of students. In Akeem's case, one student was reluctant to participate in any way, so Akeem appealed to the student's strong desire to be onstage and designed an opportunity for the student to write, and perform, a rap about police–community relationships.

Research Committee	MC and Entertainment Committee	Dance and Music Committee
◆ Gather data and statistics about community–police relationships in the Brownsville neighborhood to give to the Public Speaking Committee so they can include it in their speeches. ◆ Gather personal anecdotes by interviewing peers about police interactions. ◆ Take clear notes that their peers can follow. **Skills needed:** – *Ability to find relevant information that is current and reliable* – *Ability to take clear, logical notes* – *Ability to determine whether sources are biased or not* – *Willingness to interview peers and others about their experiences with police*	◆ Write and perform original songs at the Town Hall Meeting. ◆ Introduce speakers and special guests. **Skills needed:** – *Creative writing ability* – *Willingness to write and rewrite several songs to find the best ones to perform* – *Comfort in front of a large crowd* – *Experience with "FL Studio," "GarageBand," or other beat-making software a plus*	◆ Research songs to play at the meeting with particular attention to them and relevance to the topic of police–community relations. ◆ Find lyrics to multiple songs. Analyze songs and write why they should be part of our Town Hall. ◆ Choreograph a dance to go with the music. ◆ Perform in front of an audience. **Skills needed:** – *Dance or choreography experience* – *Deep knowledge of music* – *Willingness to identify multiple possible songs and explain their relevance to our topic*

Again, the key to the success of this work is to return to the students in the room and to listen to their needs as you author curriculum together.

Create a Social Action Headquarters

Akeem and Aaron redesigned the classroom space in order to remind the students of all that needed to be done in preparation for their town hall meeting. One board was devoted to a large calendar on which upcoming deadlines and to-do lists were sketched in. The final meeting was highlighted to remind everyone to work with urgency. Another wall had numerous color photographs of relevant public officials and their respective roles and responsibilities, as well as their contact information so that the communications team could reach out to their offices and invite them to the event. The classroom bulletin board held the questionnaire results so that the survey team could analyze them and prepare their presentation for the event.

EDUCATOR SPOTLIGHT

Aaron's commitment to Brownsville traces back a decade, beginning with community activist work with adults; however, he found the greatest success with activism work when he worked with young people. When Michael Bloomberg was in his third term as mayor, his administration had begun cutting funding from the New York City Housing Authority (NYCHA), which caused the closing of after-school programs. Aaron began to approach the youth who had been affected. He explains, "I said to myself, this is where the work is. I would walk up to these young men on the corner and ask them, 'What's your plan in life?' Of course they have dreams and aspirations." Soon Aaron had incorporated a 501.c.3 nonprofit organization called Do yoU's Enlightenment & Cultural Empowerment Services (DUECES). As DUECES grew and began to serve more young people, Aaron developed greater firsthand knowledge of the intricacies of city government. He won grants from the Mayor's Fund for Public Health, developed contacts within the local community board, and worked for a state senator. Aaron summarizes his vision for youth-empowerment work by referring to his own struggles growing up, "When I was younger, these opportunities did not exist for me. Everything I was told to do—go to school, go to college—didn't work. I *asked* for opportunities and was denied. I *demanded* opportunities and was denied. So, I *created* the opportunities I needed. I want kids to know that they can do this too. They need to know this at a younger age, not wait until they're twenty-five like I was."

Students were literally immersed in their activism and regularly reminded that their work was more than an academic exercise, that it was deeply connected to the community outside of the school.

Involve Families and Communities

A wealth of experiences and collective wisdom is compressed into our local communities; unfortunately, it often goes unnoticed and untapped. At the heart of our work in this chapter is the breaking down of the four walls of the classroom in order to show that the world and the classroom are one. All students benefit when they see that their work exists for a purpose beyond teacher approval. Try to find as many ways as possible to make the classroom permeable. We mentioned earlier how Aaron had community elders serve as chaperones for their trips, and how he and Akeem used the local library as a research hub. Begin with your students' parents and families, ask them for their labor and their expertise, but also ask them to help you bolster your network. Ask them who they know that might be interested and able to contribute to a school project. Go beyond asking your parents and families for permission to do a unit, and instead invite them into the unit as accomplices.

When approaching parents and families about classroom activism, it will be important for you to be fully transparent. Write them an introductory letter about the unit and send periodic updates along the way. Don't neglect to involve parents and families early on; they could become an impediment if they feel that your topic is too controversial, or if they don't see how the work supports academics. If you have parents or families who are anxious about whether the activism you are doing is sufficiently academic, you may want to include the academic standards their students will be practicing. Akeem's planning document in the next section below gives us a sense of how he aligned his activism work with the Common Core standards.

Be Ready for Anything

The biggest thing to be ready for is that the issues kids care about may not be the same ones you care about. So, your first hurdle is often that of stepping back from the curriculum you had in mind. It's up to us, as teachers, to keep ourselves from getting carried away by an issue or event and foisting it on the class, to avoid assuming that they share the same interests rather than learning about what matters to them. It's difficult, but we have to be cautious about letting our own enthusiasm about potential activism become a new curriculum. Remember: the kids are the curriculum. Take the time to interview them, to sit together and brainstorm, to explore identity maps again—anything that will allow students to voice issues of concern that are authentic to them. Your project will be that much more effective with their full buy-in.

While the students are the curriculum, as teachers we do have to answer to administrators who may have concerns about whether the activism we are embarking on, however noble it might be, is suitably academic. As you pitch your activist ideas to your administrative team, you may want to emphasize the academic standards that the students will practice and the essential questions they will explore. Akeem and Aaron emphasized the following objectives, enduring understandings, essential questions, and standards when approaching the principal and assistant principal.

UNIT OBJECTIVES
- to foster student engagement in reading and writing
- to foster civic engagement
- to help students realize their civic power and responsibilities

ENDURING UNDERSTANDINGS
- We can use our academic skills to affect real change in our world.
- How we write and create depends on the audience we are communicating with.
- Democracy requires informed, engaged citizens who ask the right questions and go looking for answers.

(continues)

(continued)

ESSENTIAL QUESTIONS

- How can we identify problems in our community and design concrete actions to respond to those problems?
- How can reading, writing, and speaking skills be used to make change?
- Who holds power in my community and how do I convince them to take action?
- Who holds power in my community and how do I join forces with them?

READING SKILLS

- CCSS.ELA-LITERACY.RI.8.1—Cite the textual evidence that most strongly supports an analysis of what the text says explicitly as well as inferences drawn from the text.
- CCSS.ELA-LITERACY.RI.8.2—Determine a central idea of a text and analyze its development over the course of the text, including its relationship to supporting ideas; provide an objective summary of the text.
- CCSS.ELA-LITERACY.RI.8.9—Analyze a case in which two or more texts provide conflicting information on the same topic and identify where the texts disagree on matters of fact or interpretation.
- CCSS.ELA-LITERACY.RI.8.8—Delineate and evaluate the argument and specific claims in a text, assessing whether the reasoning is sound and the evidence is relevant and sufficient; recognize when irrelevant evidence is introduced.

WRITING SKILLS

- CCSS.ELA-LITERACY.W.8.1.A—Introduce claim(s), acknowledge and distinguish the claim(s) from alternate or opposing claims, and organize the reasons and evidence logically.
- CCSS.ELA-LITERACY.W.8.2—Write informative/explanatory texts to examine a topic and convey ideas, concepts, and information through the selection, organization, and analysis of relevant content.
- CCSS.ELA-LITERACY.W.8.7—Conduct short research projects to answer a question (including a self-generated question), drawing on several sources and generating additional related, focused questions that allow for multiple avenues of exploration.

SPEAKING SKILLS

- CCSS.ELA-LITERACY.SL.8.4—Present claims and findings, emphasizing salient points in a focused, coherent manner with relevant evidence, sound valid reasoning, and well-chosen details; use appropriate eye contact, adequate volume, and clear pronunciation.

FORMATIVE ASSESSMENT

- student journaling (students should spend some time entry-writing each class session)
- participation in class discussion

Finally, remember that the work you and your students take on may hit close to home for them. When the police officers whom Aaron had invited to his classroom arrived, there was still tension. One student declared that he would not talk to the officers and left the room as soon as they entered. Aaron found him in the hallway and explained that the only way to make a change on this issue that they collectively had determined was so important to the community was to engage in these sorts of conversations. It was only then that the student agreed to return to the room. Another boy reluctantly agreed to stay in the room but sat silently in the back, watching the conversation with guarded suspicion. Aaron saw these reactions as visceral responses to traumas from their own lives. He knew that many in this community had seen fathers and uncles taken away by police, or had been frisked or questioned themselves. He knew that the responses of these students were not intended as disrespect or misbehavior, and he treated them with empathy as he listened to their needs.

As you embark on activism with your students, expect emotional moments. Look for students who are vulnerable or who respond in surprising ways, and listen to what their actions might say about how they are wrestling with these issues. Perhaps they are telling you they can continue with support, or perhaps they are telling you that they need to step away from the project.

Practice What You Teach

This might be the toughest "Practice What You Teach" section of the entire book: it really is an exhortation for us all to *act*. Our days are so filled with classroom preparation and instruction, our evenings with grading, our weekends with family responsibilities—the hours in the day are too few to do all that we want. We already give much of our time to our job and yet, here, we're going to ask more of you, we're going to ask that you engage in some form of activism yourself. In order for us to effectively teach civics, we ourselves need to be involved in civic institutions. How can we teach the different tiers of local government if we don't have firsthand knowledge of them ourselves? So, in all the busyness of your overstuffed life, we're going to ask you to fit in one more thing, some form of service to a cause that matters to you—something that requires something from you but whose rewards are measured in social connection and a reminder of your natural affinity for other people.

The COVID-19 pandemic forced nations, towns, communities, and families to endure greater and greater isolation. Often we felt the presence of others just enough to pique our loneliness, a condition that impoverishes our thinking and the democracy that depends on our participation. Twenty years ago Robert Putnam's *Bowling Alone: the Collapse and Revival of American Community* presciently cautioned: "Social dislocation can easily breed a reactionary form of nostalgia" (2000, 401). It is incumbent on us all to devote ourselves to our communities now, to act on behalf of the causes we value *now*, to make change with those around us *now*, and not to resign ourselves to shaking our fists at a computer screen or newspaper headline.

While we may find ourselves communicating with our loved ones, our colleagues, and our students over the phone, through the internet, or by mail, we can still participate in a cause. Communication challenges are not new, nor are the inequities and system-failures that cause them. We think of the teachers who drove through neighborhoods to "see" their students, the literacy coaches delivering devices again and again, the students reaching out to each other in every conceivable way, and we know that we can reach across barriers to help each other.

Consider the questions in Figure 5.7, then, and then challenge yourself to make a plan to tackle an issue that you care about and would like to see addressed. Your actions will directly inform your teaching, your anecdotes will serve as a model for your kids, and your dedication will extend your social network and magnify your impact. This is an investment, for you will surely see dramatic returns as you connect with like-minded citizens.

Finding a Cause

- What issues in the world right now are you emotionally invested in?
- What do you hope to change?
- What issues do you have a personal stake in?
- What skills and talents can you contribute?

Self-Assessing Civic Knowledge

- What is the smallest, most hyper-local government position in your community? Who holds it? What are they responsible for?
- How is your school board chosen? Who's on it? What issues are they currently considering?
- Who is serving on your municipal council? How were they chosen? What issues are they currently considering?

Self-Assessing Strength of Your Social Network

- What local institutions are you a member of?
- Are there actions that you'd like to take with friends that are dear to you?
- How often do you make common cause with people outside of your immediate family?
- How many organizations are you an active member of?
- How well do you know your neighbors?
- How many informal relationships do you have to people in your community who you see regularly and with whom you exchange pleasantries but not necessarily deep conversations?
- Do people generally trust one another in your community? How do you know?
- In what ways do you contribute/volunteer toward the well-being of other people in your community?

FIGURE 5.7 Evaluate your own civic engagement with these questions. How would you like to push yourself to become more involved in your community?

FEEDBACK AND ASSESSMENT STRENGTHEN ENGAGED CITIZENS

We began this book with attention to identity work because it matters that kids think about themselves and what they bring to the texts in front of them and to all their interactions with the world. It matters that we, as their teachers, do this as well. We all bring our own stories, our histories, our biases, all the parts of ourselves, including the parts that are known and less known to us, to everything that we do and everything we respond to, including how we offer opportunities for reflection and assessment.

When we think about our own identities, including what we're aware of and what we have language for, we realize that we have undergone seismic shifts over the course of our lives and studies. We remember what it was to become aware of our sexual identities and to come out. We remember realizing that our cultures were significant and often different from those of other students and teachers. We remember becoming aware of inequity and suffering, not only as bystanders but also through lived violence and brutal events. We remember realizing that we have internalized oppressive racist and sexist discourse that haunts our language and shades our perceptions. We have colleagues, family, and friends who support us and challenge us. We take time often to reflect, to regroup, to realize that our thinking has changed. Our students need those same opportunities.

In this chapter, we'll help you to:

- consider what we mean by assessment
- use assessment practices that support students' growth as engaged citizens
- use assessment to improve our own curriculum and instruction
- be brave, be innovative, be progressive, be kind, be research-based.

Consider What We Mean by *Assessment*

Assessment itself is a civic virtue. Citizens are assessing all the time—judging that candidate's speech, that ad's effectiveness, that phrase that a colleague just used. It's also a civic virtue to assess one's own thinking. The kind of long writing described in Chapter 4, then, is assessment as a civic virtue. The thinking you do about your students and your curriculum, and the curriculum that is the world, is a civic virtue.

Mostly, though, when we hear questions about assessment from teachers or graduate students, they're often some variation of "How will I grade?" We dread this question, even though we deeply understand it. We have to provide grades in graduate courses we teach. We have to write teacher and student recommendations. We review peer-reviewed journal articles and curricula, using rubrics we didn't create and don't often love. We grade student work—work that happens in classrooms we work in, inside curricula we love, in standardized state and national exams that we did not create but that are very high stakes for students and teachers. Grades have become so ubiquitous that it can be easy to think they're necessary.

However, even if we're working within systems that may require grades, the big thing for us all to think about in terms of assessment is this: *Kids don't get better at something because they get a grade.* They get better because they get feedback. So, as much as possible, we want to maximize the time and intellectual energy that we put into feedback, and minimize the time and intellectual energy that we put into grading. Ideally, our assessments function as feedback and dovetail with our grading criteria.

In "Teachers, We Cannot go Back to the Way Things Were," Bettina Love pleads with educators, as we regroup and rethink after COVID-19, not to return to the kinds of assessment practices that undervalued students of color and over-valued normativity. Love notes that in the midst of the crisis, she found: "Schools are relying on different indicators of achievement other than standardized testing to measure improvement, such as parent engagement, teacher-outreach levels, and interactive lessons. Teachers are making the social-emotional learning of their students their top priority" (2020, 2). We don't want to step back from that work—we want to step into it. That means learning to value students' individual voices and registers and ways of being. It also means looking hard at how our current grading practices work.

To step into assessment and grading that values all students, that looks for students' strengths, that strives to hear students' voices, we often have to step away from punitive grading practices. Two of the most influential thinkers in grading reform are Doug Reeves and Tom Guskey. We list some of their resources on page 167. They each have a huge amount to say about punitive grading practices, the dangers of averaging, and the annihilating factor of giving zeros. Doug is especially wary of what has happened as a result of technology "helping" us with grading. All too often, that technology seems to superimpose averaging, zeros, equal weighting—all sorts of retrograde practices. It's important to clarify your beliefs, values, and practices (and base them on research), and to align your software use to those values and practices, rather than the reverse.

We also suggest that you read Dan Pink's *Drive* (2009), or watch his TED Talk, "The Puzzle of Motivation" (2009), to hear about research on motivation and on the danger of short-term motivators, like grades, in contrast to internalized motivators, like connections with others, a feeling of worth, and efficacy. It turns out that it's simply not true that good grades motivate us to work at high levels or that bad grades motivate us to try harder. In fact, bad grades tend to turn kids off from learning and from a particular content, often permanently. Motivation based on good grades is a short-term, low-level, compliance mindset that inhibits innovation, experimentation, and the willingness to fail, as Kim Marshall describes in his article, "Doug Reeves Takes on Five Myths about Grading" (2017).

If you pause to think about when and how you've really learned in your own life, you'll probably realize that it's not those "getting-good-grade" moments that taught you big lessons or made you who you are. In his TED Talk, "How the Worst Moments in Our Life Make Us Who We Are" (2014), Andrew Solomon talks about how we learn in those painful moments when we want to change things. Similarly, in her book *The Rise: Creativity, the Gift of Failure, and the Search for Mastery* (2014), Sarah Lewis talks about how important a willingness to fail is to striving and accomplishment. So, yes, good grades may motivate students to get good grades. But our goal is to motivate students to tackle new thinking, push through discomfort, and discover new aspects of themselves.

We also want to involve students in assessment and to think about student work as a form of feedback. To learn more about the significance of this approach, look to John Hattie's research. Nancy Frey and Douglas Fisher have written with Hattie (2018) about creating "assessment-capable learners," students who are taught assessment literacies and inculcate self-assessment processes. Hattie also shows the effect size of feedback followed by immediate practice, and he looks at two critical qualities of feedback—the ability to help students understand "what's next" and the ability to process students' work as feedback on our teaching.

What can be especially hard to look at inside of this work are our own biases. Remember what Kendi tells us: we swim in racist waters, we breath racist air. We have unwittingly internalized assumptions and prejudices. We see some students as "better," as "trying," as "achieving," because they fit a picture of better-trying-achieving students that we learned from sources we can't even remember—television shows, our own teachers, the books we've read, the norms we see around us, our own upbringing, the people and groups we are a part of and those we are not. In *We Want to Do More Than Survive: Abolitionist Teaching and the Pursuit of Educational Freedom,* Bettina Love asserts the essential injustice that has run through the American school system, one that has systematically branded young Black and Brown-skinned students as defiant or disruptive, that has held onto and propagated stereotypes that damage young people. In her anguished and searing prologue, "We Who Are Dark," Love asks, "How do you matter to a country that is incapable of loving dark bodies and, therefore, incapable of loving you?" (2019, 3). We know we have judged and misjudged, assumed and interpreted. We know that some students make us comfortable and some do not. It's horrifying and humbling to think about. We vow to do better.

Use Assessment Practices That Support Students' Growth as Engaged Citizens

It's all very well and good to think more expansively about assessment, but how does that translate into the specific work we do with students? And how can we make these ideas work in a reality that typically requires grades? Let's take a look at how we can put these understandings into action that supports our students as people, as learners, and as engaged citizens.

Provide Opportunities for Kids to Think About Their Thinking

In our international work, we have been fortunate to work with CPRE (Consortium for Policy and Research in Education), especially with educational policy advisor Tom Corcoran. On one trip, when we were visiting science classrooms in Jordan, Tom advised us to not just look at the first ten minutes of class. "Study what happens in the last ten minutes," he told us. "Clean-up is not reflection," he said. According to Tom, those final minutes of class are when learning is consolidated or it flies away. He spoke about the significance of kids having time to write, think, and talk about the skills they are learning, the content they are coming to understand, and most of all, the ways their thinking is changing.

Some Resources for Thinking About Grading, Assessment, and Feedback

Bettina Love, "Teachers, We Cannot Go Back to the Way Things Were" (2020)

> www.edweek.org/ew/articles/2020/04/30/teachers-we
> -cannot-go-back-to-the.html

Douglas Reeves, "Leading to Change/Effective Grading Practices" (2008)

> www.ascd.org/publications/educational-leadership/feb08
> /vol65/num05/Effective-Grading-Practices.aspx

Douglas Reeves, "Elements of Effective Grading: A Video Interview with Doug Reeves from Creative Leadership" (2016)

> www.youtube.com/watch?v=dLYpqxQLRt4

Thomas Guskey, "Five Obstacles to Grading Reform" (2011)

> www.ascd.org/publications/educational-leadership/nov11/vol69
> /num03/Five-Obstacles-to-Grading-Reform.aspx

Thomas Guskey, "How Classroom Assessments Improve Learning" (2003)

> http://tguskey.com/wp-content/uploads/Assessment-2-How
> -Classroom-Assessments-Improve-Learning.pdf

John Hattie, "John Hattie on Visible Learning and Feedback in the Classroom" (2018)

> www.youtube.com/watch?v=Vpq09eY4pZo

Visible Learning, "Feedback in Schools by John Hattie," (2018)

> https://visible-learning.org/2013/10/john-hattie-article-about
> -feedback-in-schools

Nancy Frey, Douglas Fisher, John Hattie, "Developing Assessment Capable Learners" (2018)

> www.ascd.org/publications/educational-leadership/feb18/vol75
> /num05/Developing-%C2%A3Assessment-Capable%C2%A3
> -Learners.aspx

It's a civic virtue for students to think about their thinking. Opening themselves up to the possibility of change, pausing to reflect on how they are affected by new learning, sharing their thinking with others, and being responsive to the thinking of others—those are civic skills.

Marc has especially focused on and taught us about rituals that help students think about their thinking. Every Friday his students write long, in a special journal, about how their thinking is changing in response to the curriculum—and that ritual has become significant across the curriculum and the grades at his school. In the spring of 2020, the eighth grade at IS 289 created an interdisciplinary study of race, racism, and racial consciousness. In science, with science teacher Jaclyn Maricle, they studied the scientific origins of skin color and the not-so-scientific origins of race theory, and the current debunking of nineteen- and early twentieth-century science. In history, with social studies teacher Patrick Hector, they studied the religious and pseudoscientific justifications for slavery, and the cascading visibility of these racist theories. In ELA, with literacy teacher Christina Dizebba, they studied critical race theory and intersectionality. The kids did a lot of note-taking across the disciplines. But it was in their long writing (see Figure 6.1) that you could really see kids thinking hard about how their thinking was changing.

The big lesson that we take away from this kind of writing is that kids need protected time to think about their thinking. Long writing is one way for this to happen. When we build in rituals for calm, quiet, intensely personal reflection on student learning, we help them self-assess the evolution of their thoughts and feelings.

A lot of kids who start out writing short, and awkwardly, begin to write longer and more fluidly over time. Eduardo Briceño's work on the Learning Zone and the Performance Zone is important to understanding why kids get better at this work over time. In his TEDx Talk at Manhattan Beach, "The Power of Belief: Mindset and Success"(2012), Briceño talks about ways of thinking about yourself that help you live in a state of changeability. (The comments on this talk's YouTube page speak volumes: many of them are from students, noting that they wished they had been taught about this in school.)

In another TED Talk, "How to Get Better at the Things You Care About"(2016), Eduardo Briceño delineates what he calls the Learning Zone and the Performance Zone. Using the metaphor of Cirque du Soleil, Briceño describes their performances as the Performance Zone. Learning can't happen in the performance zone, he warns, because the stakes are too high—there is no margin for error. Cirque du Soleil performers perform without safety nets, literally. Instead, learning happens when the stakes are low, and there are safety nets.

Briceño's work on the Learning Zone and Performance Zone is important for teachers and students. All too often, school happens in the Performance Zone—or kids perceive it that way. Lowering the stakes helps kids learn more. If we con-

"How to Get Better at the Things You Care About"

www.ted.com/talks /eduardo_briceno _how_to_get_better _at_the_things_you _care_about

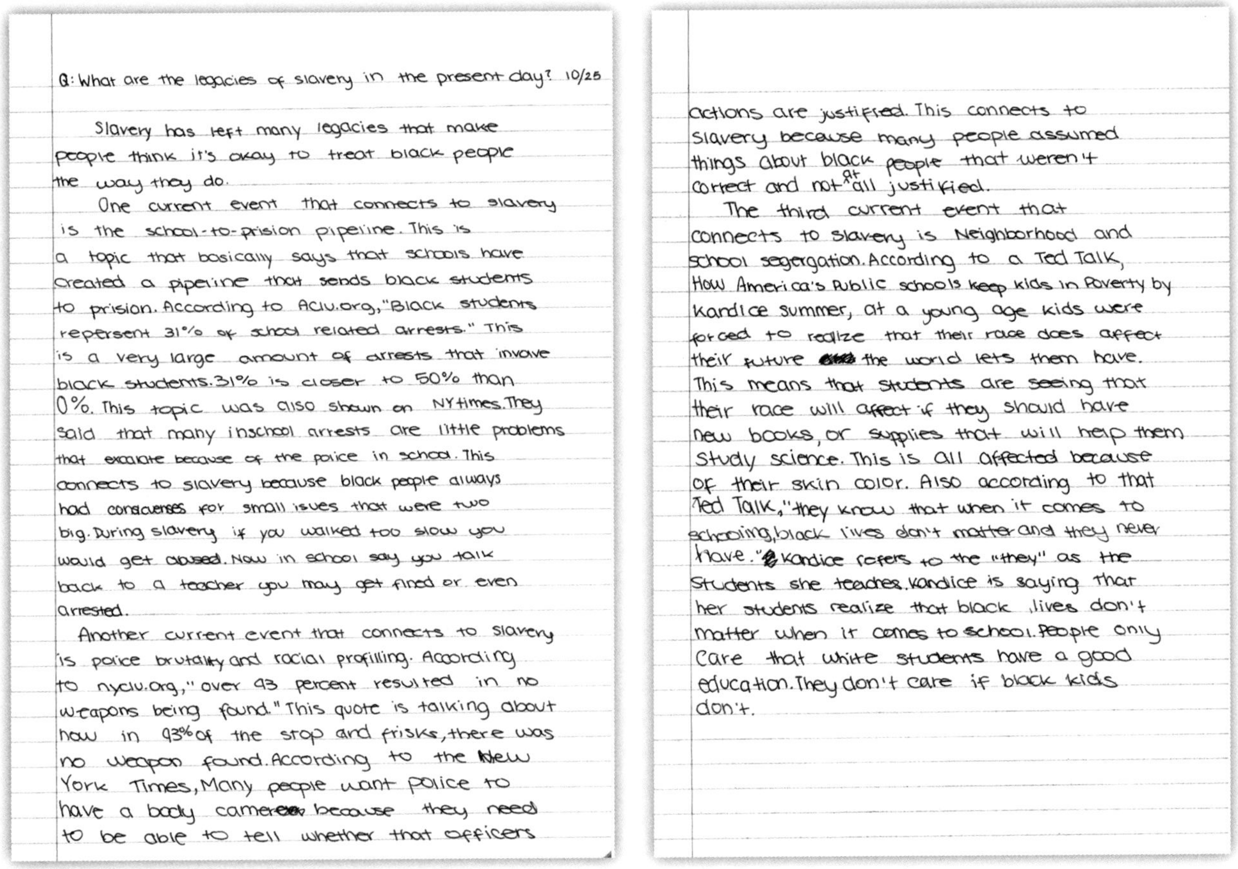

Q: What are the legacies of slavery in the present day? 10/28

Slavery has left many legacies that make people think it's okay to treat black people the way they do.

One current event that connects to slavery is the school-to-prision pipeline. This is a topic that basically says that schools have created a pipeline that sends black students to prision. According to Aclu.org, "Black students represent 31% of school related arrests." This is a very large amount of arrests that involve black students. 31% is closer to 50% than 0%. This topic was also shown on NYtimes. They said that many inschool arrests are little problems that escalate because of the police in school. This connects to slavery because black people always had consequences for small isues that were two big. During slavery if you walked too slow you would get abused. Now in school say you talk back to a teacher you may get fined or even arrested.

Another current event that connects to slavery is police brutality and racial profiling. According to nyclu.org," over 93 percent resulted in no weapons being found." This quote is talking about how in 93% of the stop and frisks, there was no weapon found. According to the New York Times, Many people want police to have a body camera because they need to be able to tell whether that officers

actions are justified. This connects to slavery because many people assumed things about black people that weren't correct and not at all justified.

The third current event that connects to slavery is Neighborhood and school segregation. According to a Ted Talk, How America's Public schools keep kids in Poverty by Kandice Summer, at a young age kids were forced to realize that their race does affect their future and the world lets them have. This means that students are seeing that their race will affect if they should have new books, or supplies that will help them study science. This is all affected because of their skin color. Also according to that Ted Talk," they know that when it comes to schooling, black lives don't matter and they never have." Kandice refers to the "they" as the students she teaches. Kandice is saying that her students realize that black lives don't matter when it comes to school. People only care that white students have a good education. They don't care if black kids don't.

FIGURE 6.1 Students use writing to synthesize their research with their own experiences.

sider "long writing" for example, what's important about it has nothing to do with grading. What's important about it is that it is ritualized. At the same time, we teachers study this long writing to gain insight into students' shifting understandings.

Long writing, when it is low-stakes and happens often, is a beautiful way for kids to develop more fluency with writing in order to think—but it is not the only way for kids to show their thinking. With Universal Design for Learning (UDL) in mind, as well as the ethical imperative for students to have multiple ways to show their learning, it's important to offer alternatives to writing. One simple option, especially in secondary school, is for kids to film or record themselves talking about their thinking. They can either upload their recordings to a classroom drive or create a QR code for their notebook. That can also be a step *toward* writing, as Douglas Reeves, author of *Reason to Write* (2002), has shown that writing, any kind of writing in the content areas, has a deep impact on content understandings. In Carol Lloyd's article, "Writing on the Wall," Reeves argues that "nonfiction writing is the most highly leveraged kind of learning—it improves kids' reading, math, social studies, music, and PE. It's 'thinking through the end of a pen.' Writing improves thinking" (2014).

EDUCATOR SPOTLIGHT

The science department at Tompkins Square Middle School (TSMS) in Manhattan started giving their students the option of videotaping themselves talking about their current understandings, rather than writing, as exit tickets in their classrooms, and/or as an option for homework. Immediately it became clear that a group of students knew a lot more science than was clear from their writing. TSMS suggests that we be careful to offer options for kids to "speak" their ideas as well as write them. And with the proliferation of voice-to-text software, kids also have multiple ways to initiate a draft, other than keyboarding. They can speak their draft, then go back in and revise it, finding alternate pathways into writing and steps along the way for consolidating their understanding.

Kids' notebook work will offer a dual value in your classroom. Your students will become more skilled in note-taking and in writing to think. And you'll have a window into that thinking. In the classrooms we work in, the notebook is one of our primary sources of information for assessment, and one of the primary ways that kids make sense of what they are learning.

Figure Out What You Value, and Watch for It

In his 2013 Teachers College lecture, "Grading and Assessment: What Works," Doug Reeves advised that schools spend more time thinking about what impact they most want their curriculum to have. He suggested conceptualizing that impact as a set of values that the school could then try to measure. From there, it's all the more important to have local markers of growth in that school, and signs of student prowess, as the state test isn't going to be a very useful assessment for English learners. For instance, a school in Danbury, CT, with many bilingual students most valued that kids were becoming multiliterate. The students developed literacy in their home languages while becoming proficient in English as well. This school, then, might emphasize publishing student writing in multiple languages in ways that the state assessment would not. A school in Seattle thought that the greatest impact of their reading curriculum was that kids were changed by their books, especially that they developed more empathy. And so they invited kids to keep tallies, not of how many pages or books they had read, but of how often they had stood up for someone, or connected with someone. They looked for signs that reading was making the students different. Marc's school, IS 289, looks for how kids have cultivated concerns for social justice, and those concerns reveal themselves in the art and music they produce, as evidenced by the opera the seventh grade produces.

One way to think about assessment, then, is to think big. Think conceptually. Ask yourself: "What kinds of behaviors and habits are we hoping kids will display as a result of this work? What would signs of growth look like? Can we see it in their writing? In what they read? In their music and art? In the way they treat each other? In the questions they ask?"

Let's take some of the civic virtues taught across this book. If you teach kids and teachers to articulate and value their identities, and to be sensitive to the biases that citizens in your communities experience—the suffering of microaggressions, the fear in response to breaking news, the internalizing of oppressive discourse— then you can also invite students and teachers to watch for and document times when students speak up on behalf others, times when they recognize the varied and sometimes urgent needs inside the community, times when they speak back to damaging stereotypes. If you teach kids to build background knowledge, read multiple sources, question texts, and read closely and critically, then you can research and watch for how they begin to internalize those habits. For instance, you can study how/if kids borrow texts in anticipation of a new research topic, how they choose texts, browse and preview text sets, contribute to text sets, and so on.

FIGURE 6.2 When thinking about assessment, think big by asking questions.

Develop Checklists and Progressions for Self-Assessment and Feedback

Along with thinking big in terms of civic virtues, it's also useful to go more granular when addressing particular academic skills. There is a whole set of specific critical reading and writing skills that are key to developing content understandings and civic virtues. The goal is to monitor kids' progress with these skills so that you can give kids feedback and adjust, develop, and implement curriculum. Checklists and progressions can be really helpful in providing kids with ways to self-assess, goal-set, and strive to improve. A progression that is also a rubric can also help you to give contained and clear feedback, next steps, and notification of where kids are along a skill progression.

We have been tremendously lucky to have had opportunities to listen to, read, and study with people like Doug Reeves, Ray Pecheone from SCALE (Stanford Center for Assessment, Learning, and Equity), and Paul Deane and his team at CBAL (Cognitively Based Assessment *of, for,* and *as* Learning at ETS.

From Doug Reeves we've learned to try to live up to the mantra in grading: "Do No Harm." Doug has shown how damaging punitive grading practices are to kids' achievement, esteem, and future engagement with the discipline. When kids seem to be failing something, Doug suggests that we give renewed opportunities for learning and success until the kid isn't failing that thing. It's simple and radical. If you take one thing from Doug's research, and from Dan Pink's research on motivation, it's to be very cautious about giving bad grades. Know that they can be damaging in lasting ways.

Probably the biggest innovation we suggest in response to Reeves' and Hattie's research is to shift assessment to earlier in the process. Instead of assessing at the end of a project, assess midway so that your feedback is more likely to affect kids' performance. Invite students to self-assess as well, before you assess, so that your feedback is not only on kids' performance so far but also on their assessment literacies.

To help students with assessment literacy, especially with meaningful self-assessment and goal-setting, there are a few kinds of tools that can be very helpful. Mary has written extensively about these tools, in a chapter coauthored with Lucy Calkins and Diana Akhmedjanova in the 2019 *Handbook of Formative Assessment in the Disciplines.* Essentially, a combination of checklists, calibrated student exemplars, and student-facing progressions can make a tremendous difference in kids being able to self-assess, set goals, and work independently to meet those goals. A rubric on its own, while it may (or may not), act as a useful progression, rarely leads to increased student performance. In our work with Ray Pecheone, we learned a lot about why.

First, Ray taught us that while rubrics may be helpful for teachers, checklists are helpful for kids. "Why would you show kids the part of the rubric that you don't want them to be on?" was a question that Ray posed to us and our colleague, Audra Robb, who was working on performance assessments at the time in a collaboration between TCRWP and the NYC DOE. It's a good question. Now we often show kids only the part of the rubric we want kids to use—that is, the portions for *meets standards* and *exceeds standards,* or *getting started* and *going deeper,* or whatever your language is for *proficiency* and *exceeds proficiency.* Kids' goals then are to get on the rubric, and to know how to move up.

In working with Ray, and innovating in classrooms around checklists, it turned out that checklists written in the first person, as in "I kept track of references in my notes as I researched," were especially effective. Something about the *I* voice helps the user feel accountable. We also found it helpful for kids if we added tips into the checklist, tucking in phrases such as, "I did this by jotting down the author and title, or taking a picture of the source and inserting it in my notes." You can read more about the power of checklists in Atul Gawande's *The Checklist Manifesto* (2011), a history and celebration of why checklists can transform practice, from preventing infection in hospitals to increasing flight safety through preflight protocols for pilots. When you think about pilots, it becomes clear why checklists can be so helpful. You don't really want your pilot to have a rubric. *Approaching standards* is not something you want as an option in a preflight fuel check.

Avoid Deficit Language and Articulate Positive Next Steps

Another crucial lesson that we learned with Ray, that our more recent reading of Bettina Love has reinforced, was to avoid deficit language. If you think of your rubric as a progression, then no part of it can be something like, "misunderstands the text," or "includes information that is inaccurate." You're going to show kids a first step, which is an entry point onto the rubric. So the entry-level stage has to be good work that is simply novice level. Then to get to the next stage, kids need to see some positive steps they can take, which can't be things like "includes inaccuracies."

Figures 6.3 and 6.4 show an example of how we've learned to shift from deficit to readiness/growth language, with a high-level secondary rubric on keeping track of references:

What we used to do—don't do this!!!		
Approaching Standards	**Meets Standards**	**Exceeds Standards**
I don't keep track of all my sources. The information I keep about my sources is partially inaccurate.	I often keep track of my sources, being sure to note the author and title. I include references for at least five sources, and I include mostly accurate information on those sources.	I always keep track of my sources, including all relevant information, such as author, title, date, and publisher. I include references for more than five sources, and the information I include is accurate and has no spelling errors.

FIGURE 6.3 There are a lot of problems with old-school rubrics. First, you can't use them as progressions because you won't want to coach kids to get on the rubric by being "partially inaccurate," nor do you want them to "move up" by being "mostly accurate," or by counting how many sources they include. Nor do you want kids to think that the way to do more innovative work is to simply do more of something. Whenever you find yourself using words like *partial* or *don't* or *sometimes* or *often*, pause. Chances are that the paradigm of the tool you are making is stuck in a deficit model. Look, as well, to see if we are being creative and visionary in the behaviors we are embracing—are we striving for inclusivity and recognition?

What we try to do now—try this!		
* (Getting Started)	** (Going Deeper)	*** (Critical Agency)
I do my best to keep track of sources as I research. I do this by: ❑ jotting the author and title ❑ jotting the page number.	I not only keep track of sources as I research, I develop systems for returning to these sources. I might do this by: ❑ jotting the authors, titles, and date of publication in my notes or by inserting photographs, URLS, or QR codes so I can find texts again ❑ noting important page numbers or sections I might want to return to ❑ starting a list of resources I've read and want to read next.	I not only develop systems for keeping track of sources, I also develop systems for *evaluating* sources. I might do this by: ❑ developing an annotated bibliography ❑ jotting comments about sources inside my notes ❑ using citation tools to create a digital bibliography/reference tool.

FIGURE 6.4 Here you see a growth mindset, with practical steps for kids that help them find ideas for raising the level of the work. It's a generative progression.

One more note: If you can layer your checklists and rubrics/progressions with student exemplars that are calibrated to the levels in your progression, then kids are more likely to be able to use these tools to improve their work. It's not enough to simply describe the work—kids often need a vision of what powerful work looks like (see Figure 6.5). Then they are better able to work independently and with peers, instead of depending on us to raise the level of their work.

Try this work out in your classroom. In all the work we've done with colleagues and in classrooms, the reframing and reworking of rubrics into student-facing checklists and authentic progressions has been some of the most important. Figure 6.6 shows a quick model of a progression for taking charge of building background knowledge.

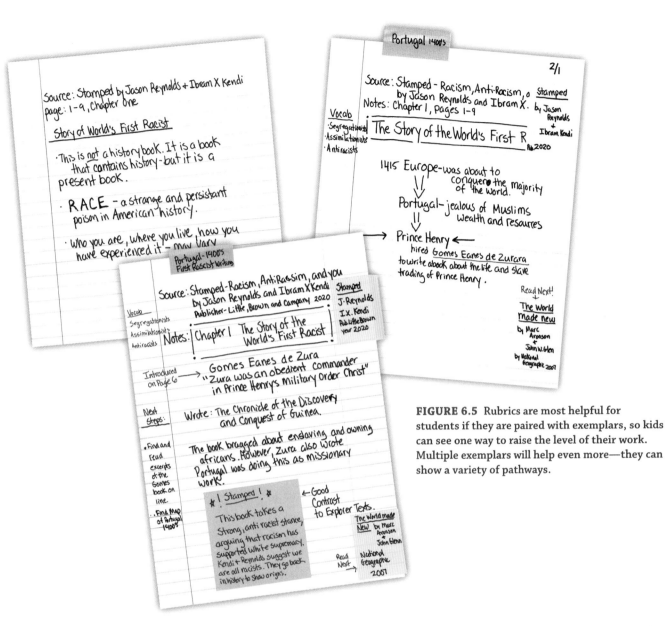

FIGURE 6.5 Rubrics are most helpful for students if they are paired with exemplars, so kids can see one way to raise the level of their work. Multiple exemplars will help even more—they can show a variety of pathways.

*	**	***	****
I read the texts assigned to me when they are assigned in class.	I not only read texts assigned to me, I read around these texts, seeking related information.	I not only read texts and related information, I seek out alternate perspectives and voices.	I actively seek, read, evaluate, and contribute a range of texts and perspectives to class and study groups. I preview content ahead of my studies when possible.

FIGURE 6.6 Progressions can help students self-assess and move forward. Here, you might note the use of stars rather than normative language such as "meets standards," or "grade level."

Another Use for Assessment: Improving Our Own Curriculum and Instruction

Assessment can also be something we use to reconsider our own instruction, versus something we use to assess kids. We deeply appreciate the *Culturally Responsive Curriculum Scorecard*, created by the Metropolitan Center for Research on Equity and the Transformation of Schools at NYU (2020), in conjunction with the Education Justice Research and Organizing Collaborative. The scorecard prompts us to think about and question our representation, stereotypes, kinds of narratives, and methods for affirming identities in our curriculum. It's humbling and motivating to evaluate curriculum this way. At the same time, we educators have to be careful of assuming that we can make a quick fix. Building more culturally responsive and sustaining classrooms doesn't happen simply by increasing the percentage of brown and Black faces on the books in our rooms. Who can forget the horrifying moment when Barnes and Noble attempted to simply color in the faces on the covers of white canonical texts, as if a pigment shade on the cover would make these texts mirrors for students of color?

Culturally Responsive Curriculum Scorecard

https://research
.steinhardt.nyu.edu
/scmsAdmin/media
/users/atn293/ejroc
/CRE-Rubric-2018
-190211.pdf

You can also study student work and look at it as giving you feedback on response to instruction. For instance, you might think about kids who read below benchmark, or language learners, or seemingly disengaged learners, or academic introverts, or vulnerable students, or highly engaged and avid readers, or already-expert students—and you can study the work of one or two of each of these students at the start of your study, later in the study, and near the end, to see how different kinds of learners are experiencing the curriculum or responding to instructional methods.

Essentially, you're using performance assessments, then, to give you information about which kids are flourishing in the curriculum and which are not. The results can be surprising. We've done this work by studying notebooks, filming study group conversations, or filming kids talking about their current understandings, and sometimes found that the kids who came into the unit of study already strong readers or writers, or already knowing a lot about the topic, didn't really grow that much across the unit. They enjoyed it. They performed well. But their rate of growth wasn't spectacular. When you find results like these, you can look to your progressions and exemplars, your coaching and tips, to see what might better support these students. Or you might find that some kids who read below benchmark didn't flourish. Or you might find that kids who identify as BIPOC didn't flourish. Then you can look to your range of texts and the kinds of pathways kids had to show their learning, and to the ways of being that you value, and consider what adjustments you can make to better support these students.

Be Brave, Be Innovative, Be Progressive, Be Kind, Be Research-Based

The main thing is, make sure that your assessment systems help kids be seen, be proud, and outgrow themselves. Make sure your tools and ways of measurement help you give feedback. Make sure they help kids self-assess and strive independently. Mostly, make sure your systems work for you, your students, and your community. Be kind, be thoughtful, be careful. Follow research. Assessment isn't just something we do to kids.

It's a civic virtue at its best, and the opposite at its worst.

Dear Friends,

Thank you for reading our book.

I first entered Pablo's humanities class at School of the Future, and Marc's social studies class at IS 289 over ten years ago. I was there as the staff developer, and I knew right away that I would be the one learning the most from these relationships. Sometimes you can tell, as soon as you meet someone, or see them work, or watch them talking with their students, that this is a place where love and daring meet.

We have so much to learn from each other. And our kids need us to keep thinking about what we care about the most in education. We didn't get into teaching because we love rubrics, or because we wanted to prove our kids could meet benchmark on a state assessment. We got into education because we care about kids and we care about the world.

Sometimes, in the last few years, it has been hard to have faith in our political system. It's hard feeling unhappy with your political leaders. It's hard to see kids and families feel frightened, and to realize that they should be frightened, because their security is threatened. It's hard to see the language in politics, in the news, in social media, and in schools, shift to normalize what we would have considered shocking hate speech just a few years ago.

I believe in what Dr. King said, that "the arc of the moral universe is long, but it bends toward justice" (1964). And my coconspirators, Pablo and Marc, have also led me to believe what former Attorney General Eric Holder said—that "the arc bends towards justice, but it only bends towards justice because people pull it towards justice. It doesn't happen on its own" (Holder 2016).

We hope you will fill your students with the belief that they can continually pull the arc toward justice, and that you can as well. I do believe, when we look at the incredible activism and outrage of young people, and the vast love of teachers for young people, and the work that teachers do to empower their students, that the future is full of hope.

I hope you feel the same.

All the best,

Mary

Dear Reader,

Crises call upon us to reflect on societal weaknesses and on the lessons we can take from those who preceded us. Of course, there are always those among us who are unwilling, or unable, to reflect, and thus it falls to the educators who have devoted themselves to lives of truth-seeking to steer the course. You and your students are the instruments of transformation that could determine the direction this country, this world, takes in the decades ahead. The novelist Arundhati Roy refers to our current crisis as a "portal," one that we can choose to walk through, "dragging the carcasses of our prejudice and hatred, our avarice, our dread, our data banks and dead ideas, our dead rivers and smoky skies behind us. Or we can walk through it lightly, with little luggage, ready to imagine another world. And ready to fight for it" (2020).

It's time to shed the old and fight for the new.

We've taken on a great mission here, and though the way forward might be obscured, our north star must be love: a love for truth and for our students.

I started with Baldwin and will end with him, a man whose searing love for the world revealed painful, necessary, truths: "Love takes off the masks that we fear we cannot live without and know we cannot live within. I use the word 'love' here not merely in the personal sense but as a state of being, or a state of grace—not in the infantile American sense of being made happy but in the tough and universal sense of quest and daring and growth" (1993, 95).

Thank you for taking on this brave and necessary work.

Our quest is only beginning.

Yours in struggle,

Pablo

Dear Educator,

Former President Barack Obama, at the dedication of the National Museum of African American History and Culture, spoke to this work, "And, yes, a clear-eyed view of history can make us uncomfortable, and shake us out of familiar narratives. But it is precisely because of that discomfort that we learn and grow and harness our collective power to make this nation more perfect" (2016). Don't we miss leaders who talk us through discomfort and not create it?

How often have we been asked, "What is your role in this country?"

Our role is teaching. We teach the future. Teaching is political. We need to teach how to participate and harness our collective power to ensure that this nation evolves and becomes more perfect.

My wish for all of you is that you find a Mary and a Pablo to share your journey with.

Thank you, Educators, for your commitment to this work which will nourish the activism of the incredible young people who sit before you.

Journey on!

Marc

REFERENCES

ABC News. 2016. "Colin Kaepernick Takes a Knee for National Anthem." YouTube video, September 2. www.youtube.com/watch?v=bBdoDOXMWkg.

Acevedo, Elizabeth. 2015. "Afro-Latina." SlamFind. YouTube video, September 21. https://youtube.com/watch?v=tPx8cSGW4k8.

Adam Ruins Everything/truTV. 2017. "Why Proving Someone Wrong Often Backfires." YouTube video, August 24. www.youtube.com/watch?v=Q8NydsXl32s.

Adichie, Chimamanda Nigozi. 2009. "The Danger of a Single Story." Filmed July 2009 at TEDGlobal 2009, Oxford, England. www.ted.com/talks/chimamanda_ngozi_adichie_the_danger_of_a_single_story/up-next.

AFL–CIO. 2020. "Lowell Mill Women Create the First Union of Working Women: AFL–CIO." AFL–CIO. https://aflcio.org/about/history/labor-history-events/lowell-mill-women-form-union.

Ahmed, Sara K. 2018. *Being the Change: Lessons and Strategies to Teach Social Comprehension.* Portsmouth, NH: Heinemann.

———. 2020. "When the World Hands You a Curriculum." Speech presented at Teachers College Reading and Writing Project, New York, January 15.

Alexander, Michelle. 2010. *The New Jim Crow: Mass Incarceration in the Age of Color Blindness.* New York: The New Press.

Allen, John R. 2020. "White-Supremacist Violence Is Terrorism." *The Atlantic*, February 24. www.theatlantic.com/ideas/archive/2020/02/white-supremacist-violence-terrorism/606964/?utm_campaign=Brookings%2BBrief&utm_source=hs_email&utm_medium=email&utm_content=83815417.

Allington, Richard L. 2012. *What Really Matters for Struggling Readers: Designing Research-Based Programs.* Boston, MA: Pearson.

AllSides. 2020. "How to Spot 11 Types of Media Bias." AllSides, January 30. www.allsides.com/media-bias/how-to-spot-types-of-media-bias#FinalNotes.

Always®. 2020. "Our Epic Battle #LikeAGirl." Video. www.always.com/en-us/about-us/our-epic-battle-like-a-girl.

Amis, Kingsley. 1999. *The King's English: a Guide to Modern Usage.* New York: St. Martin's Griffin.

Anderson, Carl. 2018. *A Teacher's Guide to Writing Conferences.* Portsmouth, NH: Heinemann.

Angelou, Maya. 2015. Facebook post, November 16. www.facebook.com/MayaAngelou/posts/do-the-best-you-can-until-you-know-better-then-when-you-know-better-do-better-ma/10153989278579796/.

Bad News. 2020. "Can You Beat My Score? Play the Fake News Game!" Bad News. www.getbadnews.com/#intro.

Baker-Bell, April. 2020. *Linguistic Justice: Black Language, Literacy, Identity, and Pedagogy.* New York: Routledge.

Baldwin, James. 1993. *The Fire Next Time.* New York: Vintage Books.

Banks, Lynne Reid. 1980. *The Indian in the Cupboard.* Indian in the Cupboard Series, #1. New York: Avon.

Baumgartner, Jody, and Jonathan S. Morris. 2006. "*The Daily Show* Effect." *American Politics Research* 34 (3): 341–67. https://doi.org/10.1177/1532673x05280074.

BBC. 2018. "A Brief History of Fake News." Video. January 22. www.bbc.com/news/av/stories-42752668/a-brief-history-of-fake-news

BBC One. 2017. "The Supporting Act." Short film. December 12. www.bbc.co.uk/mediacentre /latestnews/2017/bbc-one-christmas-short-film.

Beaty, Daniel. 2010. "Knock, Knock." YouTube video, March 15. www.youtube.com /watch?v=9eYH0AFx6yI.

———. 2014. *Knock Knock: My Dad's Dream for Me.* New York: Little, Brown and Company.

Beers, Kylene, and Robert E. Probst. 2017. *Disrupting Thinking: Why How We Read Matters.* New York: Scholastic.

Belleza, Rhoda, ed. 2012. *Cornered: 14 Stories of Bullying and Defiance.* Philadelphia: RP Teens.

Bishop, Rudine Sims. 1990. "Mirrors, Windows, and Sliding Glass Doors." *Perspectives: Choosing and Using Books for the Classroom* 6 (3).

Blakemore, Erin. 2017. "The Secret Student Group That Stood Up to the Nazis." *Smithsonian Magazine,* February 22. www.smithsonianmag.com/smart-news/the-secret-student -group-stood-up-nazis-180962250.

Bomer, Katherine. 2017. *The Journey Is Everything: Teaching Essays That Students Want to Write for People Who Want to Read Them.* Portsmouth, NH: Heinemann.

Bomer, Randy, and Katherine Bomer. 2001. *For a Better World: Reading and Writing for Social Action.* Portsmouth, NH: Heinemann.

Brainard, Joe, and Ron Padgett. 2001. *I Remember.* New York City: Granary Books.

Branch, John. 2012. "Snow Fall: The Avalanche at Tunnel Creek—Multimedia Feature." *The New York Times,* December 26. www.nytimes.com/projects/2012/snow-fall/index .html#/?part=tunnel-creek.

Briceño, Eduardo. 2012. "The Power of Belief—Mindset and Success." TEDx. YouTube video, November 18. www.youtube.com/watch?v=pN34FNbOKXc.

———. 2016. "How to Get Better at the Things You Care About." TED Talk, November. www.ted.com/talks/eduardo_briceno_how_to_get_better_at_the_things_you_care _about.

Brock, Rose, ed. 2018. *Hope Nation: YA Authors Share Personal Moments of Inspiration.* New York, NY: Philomel Books.

Bronski, Michael, and Richie Chevat. 2019. *A Queer History of the United States for Young People.* Boston: Beacon Press.

Brown, Brené. 2010. "Transcript of 'The Power of Vulnerability.'" TED Talk, June. www.ted .com/talks/brene_brown_the_power_of_vulnerability/transcript?language=en.

———. 2012. *Daring Greatly: How the Courage to Be Vulnerable Transforms the Way We Live, Love, Parent, and Lead.* New York: Avery.

Bryant, Kobe. 2015. "Dear Basketball." *The Players Tribune,* November 29. www.theplayerstribune .com/en-us/articles/dear-basketball.

Business Insider. 2018. "Anchoring Effect: Guessing How Many Jelly Beans Are In a Jar: Why Are We All So Stupid?" YouTube video, October 23. www.youtube.com /watch?v=igv_O-azRUc.

Cain, Susan. 2012. *Quiet: The Power of Introverts in a World That Can't Stop Talking.* New York: Crown Publishing Group.

———. 2017. *Quiet Power: The Secret Strengths of Introverted Kids.* New York: Random House.

Calkins, Lucy. 2001. *The Art of Teaching Reading.* New York: Longman.

———. 2020. *Teaching Writing.* Portsmouth, NH: Heinemann.

Calkins, Lucy, Diana Akhmedjanova, and Mary Ehrenworth. 2019. "Creating Formative Assessment Systems in the Teaching of Writing and Harnessing Them as Professional Development." In *Handbook of Formative Assessment in the Disciplines,* edited by Heidi L. Andrade, Randy E. Bennett, and Gregory J. Cizek. New York: Routledge.

Canada, Geoffrey. 2010. *Fist, Stick, Knife, Gun: A Personal History of Violence.* Boston, MA: Beacon Press.

Capellaro, Catherine. 2005. "Bargaining for Better Schools: An Interview with Héctor Calde-rón." *Rethinking Schools.* http://rethinkingschools.aidcvt.com/special_reports/quality_teachers/beau194.shtml

Center for Asian American Media. 2017. *Resistance at Tule Lake.*

Center for Constitutional Rights. 2012. "Stop and Frisk: The Human Impact." July. https://ccrjustice.org/sites/default/files/attach/2015/08/the-human-impact-report.pdf.

———. 2015. "Stories of Stop and Frisk." August 5. https://ccrjustice.org/stories-stop-and-frisk.

Center for Information Technology and Society—UC Santa Barbara. 2020. "How Is Fake News Spread? Bots, People like You, Trolls, And Microtargeting." www.cits.ucsb.edu/fake-news/spread.

Chabon, Michael. 2012. *The Amazing Adventures of Kavalier & Clay: A Novel.* New York: Random House.

Cherry-Paul, Sonja, and Dana Johansen. 2019. *Breathing New Life into Book Clubs: A Practical Guide for Teachers.* Portsmouth, NH: Heinemann.

Clark, Roy Peter. 2006. *Writing Tools: 55 Essential Strategies for Every Writer.* New York: Little Brown.

———. 2010. "A Toolkit for Revision." Speech presented at Teachers College Reading and Writing Project, New York, August 3.

Clements, Katie, and Audra Kirshbaum Robb. 2018. *Literary Nonfiction.* Portsmouth, NH: Heinemann.

Clements, Ron, and John Musker, dirs. *Moana.* 2016. Animated film. Burbank, CA: Disney.

ClickHole. 2014. "Litany Of Lies: A Third-Grader's Reading Log EXPOSED." April 9. news.clickhole.com/litany-of-lies-a-third-grader-s-reading-log-exposed-1825121189.

Confessore, Nicholas, and Gabriel J. X. Dance, Richard Harris, and Mark Hansen. 2018. "The Follower Factory." *The New York Times,* January 27. www.nytimes.com/interactive/2018/01/27/technology/social-media-bots.html.

Cruz, M. Colleen. 2015. *The Unstoppable Writing Teacher: Real Strategies for the Real Classroom.* Portsmouth, NH: Heinemann.

Cummins, Sunday. 2018. *Nurturing Informed Thinking: Reading, Talking, and Writing across Content-Area Texts.* Portsmouth, NH: Heinemann.

Dale Peterson for Alabama Agriculture Commission Campaign. 2010. "We Are Better Than That!" YouTube video, May 16. www.youtube.com/watch?v=jU7fhIO7DG0.

Dalles Daily Chronicle. 1892. "A Celestial Horde: Hiding in Sequestered Nooks, Ready for the Break—Only One More River to Cross." *The Dalles Daily Chronicle,* April 30.

Damour, Lisa. 2017. *Untangled: Guiding Teenage Girls Through the Seven Transitions into Adult-hood.* New York: Ballantine Books.

——— 2017. "Stress and Change." Speech presented at Teachers College Reading and Writing Project, New York, November 8.

———. 2019. *Under Pressure: Confronting the Epidemic of Stress and Anxiety in Girls.* New York: Ballantine Books.

Daniels, Harvey "Smokey", and Sara K. Ahmed. 2015. *Upstanders: How to Engage Middle School Hearts and Minds with Inquiry.* Portsmouth, NH: Heinemann.

Dear Black Women. 2018. "We Speak Their Names: Black Women Abolitionists, A June-teenth Celebration." Dear Black Women, June 19. www.dearblackwomenproject.com/todays-affirmation/we-speak-their-names-happy-juneteenth.

Del Valle, Mayda. 2009. "Tongue Tactics." YouTube video, August 4. www.youtube.com/watch?v=sa7IfuXT_Bc.

Democracy Now! 2019. "What to the Slave Is 4th of July?: James Earl Jones Reads Fredrick Douglass's Historic Speech." *Democracy Now!* Video, July 4. www.democracynow.org/shows/2019/7/4.

Dewey, John. (1916) 1968. *Democracy and Education: An Introduction to the Philosophy of Education.* New York: The Free Press.

DiAngelo, Robin J. 2018. *White Fragility: Why It's so Hard for White People to Talk about Racism.* Boston: Beacon Press.

Direct TV. 2014 "Don't Attend Your Own Funeral." YouTube video, June 13. www.youtube.com/watch?v=G8JvwvA3J4w.

Douglass, Frederick. 1855. "The Anti-Slavery Movement." Lecture presented in Rochester, New York before the Rochester Ladies Anti-Slavery Society.

Ebarvia, Tricia. 2018. "We Teach Who We Are: Unpacking Our Identities." Tricia Ebarvia, July 29. https://triciaebarvia.org/2018/07/27/we-teach-who-we-are-unpacking-our-identities/#more-5826.

Ehrenworth, Mary. 2014. "Parents as Writing Partners." *Educational Leadership*, April.

Ellick, Adam B., and Adam Westbrook. 2018. *Operation Infektion: A Three-Part Video Series on Russian Disinformation. The New York Times*, November 13. www.nytimes.com/2018/11/12/opinion/russia-meddling-disinformation-fake-news-elections.html.

Elliott, Andrea. 2013. "Invisible Child: Girl in the Shadows: Dasani's Homeless Life." *The New York Times,* December 8. www.nytimes.com/projects/2013/invisible-child/index.html.

Emdin, Christopher. 2017. *For White Folks Who Teach in the Hood . . . and the Rest of Y'all Too: Reality Pedagogy and Urban Education.* New York: Random House.

Escoloedo, Belissa, Zariya Allen, and Rhiannon McGavin. 2014. "Somewhere in America." Brave New Voices. YouTube video, July 25. www.youtube.com/watch?v=OadZpUJv8Eg.

España, Carla, and Luz Yadira Herrera. 2020. *En Comunidad: Lessons for Centering the Voices and Experiences of Bilingual Latinx Students.* Portsmouth, NH: Heinemann.

ESPN. 2019. "Terrell Owens Confronts Stephen A. over Colin Kaepernick Criticisms." YouTube video, November 21. www.youtube.com/watch?v=6ilnqIZfLw0.

Evans, Taina, and Naheem Morris. 2020. "Oral History Interview with Eric Osorio on 2015 December 15." Brooklyn Public Library. www.bklynlibrary.org/digitalcollections/item/85d7dc37-e269-43df-a327-ee5eb1d0c185.

Facing History and Ourselves. 2020. "Can You Solve This?" www.facinghistory.org/resourcelibrary/video/can-you-solve.

———. 2020. "Contracting." www.facinghistory.org/resource-library/teachingstrategies/contracting.

———. 2020. "Defining Confirmation Bias." www.facinghistory.org/resource-library/video/defining-confirmation-bias.

factitious. 2020. "Factitious." http://factitious.augamestudio.com/#.

Fayyad, Abdallah. 2018. "The Criminalization of Gentrifying Neighborhoods." *The Atlantic*, January 4. www.theatlantic.com/politics/archive/2017/12/the-criminalization-of-gentrifying-neighborhoods/548837.

Fishman, Charles. 2011. *The Big Thirst: The Secret Life and Turbulent Future of Water.* New York: Simon & Shuster.

Florio, Angelica. 2019. "Brownsville and Bed-Stuy Voiced Concerns About Police–Community Relations and Over-Policing." *Bushwick Daily,* March 18. https://bushwickdaily.com/bushwick/categories/community/5937-brownsville-and-bed-stuy-voiced-concerns-about-police-community-relations-and-over-policing.

Fox News. 2007. "The Bill O'Reilly and Geraldo Rivera Bust Up." YouTube video, April 4. www.youtube.com/watch?v=FhwwbNA3hjg.

Frazin, Shana, and Katy Wischow. 2020. *Unlocking the Power of Classroom Talk: Teaching Kids to Talk with Clarity and Purpose.* Portsmouth, NH: Heinemann.

Frey, Nancy, Douglas Fisher, and John Hattie. 2018. "Developing 'Assessment Capable' Learners." *Educational Leadership*, February.

Fritz, Jean, and Hudson Talbott. 2004. *The Lost Colony of Roanoke*. New York: G.P. Putnam's Sons.

Gawande, Atul. 2011. *The Checklist Manifesto: How to Get Things Right*. New York: Henry Holt.

Gladwell, Malcolm. 2010. *What the Dog Saw and Other Adventures*. New York: Back Bay Books/Little Brown and Co.

———. 2015. "Thresholds of Violence: How School Shootings Catch On." *The New Yorker,* October 19. www.newyorker.com/magazine/2015/10/19/thresholds-of-violence.

Gonzalez, Emma. 2018. "March for Our Lives Speech." Guardian News, March 24. www.youtube.com/watch?v=u46HzTGVQhg.

Goodwin, Liz. 2018. "'Children Are Being Used as a 'Tool' in Trump's Effort to Stop Border Crossings." *Boston Globe,* June 10. www3.bostonglobe.com/news/nation/2018/06/09 /borderseparations/Z95z4eFZjyfqCLG9pyHjAO/story.html?arc404=true.

Greene, Maxine. 1993. "Imagination, Community and the School." *The Review of Education* 15 (3–4): 223–31. https://doi.org/10.1080/0098559930150303.

———. 2000. "Lived Spaces, Shared Spaces, Public Spaces." In *Construction Sites: Excavating Race, Class and Gender among Urban Youth,* edited by L. Weiss and M. Fine. New York: Teachers College Press.

———. 2018. *The Dialectic of Freedom*. New York: Teachers College Press.

Guskey, Thomas R. 2003. "How Classroom Assessments Improve Learning." *Educational Leadership*, February.

———. 2011. "Five Obstacles to Grading Reform." *Educational Leadership*, November.

Gutmann, Amy. 1999. *Democratic Education*. Princeton, NJ: Princeton University Press.

Harfoush, Rahaf. 2018. Speech presented at Teachers College Reading and Writing Project, New York, November 7.

———. 2019. *Hustle and Float: Reclaim Your Creativity and Thrive in a World Obsessed with Work*. New York: Diversion Books.

Hattie, John. 2018. "John Hattie on Visible Learning and Feedback in the Classroom." Taylor and Francis Books. YouTube video, November 14. www.youtube.com /watch?v=Vpq09eY4pZo.

Hill, Hank. 2002. "What in the Name of High School Football?" *Literary Cavalcade,* Nov/Dec, 55(3).

Hillocks, George. 2011. *Teaching Argument Writing, Grades 6–12: Supporting Claims with Relevant Evidence and Clear Reasoning*. Portsmouth, NH: Heinemann.

Holder, Eric. 2016. "Interview with Eric Holder." CBS News, September 20. www.cbsnews .com/video/how-far-have-we-come-on-the-arc-of-justice/

Hollie, Sharroky. 2011. *Culturally and Linguistically Responsive Teaching and Learning: Classroom Practices for Student Success*. Huntington Beach, CA: Shell Education.

Horton, Myles, and Paulo Freire. 1990. *We Make the Road by Walking: Conversations on Walking and Social Change*. Philadelphia: Temple University Press.

Howard, Tyrone C. 2010. *Why Race and Culture Matter in Schools: Closing the Achievement Gap in America's Classrooms*. New York: Teachers College Press.

Howard, Zora. 2013. "Bi-Racial Hair." Multiethnic Multiplex. YouTube video, April 28. www.youtube.com/watch?v=S2VcRWbAd74.

In This Together Media, ed. 2018. *Nevertheless, We Persisted: 48 Voices of Defiance, Strength, and Courage*. New York: Alfred A. Knopf.

Institute for Propaganda Analysis. 1971. *The Fine Art of Propaganda*. New York: Octagon Books.

Ishak, Natasha. 2019. "Bushwick Named in New Gentrification Report on Over-Policed Communities of Color." *Bushwick Daily,* May 10. https://bushwickdaily.com /bushwick/categories/news/5798-bushwick-named-in-new-gentrification-report-on -over-policed-communities-of-color.

Jay Z and Molly Crabapple. 2016. *A History of the War on Drugs*. Video accessed in "Jay Z: 'The War on Drugs is an Epic Fail'" by Asha Bandele. *The New York Times*, September 15. www.nytimes.com/2016/09/15/opinion/jay-z-the-war-on-drugs-is-an-epic-fail.html.

Jensen, Kelly, ed. 2018 *(Don't) Call Me Crazy: 33 Voices Start the Conversation about Mental Health*. Chapel Hill, NC: Algonquin Young Readers, an imprint of Algonquin Books of Chapel Hill.

Jones, Tayari. 2018. "There's Nothing Virtuous About Finding Common Ground." *Time,* October 25. https://time.com/5434381/tayari-jones-moral-middle-myth.

Kaepernick, Colin. 2018. "Colin Kaepernick, Amnesty International Ambassador of Conscience" (full speech). Amnesty International. YouTube video, April 25. www.youtube.com/watch?v=5B8VU3JykvI.

Kahneman, Daniel. 2013. "Anchoring, with Daniel Kahneman." Farrar Straus & Giroux. YouTube video, February 1. www.youtube.com/watch?v=HefjkqKCVpo.

Kendi, Ibram X. 2016. *Stamped from the Beginning: The Definitive History of Racist Ideas in America*. New York: Nation Books.

Khan Academy. 2020. "Cognitive Biases." Video. www.khanacademy.org/partner-content/wi-phi/wiphi-critical-thinking/wiphi-cognitive-biases/v/anchoring.

———. 2020. "Women's Labor." www.khanacademy.org/humanities/us-history/the-early-republic/culture-and-reform/a/women-in-the-workplace-and-household.

Khan, Brooke, and Iratxe López de Munáin. 2019. *Home of the Brave:15 Immigrants Who Shaped U.S. History*. New York: Simon & Schuster.

King, Dr. Martin Luther. 1964. "Baccalaureate Commencement Address." Presented at Wesleyan University, Middletown, CT, June 7.

Kino Lorber. 2015. *Stop*. YouTube video, December 29. www.youtube.com/watch?v=02Hp-KZ9ov4.

Knight Commission on Trust, Media, and Democracy. 2019. *Crisis in Democracy: Renewing Trust in America*. Washington, D.C.: The Aspen Institute.

Kuklin, Susan. 2019. *We Are Here to Stay: Voices of Undocumented Young Adults*. Somerville, MA: Candlewick.

Kurlansky, Mark. 2011. *World Without Fish*. New York: Workman.

Ladson-Billings, Gloria. 2009. *The Dreamkeepers: Successful Teachers of African American Children*. San Francisco: John Wiley & Sons.

Le Guin, Ursula K. 1973. "The Ones Who Walk Away from Omelas." *New Dimensions 3*. New York: Nelson Doubleday.

Lehman, Christopher. 2012. *Energize Research Reading and Writing: Fresh Strategies to Spark Interest, Develop Independence, and Meet Key Common Core Standards*. Portsmouth, NH: Heinemann.

Lehman, Christopher, and Kate Roberts. 2013. *Falling in Love with Close Reading: Lessons for Analyzing Texts—and Life*. Portsmouth, NH: Heinemann.

Lewis, Sarah. 2014. *The Rise: Creativity, the Gift of Failure, and the Search for Mastery*. New York: Simon and Schuster.

Lloyd, Carol. 2014. "Writing on the Wall." *Great Schools,* March 10. www.greatschools.org/gk/articles/falling-writing-standards.

Look Different. 2020. "Look Different." MTV. www.mtvact.com/features/Look-Different.

Lopez, Carmen. 2020. "Oral History Interview Conducted with Allahlife Gallishaw on 2016 October 27." Brooklyn Public Library. www.bklynlibrary.org/digitalcollections/item/4b15c712-7dd9-4e92-b332-dc8a23d273e2.

Love, Bettina. 2019. *We Want to Do More Than Survive: Abolitionist Teaching and the Pursuit of Educational Freedom*. New York: Penguin Random House.

———. 2020. "Teachers, We Cannot Go Back to the Way Things Were." *Education Week*, April 19. https://www.edweek.org/ew/articles/2020/04/30/teachers-we-cannot-go-back-to-the.html.

Lyiscott, Jamila. 2018. "Why English Class Is Silencing Students of Color." TED Talk, April. www.ted.com/talks/jamila_lyiscott_why_english_class_is_silencing_students_of_color.

———. 2019. *Black Appetite, White Food: Issues of Race, Voice, and Justice Within and Beyond the Classroom*. New York: Routledge.

———. 2020. "3 Ways to Speak English." TED Talk, February. www.ted.com/talks/jamila _lyiscott_3_ways_to_speak_english.

Lyon, George Ella. 1999. *Where I'm From: Where Poems Come From*. Spring, TX: Absey & Co.

———. 2018. "Resources." I Am From Project. February 8. https://iamfromproject.com /resources.

Marshall, Kim. 2017. "Douglas Reeves Takes On Five Myths About Grading." *The International Educator* (TIE Online). TIE. www.tieonline.com/article/2126/douglas-reeves -takes-on-five-myths-about-grading.

Mashable. 2014. "Bill Nye vs. Ken Ham—The Short Version." YouTube video, February 5. www.youtube.com/watch?v=HA3E8wpBO_I.

McCombs School of Business. 2020. "Implicit Bias." *Ethics Unwrapped*. Video. https:// ethicsunwrapped.utexas.edu/video/implicit-bias.

Merchant, Nilofer. 2018. "To Change Someone's Mind, Stop Talking and Listen." *Harvard Business Review,* February 6. https://hbr.org/2018/02/to-change-someones-mind-stop -talking-and-listen.

Metropolitan Center for Research on Equity and the Transformation of Schools at NYU. 2020. "Culturally Responsive Curriculum Scorecard—Resources—NYU Steinhardt." https://research.steinhardt.nyu.edu/metrocenter/resources/culturally-responsive -scorecard.

Miller, Lee. 2002. *Roanoke: Solving the Mystery of the Lost Colony*. New York: Penguin Books.

Minor, Cornelius. 2019. *We Got This.: Equity, Access, and the Quest to Be Who Our Students Need Us to Be*. Portsmouth, NH: Heinemann.

Miranda, Lin-Manuel and Jeremy McCarter. 2016. *Hamilton: The Revolution*. New York: Grand Central Publishing.

Morisako, Kira. 2020. "Background Story." The Newsboys Strike of 1899. https:// newsboysstrike1899.weebly.com/background-story.html.

Morris, Christelle Pissavy-Yvernault, Bertrand Pissavy-Yvernault, and Jerome Saincantin. 2019. *Lucky Luke*. Canterbury, Kent: Cinebook.

Nasaw, David. 2018. "Read All about It: The Story of the Newsies' Two-Week Strike Against Publishers Pulitzer, Hearst." *New York Daily News*, April 7. www.nydailynews.com /new-york/story-newsies-strike-titans-pulitzer-hearst-article-1.2858550.

National Academies Press. 2020. "A Framework for K–12 Science Education: Practices, Crosscutting Concepts, and Core Ideas." www.nap.edu/read/13165/chapter/1.

National Research Council. 2012. *A Framework for K–12 Science Education.* Washington: The National Academies Press.

The New York Public Library. 2020. "Love & Resistance: Stonewall 50." www.nypl.org /stonewall50.

Newkirk, Thomas. 2014. *Minds Made for Stories: How We Really Read and Write Informational and Persuasive Texts*. Portsmouth, NH: Heinemann.

News Literacy Project. 2020. "News Literacy Project." https://newslit.org.

NewseumED. 2020. "Media Literacy Booster Pack." https://newseumed.org/edcollection /media-literacy-booster-pack./

———. 2020. "Today's Front Pages." https://newseumed.org/curated-stack/archived -todays-front-pages-key-moments-history.

Noble, Sofia U. 2018. *Algorithms of Oppression*. New York: NYU Press.

Nolan, Christopher, dir. *Inception*. 2010. Film. Burbank, CA: Warner Brothers Pictures.

Now This. 2019. "Jamila Lyiscott is Fighting for Racial Justice in US Classrooms." Video. Now This, October 3. https://nowthisnews.com/videos/news/jamila-lyiscott-is-fighting-for-racial-justice-in-us-classrooms.

Obama, Barack. 2016. "Remarks by the President." *Dedication of the National Museum of African American History and Culture*. Presented at the Dedication of the National Museum of African American History and Culture, Washington, DC, September 24.

———. 2018. "Acceptance Speech." *Paul H. Douglas Awards*. Presented at the Paul H. Douglas Awards, Urbana, IL, September 7.

Oluo, Ijeoma. 2019. *So You Want to Talk about Race*. New York: Seal Press.

O'Neal, Lonnae. 2017. "The AWP Party." AWP, December 2. www.theawparty.org/ibram-kendi.

———. 2017. "Ibram Kendi, One of the Nation's Leading Scholars of Racism, Says Education and Love Are Not the Answer." The Undefeated, September 20. https://theundefeated.com/features/ibram-kendi-leading-scholar-of-racism-says-education-and-love-are-not-the-answer.

Ortiz, Paul. 2018. *An African American and Latinx History of the United States*. Boston, MA: Beacon Press.

Palmer, Parker. 2017. *The Courage to Teach*. San Francisco, CA: Jossey-Bass.

Paris, Django, and H. Samy Alim. 2017. *Culturally Sustaining Pedagogies: Teaching and Learning for Justice in a Changing World*. New York: Teachers College Press.

PBS. 2013. "Birmingham and the Children's March." Public Broadcasting Service video, April 25. www.pbs.org/video/religion-and-ethics-newsweekly-childrens-march-50th-anniversary.

———. 2018. "Why Do Our Brains Love Fake News?" Public Broadcasting Service video, February 27. www.pbs.org/video/why-do-our-brains-love-fake-news-svp949.

Peltier, Autumn. 2019. "13-Year-Old Water Advocate, Addresses UN." CBC/Radio–Canada. YouTube video, September 28. www.youtube.com/watch?v=zg60sr38oic.

Pink, Daniel H. 2009. *Drive: The Surprising Truth About What Motivates Us*. New York: Riverhead Books.

———. 2009. "The Puzzle of Motivation." Video filmed July 2009 at TEDGlobal 2009, Oxford, England. www.ted.com/talks/dan_pink_the_puzzle_of_motivation?language=en.

Practical Psychology. 2016. *12 Cognitive Biases Explained—How to Think Better and More Logically Removing Bias*. YouTube video, December 30. www.youtube.com/watch?v=wEwGBIr_RIw&feature=youtu.be.

Putnam, Robert D. 2000. *Bowling Alone: The Collapse and Revival of American Community*. New York: Simon & Schuster.

Race Forward. 2010. "How Does It Feel to Be Stopped and Frisked?" YouTube video, July 29. www.youtube.com/watch?v=UvIBIn5Xp7s&feature=youtu.be.

Reese, Debbie, Jean Mendoza, and Roxanne Dunbar-Ortiz. 2019. *An Indigenous Peoples' History of the United States for Young People*. Boston, MA: Beacon Press.

Reeves, Douglas B. 2002. *Reason to Write: Help Your Child Succeed in School and in Life through Better Reasoning and Clear Communication*. New York: Kaplan.

———. 2008. "Leading to Change/Effective Grading Practices." *Educational Leadership*, February.

———. 2013. "Grading and Assessment: What Works." Speech presented at Teachers College Reading and Writing Project, New York, January 16.

———. 2016. "Elements of Effective Grading." YouTube video, October 25. www.youtube.com/watch?v=dLYpqxQLRt4.

Reshamwala, Saleem. 2016. "Check Our Bias to Wreck Our Bias." *The New York Times,* December 16. www.nytimes.com/video/us/100000004818668/check-our-bias-to-wreck-our-bias.html.

———. 2016. "Peanut Butter, Jelly and Racism." *The New York Times,* December 16. www.nytimes.com/video/us/100000004818663/peanut-butter-jelly-and-racism.html.

Resnick, Mitchel. 2017. *Lifelong Kindergarten: Cultivating Creativity through Projects, Passion, Peers, and Play.* Cambridge, MA: The MIT Press.

Reynolds, Jason, and Ibram X. Kendi. 2020. *Stamped: Racism, Antiracism, and You.* New York: Little, Brown and Company.

Rief, Linda. 1992. *Seeking Diversity: Language Arts with Adolescents.* Portsmouth, NH: Heinemann Educational Books.

Roberts, Kate. 2018. *A Novel Approach: Whole-Class Novels, Student-Centered Teaching, and Choice.* Portsmouth, NH: Heinemann.

Rock, David. 2006. *Quiet Leadership: Six Steps to Transforming Performance at Work; Help People Think Better—Don't Tell Them What to Do!* New York: HarperCollins.

Romano, Tom. 2004. *Crafting Authentic Voice.* Portsmouth, NH: Heinemann.

Roy, Arundhati. 2020. "The Pandemic is a Portal." *The Financial Times,* April 3. https://www.ft.com/content/10d8f5e8-74eb-11ea-95fe-fcd274e920ca.

The San Francisco Call. 1901. "Chinese Exclusion Convention Comes to a Most Brilliant Close." *The San Francisco Call.*

Scholastic Art & Writing Awards. 2019. *The Best Teen Writing of 2019.* New York: Alliance for Young Artists and Writers.

Schoolhouse Rock. 1976. "Elbow Room." YouTube video. www.youtube.com/watch?v=FfoQBTPY7gk.

Seeker. 2013. "Why Facts Won't Help You Win Arguments." YouTube video, October 18. www.youtube.com/watch?time_continue=4&v=U0QLjA1GSVI&feature=emb_logo.

Selection Bias. 2013. "Selection Bias." YouTube video, November 19. www.youtube.com/watch?v=iSKerlu3Pr0.

———. 2014. "Selection Bias: A Real World Example." YouTube video, August 18. www.youtube.com/watch?v=p52Nep7CBdQ.

Sesame Street. 1970. "A Banana in Ernie's Ear." *Sesame Street.* YouTube video. https://www.youtube.com/watch?v=EJ1a0ymGCKA.

Shire, Warsan. 2017. "Home." YouTube video, March 13. www.youtube.com/watch?v=nI9D92Xiygo.

Silverman, Craig. 2018. "In Spite Of Its Efforts, Facebook Is Still The Home Of Hugely Viral Fake News." *BuzzFeed News,* December 30. www.buzzfeednews.com/article/craigsilverman/facebook-fake-news-hits-2018.

The Simpsons. 2009. "The Bear Patrol and Lisa's Tiger-Repelling Rock." *The Simpsons.* YouTube video. www.youtube.com/watch?v=fm2W0sq9ddU.

Snoop Dogg. 2016. "Snoop Dogg Says Colin Kaepernick Needs to Choose—Football or Revolutionary?" Skip and Shannon: Undisputed. YouTube video, November 30. www.youtube.com/watch?v=oGJnAKRUEJo.

Solomon, Andrew. 2014. "How the Worst Moments in Our Lives Make Us Who We Are." TED Talk, May 21. www.ted.com/talks/andrew_solomon_how_the_worst_moments_in_our_lives_make_us_who_we_are/up-next?language=en.

Southern Poverty Law Center. 2016. "The Trump Effect: The Impact of the 2016 Presidential Election on Our Nation's Schools." November 28. www.splcenter.org/20161128/trump-effect-impact-2016-presidential-election-our-nations-schools.

Southern Poverty Law Center/HBO. 2004. *Mighty Times: The Children's March.*

St. John, Noah. 2012. "The Last Mile." NPR Snap Judgment Performance of the Year. www.youtube.com/watch?v=-Lug_IxFKo8&t=2s.

Stefoff, Rebecca, and Howard Zinn. 2009. *A Young People's History of the United States: Columbus to the War on Terror.* New York: Seven Stories Press.

Stockton, Frank R., and Mark Kurlansky. 2011. *World Without Fish*. New York: Workman Publishing.

Stolper, Harold. 2019. "New Neighbors and the Over-Policing of Communities of Color." Community Service Society of New York, January 6. www.cssny.org/news/entry/New-Neighbors.

Stone, Douglas, and Sheila Heen. 2014. *Thanks for the Feedback: The Science and Art of Receiving Feedback Well (Even When It Is Off-Base, Unfair, Poorly Delivered, and Frankly, You're Not in the Mood)*. New York: Viking Adult.

Stone, Nic. 2017. *Dear Martin*. New York: Crown Publishing Group.

Tatum, Alfred W. 2005. *Teaching Reading to Black Adolescent Males: Closing the Achievement Gap*. Portland, ME: Stenhouse Publishers.

Tatum, Beverly Daniel. 1997. *Why Are All the Black Kids Sitting Together in the Cafeteria?: and Other Conversations about Race*. New York: Basic Books.

Teachers College—Columbia University. 2002. "Maxine Greene: The Arts and Shaping a Social Vision." April 10. www.tc.columbia.edu/articles/1997/december/maxine-greene-the-arts-and-shaping-a-social-vision.

Thomas, Angie. 2017. *The Hate U Give*. New York: Harper Collins.

Trusiani, Lisa. 2019. *American Trailblazers: 50 Remarkable People Who Shaped U.S. History*. Emeryville, CA: Rockridge Press.

United States Holocaust Memorial Museum. 2020. "White Rose." https://encyclopedia.ushmm.org/content/en/article/white-rose.

UDL. 2018. "The UDL Guidelines." UDL. August 31. http://udlguidelines.cast.org.

Visible Learning. 2013. "Feedback in Schools by John Hattie." September 9. https://visible-learning.org/2013/10/john-hattie-article-about-feedback-in-schools.

Wadler, Naomi. 2018. "Naomi Wadler Speech at March for Our Lives." Fox 5/Atlanta. YouTube video, March 24. www.youtube.com/watch?v=EqKy7TXKO8c.

Wagner, Tony. 2014. *The Global Achievement Gap: Why Even Our Best Schools Don't Teach the New Survival Skills Our Children Need—and What We Can Do about It*. New York: Basic Books.

Wallace, David Foster. 2004. "Consider the Lobster." *Gourmet*, August.

Walt Disney Pictures. 2015. *Pocahontas*. Burbank, CA: Walt Disney Studios Home Entertainment.

Wardle, Claire. 2017. "Fake News. It's Complicated." First Draft, May 15. https://firstdraftnews.org/latest/fake-news-complicated.

Whitehurst, Susan. 2002. *The Pilgrims before the Mayflower*. New York: Rosen Publishing Group.

Williams, David. 2020. "Barnes & Noble Cancels Plan to Put People of Color on the Covers of Classic Books after Backlash." CNN, February 6. www.cnn.com/2020/02/05/media/barnes-and-noble-diverse-editions-trnd/index.html.

Zemelman, Steven. 2016. *From Inquiry to Action: Civic Engagement with Project-Based Learning in All Content Areas*. Portsmouth, NH: Heinemann.